An Atheist's History of Belief

An Atheist's History of Belief

UNDERSTANDING OUR MOST
EXTRAORDINARY INVENTION

MATTHEW KNEALE

THE BODLEY HEAD
LONDON

Published by The Bodley Head 2013

2 4 6 8 10 9 7 5 3 1

First published in Great Britain in 2013 by
The Bodley Head
Random House, 20 Vauxhall Bridge Road,
London SW1V 2SA

www.bodleyhead.co.uk
www.vintage-books.co.uk

Addresses for companies within The Random House Group Limited can be found at:
www.randomhouse.co.uk/offices.htm

The Random House Group Limited Reg. No. 954009

A CIP catalogue record for this book
is available from the British Library

ISBN 9781847922625

The Random House Group Limited supports the Forest Stewardship
Council® (FSC®), the leading international forest-certification organisation.
Our books carrying the FSC label are printed on FSC®-certified paper.
FSC is the only forest-certification scheme supported by the leading
environmental organisations, including Greenpeace. Our paper procurement
policy can be found at www.randomhouse.co.uk/environment

Typeset in Dante MT by Palimpsest Book Production Limited,
Falkirk, Stirlingshire

Printed and bound in Great Britain by Clays Ltd, St Ives plc

For Robert Orme and Graham Bearman, of Latymer Upper School, London: two outstanding teachers of history, to whom I owe much.

CONTENTS

Contents

'Let us consider that we are all partially insane. It will explain us to each other; it will unriddle many riddles; it will make clear many things which are involved in haunting and harassing difficulties and obscurities now.'

Mark Twain, 'Christian Science'

'Imagination rules the world.'

Napoleon Bonaparte

INTRODUCTION

As the son of a Manx Methodist atheist and a refugee German Jewish atheist, I have never been much of a believer. Yet, like everyone else, I find myself surrounded by belief. Belief was in the Lord's Prayer that I murmured uneasily at school assembly, wondering if it was quite *done* for someone like me to repeat the words. Belief was in the churches, and later the mosques, synagogues and temples, that I visited on travels. For that matter a form of belief was responsible, among many other things, for my own existence, when it forced my mother to flee from Germany to England, where she met my father.

Growing up in England gave me a vague knowledge of the official version, at least of Christianity. What, I sometimes wondered, had really happened? What had caused people to come up with such strange-seeming notions as paradise, or sin? Or gods?

This book is an attempt finally to satisfy my curiosity. Broad questions such as *Why did people invent gods?* are, unsurprisingly, hard to answer with certainty, yet I have tried to offer ideas. Where possible I have sought answers from specialist scholars. When questions have been so broad that scholars – no doubt wisely – have averted their eyes, I have done what I can.

One subject this book is *not* concerned with is the history of religious institutions. I find little fascination in organisational power struggles. I wanted to know what ordinary people *believed*. Something else I was keen to avoid was religious jargon. I have tried to recount, as clearly as I could, how beliefs evolved, without recourse to terms that require looking up in a theological dictionary. In these pages you will find no mention of dualism, monism or transubstantiation.

Though I have tried to give an overall picture of people's beliefs, I will not claim that this picture is complete, or even balanced. I have concentrated on those beliefs that I was most curious about, and that seemed to fall into something resembling a story. Though I have looked at beliefs in China, India and the Middle East, as well as the religions of the Mayans, Aztecs and Incas, I have paid particular attention to Christianity, and its parent, Judaism.

This book does not look exclusively at religious belief. I have also glanced at a couple of creeds that are, supposedly, purely political, such as Marxism. I have done so because these ideologies seem, in some ways, remarkably like religions. What is more, many of their ideas were descended from earlier religious notions that one would not normally associate with twentieth-century politics.

This book does not seek to belittle religion. On the contrary, the more I have looked at intense beliefs, the more I have found them fascinating. They say so much about us. As a fiction writer, who tries to make a livelihood from imagination, I have considerable professional respect for what is, I would propose, humankind's greatest imaginative project.

It is a project that has had a huge role in shaping our past. Non-believers ignore it at their peril. Our beliefs have been a conduit for much of our finest creativity in literature, art, music and architecture. They have also inspired a surprising number of our greatest technological breakthroughs. Beliefs have frequently played a key role in shaping the course of great events. I would go so far as to suggest that human history can be rather better understood, not through the clear air of logic and scientific discovery, but through the murky waters of intense, emotional and, at times, downright odd beliefs.

Where and when can one begin to discover such beliefs? The answer is: rather earlier than one might think.

1

INVENTING GODS

Someone Who Picked Up a Piece of Mammoth Tusk

Around 33,000 years ago, in what is now Baden-Württemberg in south-west Germany, but which was then a frozen wilderness nestling between great ice sheets, somebody picked up a piece of mammoth tusk and, probably crouching by a fire to keep warm, began carving.

When finished, the figure they had made was only 2.5 centimetres, or less than an inch, tall. Tiny though it is, it is immediately striking, and also a little puzzling. It stands on two legs, in a pose easily recognisable as human, yet it has a lion's head. Precisely what was done with it remains a mystery, though it was clearly the object of much attention. Over time it became polished smooth from being held by fingers. Eventually, whether deliberately or by accident, it was broken into pieces and left deep in a cave, the Hohle Fels. Here it remained until 2002, when it was discovered, and carefully reassembled, by a paleoanthropologist, Nicolas Conard, and his team.

Why should we be interested in this tiny lion person? It is one of the very oldest examples of figurative art yet found. It also holds another first that, to my eyes, makes it much more intriguing. It is the first clear example of religious art. It provides the earliest evidence that people believed in supernatural beings. Can one really have an idea what beliefs people held 33,000 years ago? The answer, perhaps a little surprisingly, is *yes*.

Why, one might ask, should we be interested in what people believed so very long ago? Put simply, beliefs have a way of enduring. Despite the claims of religious visionaries across the ages, I would suggest that there is no such thing as a new religion. Religions are like ice cores. In each, one can find layer upon layer of past belief. Beliefs, even from 33,000 years ago, are still present in our world. This book seeks to examine some of these ice cores, to discover how their many layers came into being, and see how they continue to influence our world, sometimes in the most unexpected ways.

Before looking at what beliefs the maker of our lion person may have held, I would like to pause for a moment, and consider what one might *expect* them to be. What would people today, whether they believe in a god or not, consider to be the essential prerequisites of any religion?

Paradise would surely come top of the list. One of the chief functions of any religion, surely, is to offer an alternative to the grim prospect of our temporary existence. Almost all modern religions dangle the hope of a happy afterlife that can be reached by their faithful if they follow the rules, at least most of the time. And yet, as will be seen, heaven first appears around 4,000 years ago. This makes it, when compared to the lion-person, a distinctly newfangled invention.

What, then, of morality? This, many would say, is at the very heart of all belief. According to almost all modern religions one's behaviour is carefully supervised by gods, and one's actions will be appropriately rewarded or punished. Yet morality, too, is a relatively new innovation. It appears, in fact, to have emerged side by side with the idea of heaven.

If heaven and morality are not the key elements of all religions, then what is? The answer, I would suggest, is *reassurance*. From the earliest times every religion has given people comfort by offering ways – so their followers believe – of keeping their worst nightmares at bay. What these nightmares are, inevitably, has changed a good deal over time. As people's lifestyles have altered, so have the things they most fear. It is the changes in our *fears*, I would argue, that have caused our religious *ideas* to change. In effect, our need to quell our nightmares has inspired humankind's greatest imaginative project: an epic labour of invention that puts fiction writing to shame.

What were people's worst nightmares 33,000 years ago? How can we hope to have even a vague idea of beliefs that existed a full 28,000 years before writing was first developed, and human history set down? The simple answer is, by making comparisons. By examining peoples whose way of life was recorded in recent times, but who led a similar existence to the carver of the lion person. As we will see, humans are unoriginal creatures. Put them in similar locations, give them similar ways of spending their hours, and similar needs and fears, and they will generally come up with similar ideas about their world.

Studies of hunter-gatherer peoples in recent times have revealed something rather surprising. All across the world, from the Arctic to Australia, from Patagonia to Southern Africa, these peoples, despite having had no direct contact with one another for many tens of thousands of years, had a great deal in common. They all lived in tribes of the same size, of around 150 people. They all moved from place to place with the seasons, and in search of animals to hunt. And they were all very interested in the curious business of going into a trance. Entering a trance, in fact, lay at the centre of all their beliefs.

There was great variety in the way in which different tribes entered a trance, from taking psychotropic substances to starving their senses in silent darkness. Likewise there was variety in who did it: in some tribes many people became entranced, though it was more usual that only one or two specialists did so. These specialists are best described as shamans. The experiences such people had when they entered a trance were very similar the world over. They heard noises like the buzzing of bees, saw geometrical patterns, and had the sensation of being drawn into a great tunnel. They felt they could see themselves transformed into something else, usually an animal. They felt themselves to be flying, and often claimed to be guided by a spirit bird. They would enter a land of spirits, which were also usually animals. These animal spirits had the power to help humans, especially in three precise areas, which recur in hunter-gatherer beliefs all across the world. Firstly, spirits could help heal the sick. Secondly, they could control the movement of animals to hunt. Finally, they could improve the weather.

So, it seems, we catch a glimpse of humans' earliest angst. These fears do not seem particularly surprising. Sickness would have been a constant and incomprehensible danger. For people who had no choice but to spend much of their time outside, bad weather was not only frightening, but life-threatening. Finally, if hunter-gatherers failed to find game to hunt, they would slowly starve to death. So it is only natural that the trio of disease, animal availability and meteorological conditions would have been high on people's worry list.

Can we be sure that these recent hunter-gatherer beliefs were the same as those of the carver of the lion person in the frozen wilderness of Baden-Württemberg 33,000 years ago? It is widely accepted today that the statuette found in the Hohle Fels cave depicts a shaman who is lost in a state of trance and believes himself, or herself, to have been transformed into a lion. It is clear that the Hohle Fels statuette was no random piece of creativity as a second and larger lion-person, dating from around the same time, was found in another nearby cave. It seems these figures represented something that was well established in people's minds. So it appears that as early as 33,000 years ago people had already devised a simple form of religion. If one entered a trance and contacted animal spirits, they might help one cope with disease and bad weather, and make one's endless search for prey a little easier. A way of lessening life's frightening uncertainties had been found.

Clues as to how this early religion might have looked and felt can been found in the remarkable cave paintings of south-western France and northern Spain, some of which date from only 1,000 years or so after our lion-person was carved. The paintings are almost all of animals, and it used to be thought that they depicted hunting scenes. Rather puzzlingly, though, the creatures often lack hooves, so they seem to hang in the air. Also lacking are details of rocks or foliage. What does this signify? David Lewis-Williams, a cognitive archaeologist, came up with a notion. Having studied one of the last hunter-gatherer tribes to have kept its old ways right up to the present – the San people of south-western Africa – and then examining early-European cave paintings, he concluded that these paintings in fact represented animal spirits.

How would these first supernatural beings have been worshipped? What were early religious services like? Archaeological finds offer some ideas. People would have crept into the depths of caves, far beyond the reach of any natural light, using simple lamps made of animal fat on flat pieces of stone, with strands of juniper as wicks. These would have flickered feebly, illuminating only tiny patches of the paintings. Deep in the caves, perhaps with a small congregation gathered round them, shamans would have entered a trance and tried to contact the spirits. There could well have been music. A number of bone flutes have been found in early caves, while people may also have sung or chanted, and used stalagmites as natural bells, striking them to produce deep booming sounds. The caves lacked oxygen, which would have added to the sense of unreality for those taking part. The whole effect of music, smoke, near darkness and airlessness would, when combined with the utterings of the shaman lost in trance, have been intense.

So, even thirty millennia ago, religion was already a leading sponsor of the arts. As people endeavoured to make their world less frightening, and so to feel less helpless, they devoted their hours to making music, to carving sculptures, and to creating paintings that, to this day, remain hauntingly beautiful. It was the beginning of a remarkably fruitful association. Up to our own times religion has encouraged breathtaking art, architecture, music and literature. Whatever reservations one may have about religion, it is hard not to admire the many beautiful creations it has inspired.

Before leaving this distant era, I would like to ask one more question, one that takes us even further back, to times when evidence is negligible and conjecture can only be of the vaguest kind: why might people have devised such a strange thing as religion? What on earth could have prompted them to believe that their fate lay in the hands of beings they could not see or hear, except when lost in a state of trance? Here, unsurprisingly, no clear answer is forthcoming. Yet a little theorising is possible.

In recent decades there has been increasing interest in a

remarkable human ability: one which is on a par with our skill for using complex language, or tools. That this talent had escaped much notice before now was perhaps because it is so basic to our nature that it was almost invisible to us. It is our skill at imagining others' points of view, known as 'Theory of Mind'.

Theory of Mind is something that only humans possess to any degree. Even chimpanzees struggle to comprehend any view outside their own. Theory of Mind lies at the heart of all fiction, and, arguably, storytelling may have come into existence to provide us with a little practice. Fiction certainly offers the best means of describing what Theory of Mind is. Shakespeare's *Othello* is sometimes cited as an example, though any bedroom farce would do. In *Othello* members of the audience need to keep in their heads, simultaneously: Desdemona's point of view (innocent and unknowing), Othello's view of Desdemona (filled with jealous suspicions she has little idea of) and Iago's view of Othello (maliciously leading him astray by planting his suspicions). Plus, perhaps, Shakespeare's view of all the characters, and, finally, the member of the audience's own view of the whole effect. People can routinely balance four or five layers of others' points of view.

Why did humans develop this skill to such remarkable levels? Almost certainly because it was key to our ancestors' survival. In a hunter-gatherer tribe, where violence was likely to have been common, especially when stomachs were empty, having a good grasp of Theory of Mind would have helped people to recognise, and fend off, danger from their fellow humans. It would have allowed them to make alliances and friendships, to win the help of others in protecting and feeding themselves and, crucially, in protecting and feeding their children. It would have been a case of *survival of the most intuitive*.

This remarkable talent for Theory of Mind leads us to *imagine other people's thinking*, every waking moment of the day, whether we intend to or not. We constantly consider others' feelings towards ourselves, and try to guess the reasons for their behaviour. It seems not such a big step to suppose that, at some point long ago, our specialisation led us to start detecting humanlike personalities even outside the world of humans. We began to detect them *everywhere*. We began to see human points of view in anything that was important to our survival. We saw human moods in the sky, in the weather, in brooks we drank from, in trees that might conceal prey or give us shade. Most of all we gave human personalities to animals, whose thinking we needed to understand if we were to find and hunt them. Almost anything could be given a personality, or spirit. Naturally we sought help from these beings, just as we sought help from one another. To contact these spirits, people entered that mysterious state of trance, which they found they were also skilled at. So, it may have been, that we invented our very first gods.

There would, needless to say, be many, many more.

A New Pastime on a Bare Mountain

One day, around 9,500 BC, on a mountaintop with panoramic views – now Göbekli Tepe in modern south-east Turkey – a group of people occupied themselves doing something wholly new. It was also wholly backbreaking. They chipped away at a bed of limestone rock, using only tiny flint blades, until they had cut free a gigantic piece of stone. Thin and T-shaped, it looked like a huge, slender stone mallet. It was five metres high and weighed almost ten tons. The group then hauled the stone for several hundred metres to the mountain's summit, where they set it carefully upright, facing another just like it. The two became the centrepiece of a stone circle, dug into the ground like a kind of sunken bath and enclosed by a wall, which contained no fewer than eight more giant mallet-shaped stones.

At some point the circle was covered with earth, and, over a period of some 1,500 years, another nineteen or so circles were created, on top of one another, so they formed a large mound on the mountain's summit. On some stones there were carvings of scorpions, foxes, snakes, lions and other creatures. One was decorated with the disturbing image of a detached human arm. Some had patterns that, to modern eyes, look beguilingly – and misleadingly – like writing. Finally, around 8000 BC, after some fifteen centuries of work, the site was abandoned. It remained forgotten for another 10,000 years, until, in 1994, it was visited by the archaeologist Klaus Schmidt, who quickly realised he had found something remarkable.

The people who built Göbekli Tepe did not live there. No houses or waste tips have been found that would indicate the presence of a village. It seems they clambered up the mountainside from settlements elsewhere. They *commuted*. Why, one might wonder, did they choose to make their lives so very hard? Why, instead of struggling up a mountain, to carve out and haul vast pieces of stone, did they not just stay comfortably down below, as their ancestors had been content to do? Why not spend their hours on tasks that were easier, and more practically useful, like gathering nuts or hunting animals? What, once they had built a stone circle, did they do up there?

As is so often the case when looking back to prehistoric times, answers are elusive. In fact, in many ways, it is harder to guess what went on at Göbekli Tepe than it is to guess what occurred some 20,000 years earlier in the painted caves of Europe, whose occupants' religion is easily comparable with those of recent times. This situation may change. Only a small part of the Göbekli

Tepe site has so far been excavated, and further work may provide new clues. In the meantime, it is possible at least to point to an idea that, almost certainly, was keenly present in the minds of stone-circle makers. This was a notion that had a limited place among hunter-gatherers, but was much in vogue among the societies that gradually displaced them. It was *sacrifice*.

It is not hard to imagine where the idea originated. Humans constantly interact with one another *reciprocally*. We do each other favours and keep a rough tab of what we owe and are owed. People may sometimes choose to ignore the reciprocity system, and give without expecting anything in return, but this, I would suggest, is a little exceptional, and is usually seen as such, entitling the giver to special prestige. If this seems a rather cold-blooded account of human behaviour, ask yourself how you would feel if a friend, who is as well provided with the necessities of life as yourself, repeatedly asks you for favours, but refuses to give anything in return, or even to recognize his or her rising debt. You would probably feel used. The notches on your tabs would become so far apart that your friendship would come under strain.

It makes sense that a system which is profoundly engrained in our thinking would become extended also to the world of our invented helpers: the gods. If supernatural beings were going to save us from our nightmares then surely, like humans, they would expect something in return. As the help of the gods was, in people's imaginations, of great value, so people's payment to them, or sacrifice, also had to be of great value. It had to be difficult. And what could be more difficult than repeatedly climbing the slope of Göbekli Tepe, to chip away with tiny flint blades, and haul ten-ton slabs of limestone.

Hunter-gatherers, such as the carver of our lion-person, do not seem to have been especially interested in sacrifice. Why did the idea become so popular? The answer is almost certainly connected with what was, arguably, humankind's greatest lifestyle change. Around 9600 BC – roughly the same time that people began climbing up the slopes of Göbekli Tepe – the climate suddenly and dramatically improved. After a thousand-year mini ice age, the Middle East became green and temperate. This change allowed people to achieve something that had eluded them until then. They were able to give up their endless wandering and settle down in permanent villages. Country life had begun. People were not yet farmers, but they were close. They were *hunter-gardeners* cultivating wild crops, which they harvested with bone scythes lined with sharpened stones.

With this new lifestyle would have come new fears. Hunter-gatherers' lives may have been dangerous, but at least they were uncomplicated. They wandered from place to place, hoping to find and kill prey without being injured or killed themselves. They lived from day to day. Though people in villages would have enjoyed more regular meals, their lives may also have felt more precarious. They had to think ahead, clearing land for their wild crops to grow, while these crops, on which they soon depended, could be suddenly and unexpectedly destroyed by disease or bad weather.

Village life would have helped people come up with projects like Göbekli Tepe. For a start, village life meant that there were now many more people to work on a backbreaking sacrifice project. As Massimo Livi-Bacci has shown in his study of population, when people stop constantly moving around, and no longer have to carry their small children from place to place, they have children more frequently. Thanks to the dramatic improvement in the climate, food was now more plentiful. Consequently this era would have seen a rapid rise in population. Once harvests were brought in, people would have had something they had never enjoyed before: spare time. People had the numbers and the leisure to embark on vast ventures to keep their gods sweet.

The results were spectacular. On Göbekli Tepe people constructed what is almost certainly the very first *purpose-built temple*. They created the first monolithic stone circles, which are more than twice as old as Stonehenge. They devised what was, in effect, the first architecture. They may also have inspired, unintentionally, another remarkable first, at least in the Middle East: farming. Genetic studies show that many key crops which are eaten across the Western world today are directly descended from wild plants that still grow in a single, small area: the Karadag hills in southern Turkey. The Karadag hills, as it happens, are only twenty kilometres from Göbekli Tepe. It seems a great coincidence that a number of major farming crops should have originated so close to this remarkable place. Almost certainly, there is no coincidence at all.

The archaeologist Jacques Cauvin has suggested that Göbekli Tepe helped *cause* the discovery of farming in the Middle East. How could a set of stone circles bring about one of humankind's greatest discoveries? To answer, I first need to explain, very briefly, what farming was, and how it was altogether different from the hunter-gardening of wild crops that people had practised before. Farming was, in effect, humankind's first foray into the world of *genetic manipulation*. People nurtured rare mutant types of crops, which failed to release their seeds. This meant we could thresh them and catch every grain. For these suicidal varieties to prevail over the older, non-suicidal wild varieties – which *did* release their seeds – they needed to be planted in new locations, to reduce competition from wild crops. In effect, they had to be transported by humans. Pilgrim rock cutters clambering up to Göbekli Tepe would have done precisely this. As nobody was permanently living on the mountain, they would have needed to bring seeds there, to eat and perhaps sow. Studies of food remains from Göbekli Tepe show that farming had not begun when the site was built. The seeds are of wild varieties, not cultivated. Until recently it was widely assumed that organised religion grew from farming. In the Middle East at least, it now seems that the exact opposite was true: farming was a spin-off from organized religion. As we will see, it was the first of many technological breakthroughs that religion would inspire.

But heaving ten ton blocks of stone was not the only kind of sacrifice that people invented in their efforts to impress super-natural beings. At Çayönü , a few dozen kilometres from Göbekli Tepe, between 8000 and 7000 BC, or just after Göbekli Tepe was abandoned, something very *grisly* seems to have taken place.

Archaeological excavations have uncovered the remains of a small, rectangular building with a semicircular apse in one wall. In its day it would have looked a little like a tiny Christian church. In a side chamber was found a huge polished stone, weighing close to a ton, along with a large flint blade. Both were stained with copious quantities of blood: from sheep, wild cattle and humans. In other antechambers were almost 300 human skulls, together with numerous other human remains, most of which belonged to young adults. It is widely assumed that the inhabit-ants of Çayönü indulged in large-scale human sacrifice.

They were almost certainly not alone. At one of the world's earliest towns, the settlement of Jericho in today's Palestinian West Bank, the archaeologist Kathleen Kenyon found, in only one small portion of the site, the remains of almost 300 people. These were dispersed right through the very fabric of the settlement: under floors, between walls and in the town's stone tower. Especially disturbing was the large number of infant remains that Kenyon found. These were buried either in the walls of homes or beneath their front doors, indicating that they had been placed there for a specific purpose. Some corpses had been buried, then dug up again, and then had their skulls reburied, placed carefully in stacks, facing one another. Some had been picked out for honorary treatment, their faces re-created with plaster, with cowrie shells for eyes.

Then there is Çatalhöyük in western Turkey, which is surely one of the strangest settlements ever to have existed. The town, which peaked around 7000 BC, had no streets, so its houses formed a solid mass, and inhabitants could reach their homes only by walking over those of their neighbours, and then clambering down ladders through a hole in the roof. Though nobody has any idea what religious beliefs Çatalhöyükans may have had, the excavated remains of their town suggest an intense, even obsessive, state of mind. All houses were virtually identical, with their tiny, dark rooms, their hearths and their sleeping platforms arranged in precisely the same way. Some houses had bizarre wall paintings, painted and repainted dozens of times, of skulls and bulls, and of vultures feeding on headless humans. Others were decorated with wall reliefs of giant female breasts, whose nipples were pierced by real animal skulls. As at Jericho, human remains were found through the fabric of the town, between walls, and under floors and sleeping platforms. Male remains show a suspiciously high occurrence of wounds to their arms and skulls. The archaeologist Klaus Schmidt believes that human remains may well also be found beneath the stone circles of Göbekli Tepe.

So a shadowy picture begins to emerge of a culture of sacrifice. It seems people tried to bribe the gods into helping them – or at least into not punishing them – by sacrificing their time, their labour, their animals and themselves. On the evidence of later religions, they probably also made less dramatic, day-to-day offerings of small quantities of their food, which were burned or left out to rot.

It is time, though, to move on from vague conjecture. A new technological breakthrough was on its way, one which would allow us, for the first time, to see people's religious beliefs in clear detail: writing.

Dressing for Breakfast

Around 2100 BC at a temple in the city of Nippur, south of modern Baghdad – a religious centre that was the Mecca, or Rome, of early Mesopotamia – the chief of all the gods, and controller of weather, Enlil, dressed for breakfast. This was not a special day at Enlil's temple. No festival was taking place, bringing throngs of visitors. No god or goddess from a neighbouring city had come to pay court, their statue carried up the Euphrates in a huge, ceremonial barge. Thousands of days like this one had already occurred, and many thousands more would do so over the next two millennia.

Enlil – or rather his statue – would have been dressed in his private apartment, which was probably located on top of a kind of flat-topped Mesopotamian pyramid, or ziggurat. His wardrobe was extensive, and included loincloths, linen coats, lapis lazuli beads, silver earrings and gold rings. More remarkable than the clothes he wore, though, were Enlil's meals. Enlil would have dined four times a day, enjoying two light snacks and two full feasts. His food would have been brought by temple staff on great platters, which were placed before him, as drums were beaten and hymns sung. Enlil's feeding required considerable organisation. Towns around Nippur took turns sending him cattle by the dozen, sheep and goats by the score, as well as huge quantities of butter, cheese, grain, fruit, beer and just about anything else that could be eaten or drunk. Near Enlil's temple, special warehouses and animal pens had been built as part of a vast state apparatus to keep him amenable.

We have this portrait of Enlil's daily routine and the vast economic system it spawned thanks to the invention of writing. Yet writing itself was almost certainly a spin-off from this religious machinery. The breakthrough that made it possible – coming up with the bizarre notion of representing sound with written signs – first occurred in Mesopotamia. Steven Roger Fischer, a historian of writing, goes so far as to suggest that it may well never have occurred anywhere else, and that all subsequent writing systems across the world are likely to have descended from a single Mesopotamian original.

This first breakthrough probably took place around 3500 BC, and it happened, almost certainly, in the world's first great city, Uruk, near present-day Basra in southern Iraq. How did it happen? A clue can be found in the very earliest written documents yet found, which date from around 3100 BC. These are not history or poetry or literature. Aside from a few magic spells, they largely consist of *accountancy*. They record temple transactions and receipts for goods received. It is likely that the breakthrough behind writing was stumbled upon in a busy warehouse, filled with grain, oil, and animals for Uruk's gods.

Thanks to writing we have for the first time a relatively precise idea of what people believed, and what rituals they followed. So what was Mesopotamian religion like? One of its most noticeable aspects was that it *had no heaven*. Mesopotamians looked forward to an afterlife, but it was a miserable existence, in a dark, grey underworld. Even monarchs were destined to spend their days here, and the world's first example of great literature, the Epic of Gilgamesh, tells the story of a Mesopotamian king who tries to escape this fate, and fails. Mesopotamians were not alone in believing in a dismal afterlife. The same notion can be found in early societies all around the world, from China to Mexico, and from Central Asia to Greece and Egypt. It is quite possible that this was a universal belief. The cognitive archaeologist David Lewis-Williams has suggested that the idea originated in the cave religion of the hunter-gatherers, and was inspired by the caves themselves, which seemed to reach down deep into the earth. Animal spirits were believed to live just beyond the caves' walls, so it would make sense that dead humans also dwelt there. Such a dismal afterlife may well have troubled the dreams of the carver of our lion-person, 33,000 years ago.

A second curiosity of early Mesopotamian religion was that it was not based on morality, or at least not any morality that we would recognise today. Yes, a person could do right and wrong, and their choices would decide whether gods would treat them kindly or otherwise. Doing right or wrong, however, had little to do with a person's general behaviour or how they acted towards other people. Rather it concerned showing proper respect for the gods, by performing laboriously complex rituals without making mistakes.

Who were these gods? They were just the sort of deities you would expect to have been imagined by people struggling to grow crops in their irrigated fields. There were farming gods, of grain, of fresh water, of cattle and sheep, and of rats and mice (whom you prayed to so as to keep the hungry creatures away). There were catastrophe gods, of storms, of disease, and of fire. There were gods of the weather, of the sky, and of creation. There were household gods of home and hearth. And there were relationship gods, of sex, fertility and motherhood. One can find much the same mix in other early farming societies, naturally with some local adjustments, such as rice gods in China and maize gods in the Americas.

Our first clear glimpse of religion reveals that it already played a huge part in people's lives. Arguably, in fact, early Mesopotamia was one of the most intensely religious societies the world has ever seen. Religion was *everywhere*. It was at the heart of Mesopotamian politics. The first Mesopotamian states were ruled by priest kings, an arrangement that seems to have existed in numerous early farming societies, from the Yucatán to Rome to China, and which Lewis-Williams suggests may also have been a direct inheritance from earlier times. The new priest-kings were simply shamans with greater responsibility and greater power.

Religion was also at the heart of the Mesopotamian economy. It is no exaggeration to say that, in early Mesopotamian states, economic output was moulded around the idea of *god-bribery*. We have already seen the arrangements that went into Enlil's meals: regions offered a large part of their produce and transported it to the capital, Nippur, where it was stored in warehouses and pens, then prepared and brought to Enlil.

What is less clear is what happened to the food afterwards. Choice items no doubt went to temple staff, and much of it may have been stored for times of shortage. As for the rest, some may have gone to widows and orphans in the care of the temple. Some may have been distributed among the people of Nippur, or even returned – now less fresh – to the farmlands from where they had come. Much may have been sold. Mesopotamia's great temples were economic powerhouses, acting as banks and moneylenders and their expenses would have been considerable. What seems quite clear is that the movement of food would have been decided by priests and priest-kings. So, through religion, Mesopotamia evolved a kind of *controlled economy*.

Religion had come a very long way from the simple days of our carver of the lion-person in frozen Baden-Württemberg.

And yet, it might be asked, did it *work*? Did this vast machinery of god-placation give Mesopotamians a sense of reassurance? The answer, rather unhappily, seems to have been no. By all accounts Mesopotamia was a highly anxious place, as the historian Jean Bottéro describes:

> It was as if, in the minds of the people, everything was extremely fragile and perishable, constantly dependent on the sovereign activities of the gods . . . only their intervention, constantly renewed, could prevent things from perishing and disappearing.'[1]

Why were the Mesopotamians so anxious? I suggested earlier that a culture's religious beliefs mirror its worst nightmares, and the Mesopotamians certainly had a great deal to trouble their sleep. Irrigation farming had many risks. One might sow one's seeds too late or mistime the harvest. One's crop might be eaten by rats or locusts; it might be destroyed by disease or spoil in storage. Epidemics would have swept regularly across the land. As the population swelled, and people became increasingly dependent on a small number of crops, narrowing their diets, they would have suffered increasingly from malnutrition, iron deficiency and osteoporosis.

Mesopotamians, in fact, had more to worry about even than other irrigation farmers. The Tigris and Euphrates rivers could change their courses without warning, leaving whole populations stranded in desert wasteland (something which happened to the city of Nippur not once, but *twice*). The rivers often flooded at the wrong time – when crops were almost fully grown and could easily be drowned by too much water – requiring Mesopotamians to maintain an immensely complex system of canals and storage tanks. The floods might also be poor, or fail altogether. Famine would have been a constant, lurking threat.

The Mesopotamians' anxiousness may also have sprung from the very beliefs that should have eased their fears. Mesopotamian religion – perhaps in reflection of people's lives – was fiendishly complicated. Gods ran into the hundreds, if not thousands. Rituals to placate them were likewise convoluted, while a single mistake would be enough to render them void, and leave the gods furious – and vengeful – at being dishonoured. Early Mesopotamians were constantly watching for indications that a god was angry and that disaster threatened. They believed such signs might be found in almost anything: an odd arrangement of the stars, a sacrificed animal with the wrong kind of liver, or simply a stranger you passed in the street who had the wrong kind of face. They might be revealed by your chancing upon a broken pot, or a menstruating prostitute, or by discovering a stray cat of the wrong colour in your house.

Yet Mesoptamians did not give up. When faced by a bad sign, they valiantly attempted to conduct, without error, the ritual appropriate for placating the god in question. As an example of what this could involve, here is the procedure that had to be followed if a deformed foetus – animal or human – was born in your household (a very bad sign indeed). First, the chief of the household had to take the foetus to the riverbank. Here he would build a small reed hut, complete with a tiny reed altar, where he left an offering of beer, food, and also a little silver and gold. Next he placed the foetus on the ground and flattered the poor, dead thing, tricking it into thinking it was about to be honoured. He did this by placing a gold pin at its head, and perhaps also a little gold breastplate. When the householder was confident the foetus had been lured into a false sense of security he recited a prayer begging the god of justice, Samas, for help. Only then could he slip the foetus into the river, and hope that it would find peace. But the process was fraught with the possibility of failure. What if the reed hut had been incorrectly built, or if the offering to the god were too small? What if the foetus had not been flattered enough, or if a mistake had been made in the prayer? The whole effort would be useless.

Out of such anxiousness a new idea was born. According to Jean Bottéro, around 2500 BC Mesopotamians came up with a terrifying concept: *sin*. This notion was very different from the sin of today. It was not a moral concept. For Mesopotamians, sin was not concerned with one's behaviour. It was about making a mistake in some ritual or sacrifice that would cause a god to feel dishonoured and to mete out punishment through his or her enforcers: a kind of *supernatural police force*, known as daemons. You might not even realize that you had made a mistake. From fears that you *might have done so*, came the terrible logic of sin. Sin assumed that if you were struck by misfortune, this could only be because you had committed a transgression against a god. If your cow died or your house was blown down in a sandstorm, it was *your own fault*. Punishment was proof of guilt.

Mesopotamians became obsessed with this appalling idea, and even gave their children names such as *What is my sin?* and *What sin have I committed against a god?* If someone was struck by bad luck, their only hope was to go over the heads of the daemons and win round their controllers, the gods, with *correct* rituals and sacrifice. It was a little like bribing a malleable ciric mayor to call off the police from investigating your crimes.

Occasionally, we glimpse signs of protest against this oppressive belief. The *Poem of the Righteous Sufferer*, written around 1500 BC, paints a searing portrait of a man who feels he has honoured the god Marduk correctly in every way, yet finds his life has fallen apart.

> I, who walked proudly, learned slinking,
> I, so grand, became servile,

> My brother became my foe,
> My friend became a malignant demon,
> My slave cursed me openly in the assembly of gentlefolk
> My slave girl defamed me before the rabble,
> A pit awaited anyone speaking well of me,
> While he who was uttering defamation of me forged ahead,
> They let another assume my duties,
> They appointed an outsider to my prerogatives.
> The sources of my watercourses they blocked with muck,
> They chased the harvest song from my fields.[2]

Yet, in spite of the constant uncertainty that it inspired, ancient Mesopotamian religion was highly enduring. The same gods were worshipped in much the same way for close to 3,000 years. Over this huge period of time, did Mesopotamians become less anxious? It seems not. In fact, in later Mesopotamia angst prevailed among the very people one would have expected to be immune: the most powerful people in the Middle East. For, by the seventh century BC, northern Mesopotamians had created one of history's first superpowers and one of its most ruthless: the Assyrian Empire. Yet its all-powerful rulers could be as fearful of inauspicious signs as any village farmer.

A king, of course, could answer his fears in very different ways from a poor farmer. In the 670s BC King Essarhaddon, worried that he might miss signs sent by the gods, created a vast state machinery to seek them out. Agents across the Empire watched for any seemingly trivial yet odd occurrence that might warn of a god's anger, from an odd star in the sky to a fox falling down a well. All such information was sent on to the Assyrian capital, Nineveh, and recorded on clay tablets, in one of the world's first great libraries. Thus Essarhaddon created a kind of *CIA of the supernatural*, for which his library at Nineveh was the database.

And if there was an inauspicious sign? Like Mesopotamians 2,000 years earlier, Essarhaddon would try to placate the gods with rituals, chants and prayers, conducted by professional diviners, who would have wielded considerable power at court. The older an incantation, the more powerful it was thought to be, and for this reason the library at Nineveh contained numerous texts written in a Mesopotamian language that had been dead for a thousand years: Sumerian. Assyrian scribes continued to learn it so that its magical formulas could be recited. And if spells were not enough, the Assyrian king could replace himself, for a time, with a double, who would absorb the gods' anger and who was probably quietly disposed of when his work was done.

Why were the rulers of the world's greatest empire so full of fear? Assyrian kings had to keep constant watch for plots against them, by their generals, and often also by their closest relatives. The Empire, despite its ruthless brutality – or perhaps because of it – suffered constant rebellions from its subject peoples. The Empire's very success may have bred insecurity. From such heights, the only way to go was down. And, as events proved, Essarhaddon was right to be anxious. Within two generations of his death, the Assyrian Empire had disintegrated, and his library of the supernatural in Nineveh had been burned to the ground (a blessing for historians as its clay tablets became baked hard like so many bricks). From now on Mesopotamia had to endure the humiliating role of a land ruled by others: Persians, Greeks, Parthians and Romans.

Mesopotamian religion, too, entered a slow decline, as new rivals closed in, stealing away believers. Because, even long before Essarhaddon's time, a great sea change had begun. A new belief was emerging both to the east and west of Mesopotamia : one that would prove to be enduringly beguiling, because it offered a wholly new kind of reassurance.

2

INVENTING PARADISE

Cape Canaveral of Dead Kings

One day, around 2570 BC, at Giza in Egypt, a group of labourers set to work on a task that would have been all too familiar to the workaholics we saw on Göbekli Tepe mountain, some 7,000 years earlier. They were dragging a huge piece of stone across the ground.

How had the life of a stone hauler changed over these seven millennia? In some ways the Giza group had things easy compared to their Göbekli Tepe predecessors. Though little is known of the methods they employed, it is thought they used sleds or rollers to lighten their work. By contrast, the Göbekli Tepe workers probably had only the crudest version of such devices, if they had any at all. The Giza haulers' stone was squarer, and much less fragile than the thin, mallet-shaped pieces of 9500 BC. It was also much lighter. At two and a half tons, it weighed only a quarter as much as the stones hauled across the summit of Göbekli Tepe mountain.

Overall, though, the Giza workmen could have looked on their Göbekli Tepe predecessors with some envy, as the latters' work, though backbreaking, was at least highly occasional. The twenty stone circles on Göbekli Tepe were built, it is thought, over a period of some fifteen centuries, or across sixty generations, while each circle contained only a handful of giant stones. On average, a dozen or so stones would have been cut and moved every seventy-five years. By contrast, the project at Giza, which was probably completed in around twenty-three years, contained more than two million huge pieces of stone. In other words, for twenty-three years a huge stone would have been cut, hauled and moved into place, day and night, every *five minutes*.

These Egyptians were, of course, building the great pyramid of Pharaoh Khufu, also known as Cheops: one of the earliest great stone buildings and, to this day, still the world's largest. They were constructing a tomb for their ruler. But these stone haulers were also doing something else, of which they would have been wholly unaware. They were, in their own small way, contributing to the development of a new invention: one that would go on to catch the imagination of most of humankind: Heaven.

How so? A clue lies in the ancient Egyptian ritual known as the Opening of the Mouth Ceremony. This ritual was originally used to activate newly made statues of gods. A priest would touch the statue's lips, probably with his fingers, and, in Egyptian imagination, bring it to life, much as a midwife might clear the mouth of a newborn baby. By the era of Pharaoh Khufu, in the mid twenty-sixth century BC, not only statues were enjoying Frankenstein-like animation. The corpses of freshly dead pharaohs were being symbolically returned to life with the same ritual. Egypt's rulers had attained a remarkable promotion. Uniquely among their countrymen, they possessed a spiritual force known as *ba*. They had become living supernatural beings.

A thousand miles to the east, Mesopotamian kings could not dream of such status.

Not that the pharaohs were seen as possessing all the powers of a great god. Such a claim, after all, would have led to unrealistic expectations among their subjects. Rather, they were viewed as a kind of lesser supernatural being, floating midway between the worlds of humans and the gods. In Egyptians' eyes, they were very valuable. A pharaoh, once dead, was regarded as a kind of *lobbyist to the divine*. At dawn each morning he would fly up from his tomb and accompany the greatest of all the deities, the sun god Ra, on his daily journey across the sky. Dead pharaohs had Ra's ear, and could urge him to keep the seasons turning, to make sure the Nile flooded at the right time, and not to wreak havoc on humankind.

Naturally this cause was regarded as worth supporting. Modern, cynical eyes might regard the pyramids as monuments to pharaonic power and egotism – which no doubt, in part, they were – but it is highly doubtful that Egyptians thought of them in this way. There is no evidence that they were built by coercion. The tombs of the workmen who constructed Khufu's great pyramid are too close to the royal grave to be those of slaves, indicating that they had been free men. This notion is supported by graffiti in the workers' tombs, in which they describe themselves as the 'friends of Khufu'. So it appears that the pyramids were constructed through a huge voluntary national effort. Some Egyptians cut and heaved stones. Others worked their fields for them and sent them food . They did so because they believed this was in their own interest. By honouring dead pharaohs, and helping them in their lobbying work, Egyptians imagined they were making their own lives safer.

As a result of this belief, Giza became a kind of *supernatural Cape Canaveral* of its time, from which pharaohs ascended into the heavens. Every care was taken to help the country's dead rulers perform their vital mission. Research was undertaken to improve embalming techniques – never very successful – so that the pharaohs' bodies would be kept as intact as possible for their supernatural work. They were built replica palaces to inhabit. Riverboats, some carefully dismantled, were buried around the pyramids so pharaohs could travel across the sky in proper style. Small cities were constructed near each pyramid, for priests and their attendants, who conducted regular rituals to honour each dead ruler and to provide him with regular meals.

This vast project transformed Egypt. A complex new state apparatus was created to administer the logistics. The country became aggressively expansionist, as Egyptian armies marched into modern northern Sudan to secure gold to embellish the pharaohs' tombs. But the project also *ruined* Egypt. In spite of Sudanese gold, the cost of servicing dead pharaohs would have been cripplingly high to the Egyptian state. Worse, it would have become more so with time, as each new royal corpse required a new pyramid, and a new priest-city to honour him. The financial strain of such arrangements is thought to have been a key factor in the collapse of the early Egyptian state known as the Old Kingdom. Four centuries after Khufu's pyramid had been completed, Egypt disintegrated into famine, banditry and feuding warlord states.

But what, we may ask, does any of this have to do with the invention of heaven? Put simply, the pharaohs were the very first people who could look forward to a kind of *paradise*. There is no evidence of anybody having hopes of a happy afterlife before them. Mesopotamian kings were resigned to enduring a miserable, underground existence after they died. By contrast, Old Kingdom pharaohs, such as Khufu could look forward to a joyful eternity, flying through the sky in the company of gods.

This appealing idea soon proved infectious. Five hundred years after Khufu's death, it was not only pharaohs who could look forward to their deaths. When Egypt re-emerged from collapse in the twenty-first century BC, pharaohs' privileges had been usurped. In the Middle Kingdom, Egyptian aristocrats claimed to possess the spiritual force, *ba*, that had been the unique property of the pharaohs. They had themselves embalmed and placed in lavish tombs, and had their coffins decorated with texts copied from those of the pharaohs. They even had tiny chapels built, where their relatives could pay their respects to them, in imitation of the huge temple complexes erected to honour pharaohs.

How could pharaohs have allowed their monopoly to be broken? They had brought it upon themselves, by letting their grip on power slip away. Local magnates died like pharaohs because they ruled like miniature pharaohs. Paradise became the new fashion, so much so that in the Middle Kingdom the old royal god, Ra, became displaced as the country's most popular deity by Osiris, the king of the underworld. Osiris offered an inspiring *personal* example of how one might overcome death, in a story that every Egyptian would have known. He was murdered by his wicked brother Seth, who, just to make quite sure of matters, then cut Osiris's remains up into tiny pieces, which he scattered across the land. It was not precaution enough, though. Their sister Isis carefully gathered up Osiris's body parts, put them back together, reanimated her brother and then sired a child by him: the king of the living world, Horus.

Osiris's rites, which had been the monopoly of kings, gradually became available to everyone. Though non-pharaohs could not expect to fly through the sky in the company of gods, they hoped to find themselves in Osiris's underworld, which was now a happy, desirable destination. After a further national collapse around 1650 BC, when the Middle Kingdom fell to a revolt by what appear to have been mercenaries or slaves from Asia – the Hyksos – even Egypt's poor became paradise-obsessed. During the country's third great era, the New Kingdom, pilgrims flocked to pay Osiris homage at his cult centre, in Abydos. At the end of the holiday season, when the Nile was flooded and no farm work could be done, Egyptians held an eighteen-day festival in the god's honour, called *Khoiakh*, during which priests produced amateur theatricals re-enacting his grisly life.

By this time Egypt had not one happy afterlife, but *three*. Each was carefully tailored to its clients' notion of an ideal existence. Pharaohs continued to look forward to flying across the skies with gods. Poor Egyptian farmers, by contrast, hoped to spend their afterlife years tilling little plots of land beyond the western horizon, in the Field of Reeds, where it was always springtime and there was no danger of bad weather or plagues of locusts. Such an afterlife, needless to say, held little appeal to aristocrats. They looked forward to a leisured eternity. To be certain of this, they filled their tombs with models, known as *ushabtis*, which they believed would be brought to life to become their loyal servants when their own bodies were reanimated by the Opening of the Mouth Ceremony. Tombs of wealthy Egyptians had *ushabti* Nile boats, complete with oarsmen, and some contained whole fleets. There were *ushabti* dwarfs and musicians for entertainment, *ushabti* pet animals, and even *ushabti* concubines, for after-death pleasure. Most of all, however, nobles' tombs abounded with *usahbti* farmers, often by the hundred, so that the tomb's owner could be absolutely sure that he would not have to dirty his hands in the fields.

Egypt's New Kingdom, offers us our first clear glimpse of a fully functioning afterlife-fixated society. Egyptians prepared for their afterlife much as modern Westerners plan for their retirement. For the wealthy, preparing for one's death was not unlike moving house. This was certainly the case with Kha, a methodical man who hid his own tomb where robbers would not expect to find it, so that – almost uniquely – it remained intact until it was rediscovered by archaeologist Ernesto Schiaparelli in 1906. Inside, perfectly preserved, were Kha's wooden bed and bedsheets, his best clothes and jewellery, his work tools and even his favourite game, *sene:* a version of snakes and ladders, in which, appropriately enough, one landed on auspicious or inauspicious squares. Kha had had prepared loaves of bread, and jars of wine and oil, for his after-death meals, along with vegetables, which had been carefully mashed up, because Kha had lost almost all his teeth. There was a copy of the Book of the Dead – a kind of ancient Egyptian user's guide to the afterlife – which even contained a picture of Osiris warmly welcoming Kha to the underworld, along with his wife Meryt, who had died a few years earlier. She lay in an adjoining chamber, in a sarcophagus noticeably cheaper than Kha's own.

Not that Kha could take his admission to Osiris's afterworld for granted. New Kingdom Egyptians agreed that – pharaohs excepted – you might not get in. Success depended on your behaviour in life. So we come to the other great innovation of this time, which seems to have developed in parallel with the notion of heaven: the rise of *morality* in religion. Morality, needless to say, was far from being a new invention in itself. It is likely that it far pre-dated any form of religion. It would have emerged from the rules of behaviour that governed early hunter-gatherer societies, and which, in simpler form, even exist among groups of chimpanzees. Now it became the price of the ultimate supernatural reassurance: a never-ending happy life.

How was one's behaviour judged? At a supernatural trial, naturally. Dead Egyptians of the New Kingdom expected to face a court of no fewer than forty-two gods, in a process that Osiris himself was believed to have undergone. They had to swear to each god in turn, that they had not committed transgressions during their lifetime. After this their hearts were placed in a set of scales and balanced against the feather of truth. The goddess of Fate, Shai, then gave judgement on the deceased's character. If he or she was innocent, the two scales would balance exactly, and the deceased could proceed directly to a happy afterlife. If the heart was heavier than the feather, however, the individual guilty, and the heart would be tossed to a hungrily waiting mythical animal. Instead of enjoying a happy afterlife, the poor unfortunate would die a mortal death.

If ritual sin came to obsess Mesopotamians, it was morality that caught the imagination of early Egyptians. During the Middle and New Kingdoms, writings known as wisdom literature appeared, in which a wise older figure advises a younger son, or pupil, as to how he must conduct himself in life. The values that emerge seem, to modern eyes, decidedly old-fashioned. One should treat people fairly, be always honest and well-mannered, and behave correctly towards those higher or lower in rank. One should walk respectfully behind higher officials, speak well of one's parents, and not be greedy in life or become too friendly with women in other households.

By the New Kingdom, if not before, a clear link had been forged in the Egyptian imagination between a person's behaviour in life and their hopes of a happy eternal existence. We might wonder, was this inevitable? Why did people not opt, instead, for a happy afterlife for *everyone*, as was the case with the earlier, miserable afterlife? Why make gods supernatural snoops, endlessly judging humans' moral behaviour? Why, for that matter, did the idea of a happy afterlife, which now seems so pivotal to religion, emerge only now and not much earlier? To answer such questions, it is useful to look at some other happy heavens, because paradise – like many other discoveries – was invented not once but many times, quite separately, in different parts of the world.

Zarathustra and Friends

One day, perhaps around 1200 BC, though it may have been several centuries earlier or later, a traveller and exile, who had been wandering for many years, arrived in a new kingdom. The whereabouts of this kingdom are, like the date, unclear, though it may well have been in modern Afghanistan. As for the man, he was Zarathustra, the founder of Zoroastrianism: a religion of vast influence which endures to this day.

Zarathustra is the earliest religious founder about whose life any details are known. So we have our very first glimpse of the dispiriting career of a prophet. Zarathustra had been trained as a priest in the traditional religion of his people, nomadic Central Asian Iranians – a multigod arrangement that was a close cousin of the religions of classical Greece and Rome, and also northern India, One day, though, as he gathered water from a river, Zarathustra had a vision which turned him strongly against the beliefs he had been brought up with. He began preaching his new religion, made enemies and was forced to leave his homeland. For years he wandered, having won only a single convert to his movement: his cousin Maidhyoimanha.

It was only when he arrived in the land of King Vishtaspa that Zarathustra's luck finally changed. His breakthrough came when he converted the king's wife, Hutaosa. This was a common enough road to success for a prophet. Across the ages women frequently proved more open to radically new religious ideas than men. Doubtless with Hutaosa's help, Zarathustra then won over King Vishtaspa. Again, this would prove a standard path for a successful religion. Converting a ruler, as will be seen, would be the making of most leading religions, from Christianity and Manichaeism to Buddhism and Jainism. Even Zoroastrianism would only find true success when, centuries after Zarathustra's time, it was adopted by the kings of the Persian Empire.

With the king behind him, Zarathustra won a large number of followers, but then disaster struck. He himself was killed, apparently by a priest of the old religion that Zarathustra had rejected, and Vishtaspa's kingdom succumbed to an unknown catastrophe. His followers were forced to wander for centuries, struggling to preserve their founder's ideas.

What were these ideas and why were they thought so dangerous that they caused Zarathustra to be driven into exile and then murdered? Many of them may seem rather familiar, and with good reason, as they have been regularly plagiarised by more recent religions. Zoaroastrianism had strict and alluringly simple rules, such as that followers must pray to Their God Ahura Mazda five times each day (as would Muslims). It also, though, offered an excitingly new vision. Zarathustra saw a *dual world*, split between good and evil. The leaders of these rival forces – Ahura Mazda and Angra Mainyu – were in a constant state of struggle. Zarathustra also saw a world of *three ages*. In the first, brief age, the world, created by Ahura Mazda, was green, lush and perfect. After a vicious attack by Angra Mazda, who tried to turn it into wizened desert, but was then thwarted, the world existed in its flawed, present state. But Zarathustra insisted that if people followed Ahura Mazda, they had the chance of bringing the earth to a third and final state of renewed perfection. Jews, Christians, Manicheans and Muslims would have much the same vision. Zarathustra, or his later followers, even came up with the idea of a messiah. Born of a virgin, who would be impregnated by Zarathustra's supernaturally long-lasting sperm when bathing in a lake, he would go on to lead men into the coming perfect age.

One thing Zarathustra did *not* invent was paradise. He did, though, *reinvent* the idea. Well before Zarathustra's lifetime, central Asian Iranians already had hopes of a happy afterlife, or rather some of them did. Like early peoples across the world, they originally seem to have been resigned to a miserable after-life, in an underworld that was reached by crossing a dark river. But at some point well before Zarathustra's lifetime, this arrangement changed. A bridge was now thought to cross the dark river, and though most dead Iranians tumbled off it into the underworld, a lucky few – the aristocratic elite – walked on and reached a light-filled, happy eternity on Hara Mountain. As in Egypt, paradise first came into existence only for those in the right set.

Zarathustra offered a very different vision of paradise. Though born of privilege, he turned strongly against his roots and one can still detect in his ideas a whiff of ancient class warfare, as in his prayer, 'To Ahura Mazda is the kingdom, which they have established as pastor for the poor'. Zarathustra launched an assault on Iranian warrior aristocrats. He denounced their favourite fighting gods as working for the forces of evil. More radical still, he declared that entrance to heaven depended not on wealth or birth, but on one's behaviour during life. Dead Iranians would face a tribunal of gods and a set of scales, on which their past actions would be carefully weighed. If their good deeds proved heavier, a beautiful virgin would lead the deceased over a bridge to the mountain paradise. If the bad outweighed the good, however, then, as in a special effects film scene, the bridge would narrow to a blade, and as the hapless deceased desperately tried to creep along it to the other side, he or she would be seized by a hideous hag and flung down into an underworld of darkness, misery and dreary food.

A tribunal of gods and a set of scales to measure one's moral behaviour in life? All of this sounds very much like the afterlife selection process envisaged in Egypt, and it is quite possible that some Egyptian notions may have strayed eastwards to Iranian Central Asia. Also detectable, though, is a larger pattern. Both in Egypt and Iran paradise first emerged from the old idea of a miserable underworld for all, as a privilege only for the rich. Interestingly, one can find a similar arrangement in later times among the Mayans, the Aztecs and the Vikings. All of these cultures also envisaged a paradise for certain groups – especially elite warriors – while the rest had to make do with a miserable afterlife underground. In both Egypt and early Iran, though not in Mesoamerica or among the Vikings, there then followed another stage, when paradise was seized from the elite in a kind of popular revolution of the supernatural.

Looking at this pattern one can perhaps surmise why it was that, as religions took on the idea of heaven, they also embraced morality. Across the ages the most effective response to aristocratic claims of superiority by *birth* has been the claim of superiority by *merit*. Early Egyptians and Iranians at first accepted that only a lucky segment of the population could enter paradise, while the rest would be excluded. As aristocrats lost their monopoly on paradise, this selective arrangement remained but the selection procedure changed. Now it was people's behaviour towards one another, rather than their status and wealth, which decided matters. Exactly why, in a religion aimed at *all* members of society, selection remained is rather harder to say. It could have reflected hunger for a little social revenge. In later popular revolutions, virtue would often become a device with which to attack the old elite. The new faithful may have liked the idea of excluding from heaven some of those who had sought to exclude them. Whatever the case, from the moment it was first devised, Zoroastrian paradise, like Osiris's, was a place you feared you might not reach.

Yet what of the bigger questions? Why was paradise invented at all? And why was an idea that now seems key to religion not devised far sooner? A possible answer to both these questions is that *life was getting better*. As we have seen, in early farming societies peoples' lives were generally tough, short and full of fears. Their chief concern would have been to avoid disaster. As disaster was thought to be caused by angry gods, it made sense that people concentrated on constantly placating their deities with offerings. From the second millennium BC, however, this worldview started to change. People began to look beyond their daily survival and became preoccupied by something quite new: what would happen to them after they died. Why?

A clue, surely, lies in the fact that the first to look ahead to paradise were members of the privileged elite. Such people, one supposes, would have been the first in their societies to have a little peace of mind and leisure time. First the elite, and then the rest, became worried about their *afterlives*, one suspects, because they could afford to worry a little less about their *actual lives*. It makes sense that this change first took place on the Nile, where the annual flood was more reliable than in Mesopotamia, and where invasions and social collapse were comparatively rare, so people could hope to lead stable lives. If, as I suggested earlier, religion is chiefly a means to achieve reassurance, and so mirrors people's greatest fears, then one might see, in the invention of paradise, evidence that the quality of people's lives was slowly improving.

Once established, paradise became an immensely appealing

idea which would eventually captivate most of the world. As such, it would manage to inveigle its way into the most unlikely of places. It even hijacked a highly successful movement which, originally, was not even a religion. So we come to the strange story of Mahayana Buddhism.

Revenge of the Supernatural

In the fourth century BC, in the town of Vaishali, in the modern Indian state of Bihar, a group of Buddhist monks were given a thorough dressing-down. They had been caught indulging in practices that their fellow monks considered quite beyond the pale. They had not waited until after sunset, but had eaten their dinner just before. They had been handling money, rather than making do with begged food. They had also gone begging in places allotted to other monks. It seems a minor turf war had been going on. The Vaishali assembly roundly condemned this wickedness, yet the problem did not go away. A few decades later, another meeting held at Pataliputra (modern Patna) ended not with condemnation but with a schism between a minority of puritanical elders and the majority of monks, who felt the rules were too harsh. That split that has endured ever since.

Every movement has its fault lines, and in India at this time the greatest of these was *austerity*. Buddhism's rival movement, Jainism, split over the question of whether its monks could wear clothes or, to avoid owning any property at all, should beg naked. To fall out over such issues may seem, to modern eyes, faintly absurd, and yet those involved were, in a way, right to be concerned, as something far greater was at stake. These Buddhist councils marked the first skirmishes in a long struggle for the soul of their order. And waiting in the wings was paradise.

Not that paradise was anything new in northern India. It will have been first imported by Zarathustra's ancestors, when northern India was invaded by the Iranians' close cousins, the Aryans, who brought with them the idea of aristocratic heaven that Zarathustra so disliked. Over time, though, as the early Aryan religion evolved into Hinduism, paradise for the privileged became replaced by an altogether more original concept. This was reincarnation: the idea that souls return in a next life as another life form. Reincarnation was accompanied by a new, and equally original, moral system, karma: the notion that one's actions, good and bad, will be directly rewarded or punished. Reincarnation was, in many ways, rather more logical than the Zoroastrian, Egyptian or, later, the Christian and Islamic versions of the afterlife. All of these presupposed a kind of *inflationary heaven*, which housed a constantly growing number of souls. By contrast, early Hinduism envisaged a more stable world, of souls constantly recycled. Your soul was truly eternal, having existed long before your birth. Hinduism was also less brutally final than the paradise religions that evolved further west. The Hindu afterlife was not a one-shot affair, with a single chance of success, but a continuous process, in which, in each life, your past actions would decide the kind of creature you would become after death.

Though this may sound like an admirable arrangement, it had its critics, including Siddartha Gautama, who is better known as the Buddha, or Awakened One. It was not Hinduism's ideas that Siddartha objected to, but rather Hinduism as an institution. Even in these early times northern India had a caste system, within which the highest caste was that of the priests, or Brahmans. An early priestly manual, the *Brahmanas*, probably composed between 1000 and 800 BC, revealed a tightly closed world, in which any movement between castes was prohibited, and where the Brahmans held a monopoly over all religious ritual. Within a century or two, however, this priestly stranglehold became fiercely challenged, as a series of dissident movements attacked the religious establishment, in what was something like an early-Indian version of the Protestant Reformation. One of these movements was begun, probably in the later sixth century BC, by Siddartha Gautama.

Siddartha had a certain amount in common with Zarathustra. Like Zarathustra, he was born into a privileged family but turned strongly against his roots. Like Zarathustra, he became an exile, though in Siddartha's case the decision was voluntary. Disgusted with his own advantages, he took on the life of a wandering beggar. After fasting for many weeks, he believed he truly comprehended existence. The essence of his vision was that life is suffering, that suffering comes from desire, and that, if one could only escape desire, one might find true peace. He began to preach his ideas to others.

Exile, a moment of revelation, preaching, the founding of a movement: Siddartha's life has all the elements of the life of a prophet. Yet it is highly doubtful that he was a *religious* prophet. Though his teachings accepted the ideas of karma and reincarnation, they made no mention of gods. Some people today regard him as an atheist. He probably saw himself as someone who was advising people on a better way of leading their lives: advocating escape from desire through the wandering life of a begging monk. Had he seen what his ideas would grow into, one suspects that he would have had a nasty surprise.

His movement was, in many ways, a victim of its own success. It won converts, who followed Siddartha's advice and led lives as wandering monks. But as a puritanical movement grows, some in its ranks inevitably hope to make their lives a little more comfortable, and so it was with Buddhism. By the late fourth century BC, several generations after Siddartha's death, some Buddhist monks were, as we saw, eating dinner before sunset and begging for money rather than food. They were also *changing Siddartha*. Around this same time Buddhists decided he had been a super-mundane being, or more than mortal. Like the pharaohs of early Egypt, and, in later times, Jesus of Nazareth, Siddartha had enjoyed a divine promotion. This, though, was only the beginning. A generation later Buddhism hit the jackpot when it won the support, and perhaps the conversion, of one of India's most powerful rulers, Asoka. Buddhism, would no doubt have won many new recruits, who would, in turn, have added further pressure for the movement to become less austere.

Next came heaven. Siddartha had talked of having been awakened, and having reached, through escape from desire, a state of nirvana, meaning bliss, or peaceful fulfilment. Now nirvana was gradually turning into something very different: a form of salvation which increasingly came to look very much like paradise. So, a movement that had been inspired by the idea of *escaping* desire, became *captured by one*: the desire to find happiness after death. Siddartha's philosophy had been infiltrated by heaven. One can only speculate as to how such a thing came about, though it is likely that the movement simply adjusted to the wishes of its growing number of followers, who wanted something more satisfying than a philosophy of austerity.

Paradise, though, was not the only great change Buddhism underwent. As we have seen, the movement had split into two distinct strands. Followers of the more austere elder monks – who had insisted one should not eat till after sunset – formed Theravada Buddhism, which remained rather closer to Buddha's thinking. The large majority, though, that descended from the more easy-going, pre-sunset diners, formed Mahayana Buddhism. Mahayana Buddhists made a remarkable discovery. They noted that Siddartha had not abandoned himself to the bliss of nirvana.

Instead he had selflessly continued to wander in the world, so he might help others to find the true path. If the Buddha had done this, Mahayana Buddhists argued, then why not others? So there was born the doubtful concept of the future Buddha, or bodhisattva. This was somebody who was ready to attain nirvana but who, like Buddha, preferred, selflessly, to delay his ascent into the state of bliss, so that he might help others. Naturally such a person deserved respect, even veneration, even when still alive.

Early Indian writings are elusive, so it is hard to say exactly when Buddhism changed, but change it did. By the first century AD, statues of Buddha the supermundane appeared, and he was depicted floating above a group of leading bodhisattvas, who now looked very much like a Buddhist pantheon of gods. Around this same time, Mahayana Buddhists decided that not only professionally austere monks could attain nirvana, but *anyone*. Worshipping living bodhisattvas became a good deed, which would help the worshippers towards their own salvation. For the convenience of all, living bodhisattvas set up their own temples, where they could be worshipped. It is not hard to see that such an arrangement would have appealed to India's rich and powerful. By performing good works – and over time these became ever less demanding, until they required very little effort – rich Indians could become future Buddhas themselves. They could be worshipped at their own temples and enjoy the prospect of guaranteed nirvana salvation.

So, in the space of five to six centuries, Mahayana Buddhism had become the very thing it had begun as a protest against: an entrenched, ritualised religion organised to satisfy the spiritual needs of a rich elite. It had also changed from being a philosophy of life to a full paradise religion, with a pantheon of colourful gods, and the promise that, if its adherents followed the rules, they would reach nirvana heaven. By the early centuries AD there was little to distinguish ornate Buddhist temples from those of Hinduism, which, to add to the confusion, had stolen some of Buddhism's best ideas. There was a certain logic at work when, from around the seventh or eighth centuries AD, Indian Mahayana Buddhism became amalgamated into Hinduism, and, so, in the place of its birth, completely vanished, like a rebel corpuscle reabsorbed.

As we will see, though, it would have a surprising second life in another part of the world.

3

INVENTING DEALS
WITH GOD

One day, probably between 750 and 722 BC, and probably in Samaria, the capital of the northern Jewish kingdom of Israel (there being two Jewish kingdoms at this time) a man named Hosea began making some very alarming prophesies. Nothing is known of Hosea aside from his doomy predictions, but if the lives of other high-profile prophets are anything to go by, it was probably full of rancorous arguments, of struggles to win over influential people, of periods of exile, and of friends lost and enemies made.

Though at least Hosea was not wholly alone. Like-minded predictions were made by two other prophets, Micah and Amos, who are thought to have preached in Israel at around the same time. Still, it is hard to believe that Hosea enjoyed a quiet life. He certainly did not make matters easy for himself. His ideas were so radical that they amounted almost to a new religion, a sure road to trouble. And he had an unfortunate habit of threatening the very people he sought to persuade, as in this passage, where he has the main Jewish God, Yahweh, harangue the population of Israel with his demands (which, one can be sure, were also Hosea's):

> . . . a vulture is over the house of the Lord, because they have broken my covenant, and transgressed my law. Israel has spurned the good; the enemy shall pursue him. They made kings, but not through me. They set up princes, but without my knowledge. With their silver and gold they made idols for their own destruction. I have spurned your calf, O Samaria. My anger burns against them. How long will it be till they are pure, in Israel? A workman made it; it is not God. The calf of Samaria shall be broken to pieces. For they shall sow the wind and they shall reap the whirlwind. (Hosea 8:1–8)

Hosea was asking a great deal of the people of Israel, though he offered them little in return. Firstly, he demanded that the Israelites obey God's law. Just what this law was remains unknown, as none of it has survived, but, judging by Hosea's threatening tone, it was probably strict. Secondly, Hosea told the Israelites, who until then had happily worshipped a whole pantheon of gods, of which Yahweh was the senior, that they must now reject all gods except Yahweh. They were to be monotheists.

This prospect may not seem radical now, because we expect Jews to be monotheists, but it would have been radical at the time. Gods of this era were seen as specialists, who could help you with a precise concern, from curing your sick ox to keeping you safe on a sea journey. Who was to say if Hosea's *one size fits all* Yahweh would be as effective as the old array of experts? Abandoning the multi-god faith would also have caused considerable upset in people's daily lives. Temples to Yahweh's fellow gods, where Israelites would have been accustomed to gathering, and which would have been an important part of their social calendar, would have had to be closed down.

If the Jews of Israel did all that Hosea demanded, what could they expect in return? In essence, Hosea offered them a kind of *national supernatural protection policy*. Jews had long believed that Yahweh looked after them, but not them alone. Foreigners were also entitled to seek Yahweh's help, if they took the trouble to worship him, just as Jews could worship other gods. Now, under Hosea's new proposals, Yahweh became a *purely Jewish god*. If Jews honoured him by worshipping nobody else, he in turn would devote his full attention to their protection. It was very much a *conditional* protection, however. If the people of Israel did not obey Yahweh's new laws, and stop worshipping other gods, they would have no protection at all, but would 'reap the whirlwind'. They would be destroyed.

Why did Hosea come up with such alarming ideas? Before trying to answer this question, I would first like to ask another one: *who were the Jews?* National history may be out of place in a book about beliefs, and yet, in the case of the Jews, it is hard to avoid. Thanks to Hosea and others, the Jews' understanding of themselves as a nation, and as followers of a religion, became so profoundly intertwined that it is impossible to consider one without the other.

Did the Jews really emerge as a nation, as the Book of Exodus claims, by escaping from slavery in Egypt? Unsurprisingly, the truth concerning this event, belief in which seems to have been at the heart of Judaism from its earliest days, is hard to find. Yet an answer can be attempted. The very first historical mention of the Jews comes from an Egyptian inscription dating from between 1213 and 1203 BC, which lists a number of peoples that Pharaoh Merenptah claimed to have defeated, one of which is a tribe called Israel. After this, our next source of information comes from the Jews themselves. Their own first histories, collected in the Old Testament, are thought to date from around 950–850 BC, at the earliest, though they were much revised – one might say faked – over time. These histories contain the famous exodus story, which tells of how the Jews were taken from their homeland as slaves to Egypt, but then escaped, with the help of spectacular supernatural intervention by their god, Yahweh. It tells how, after wandering for years in the Sinai desert, their leader, Moses, agreed to a contract with Yahweh, under which Jews promised to worship only him, in exchange for his special protection. If this sounds familiar, there is, as we will see in due course, a very good reason. Finally, it tells of how, thus prepared, the Jews reconquered their old homeland in a series of spectacular and bloody victories.

Did any of this actually happen?

One thing is abundantly clear. Both archaeological finds and early Jewish writings agree that, when the Jews first properly enter history, around 950 BC, they were almost indistinguishable from their neighbours. Jews, Phoenicians and Philistines all spoke versions of the same language, had closely related writing, lived in the same kind of houses and, as I have already mentioned, worshipped the same gods. The Jews had a favourite god – Yahweh – but their neighbours, too, had their favourites. This evidence indicates that the Jews had not suddenly arrived from somewhere else, but had lived in the region for a long time. Furthermore, archaeological investigations for the centuries before 1200 BC have found no evidence of a violent invasion of the area, in which towns, such as Jericho, were razed to the ground.

And yet, from very early on, Jews seem to have had a strong sense of being different. Unlike some of their neighbours, they staunchly refused to practise human sacrifice. They insisted that their special god, Yahweh, must never be depicted in art, while other gods were routinely represented with statues or paintings. Most of all, Jews had an intense preoccupation with their origins as a people. The story of an escape from slavery in Egypt was so well established by Hosea's time that it must have already existed in Jewish imagination long before then. At first sight, none of this seems to make much sense. How could the Jews have been slaves escaped from Egypt, if they were culturally all but identical to their neighbours, and had anciently lived in the same place?

Unless, of course, the Jews were descended from *two* separate peoples who had merged together. Though this is nothing more than conjecture, it is a pattern that can be found commonly enough elsewhere in history. A settled population becomes dominated for a time by a smaller number of incomers, who gradually become subsumed by the language and culture of the majority, yet who leave a few traces of their own past. Examples include the Bulgars in Bulgaria, who left little more than their name and stories of their adventures. The same was true, to varying degrees, of the Franks in France, the Manchus in China and the Vikings in Russia, among many others. So did a large number of originally Levantine people escape from Egypt and make their way back to the Levant? One would think that such a dramatic event would have been mentioned in Egyptian records. As it happens, it was.

In the last chapter I mentioned, in passing, a mysterious people named the Hyksos, who ruled northern Egypt from around 1650 to 1550 BC, before being defeated by a southern Egyptian army. In the first century AD, the Jewish historian Josephus believed that the Jews were descendants of the Hyksos, and his claim has a good deal of logic. Archaeological work on their their capital, Avaris, indicates that the Hyksos had been a subject people of the Egyptians – employed as slaves, guest workers or frontier troops – who then rose against their masters.

The Book of Exodus, of course, makes no mention of Moses' people having ruled half of Egypt for a century under their own pharaohs, but then such details would have detracted from the story's romance. As for the parting of the Red Sea, the Hyksos appear, less excitingly, to have walked across dry land to freedom. Yet walk they did. Egyptian accounts, which are confirmed by recent archaeological studies, relate what was, for the Egyptians, a rather sorry end to a glorious campaign of national liberation. The Hyksos capital was too strong for the advancing southern Egyptian army to seize it by storm. Instead, a deal was made under which the Hyksos were allowed to leave Egypt unharmed. Perhaps – and perhaps is the word here – Hyksos refugees went on to dominate the inhabitants of the rocky, inland area between the Mediterranean and the Sea of Jordan, and then gradually faded away, until all that remained of them was a story, and a memory of having done something very special.

If this part of the Exodus story may look back to real events, what of the rest? Did the Hyksos wander for years in the Sinai desert, profligately worshipping a pantheon of Levantine gods? Did their leader make a deal with Yahweh, under which they agreed to worship only him? The simple answer is *no*. The Hyksos, during their long stay in Egypt, had long lost interest in their old Levantine gods, let alone one called Yahweh. They now worshipped Egyptian gods.

If the Moses of the Sinai story was wholly fictional, then who could have invented him? And why? These questions take us back to our doomy prophet, Hosea. As we saw, Hosea was the man who first demanded that the Jews of Israel worship only one god. Was this Hosea's own idea? It probably was. The idea of monotheism was not in itself entirely new. In the fourteenth century BC, a maverick Egyptian pharaoh, Akhenaten, tried to impose a single god, Aten, on all his subjects, but it is doubtful that Hosea would have known much about his attempt. Akhenaten ruled six centuries years before Hosea's time, and his monotheistic revolution had been a disastrous failure. It seems likely that Hosea came up with the concept himself.

What led him to come up with such an idea? The answer probably had little to do with religion and much to do with international politics. Early Jews were poor at remaining a united people. Though they first emerged into the light of history under a single, strong kingdom in the tenth century BC, this soon broke up into two states: Judah in the south and Israel in the north. Between the 740s and 722 BC, when Hosea is believed to have made his dire prophesies, both kingdoms, and especially the northern one, were in great danger. They faced the rapid expansion of one of the most brutally aggressive military powers, not only of this early age, but of *any* age: the Assyrian Empire. Assyrian kings, whom we met briefly in Chapter One, had a love of terror tactics that has invited comparisons with Adolf Hitler and the Mongol leader Genghis Khan. Assyrians were famous for killing every last inhabitant of captured cities, for deporting whole peoples to the furthest reaches of their empire, and for tying captured kings with ropes through their cheeks, to act as guard dogs in the gates of the Assyrian capital. From the 740s BC the Assyrians began moving towards the two Jewish kingdoms, brutally crushing any resistance they met along the way.

If the heart of all religion is reassurance, it is not hard to see what reassurance Hosea sought. When he warned that the kingdom of Israel might be destroyed, he knew precisely how this would happen: it would be torn apart by Assyrian terror. Clearly a strong patriot, Hosea feared for his nation's survival, and this fear, arguably, inspired his religious vision. Even at this moment of danger, the Jews of the kingdom of Israel were divided, and their response to the Assyrian threat was disastrously indecisive. Though one ruler of Israel, Menahem, had tried to placate the Assyrians by paying tribute, he was toppled by another, Pekah, who urged resistance, and, worse still, *stopped paying*.

Hosea may have thought that a single god would help unite Israel's Jews as a people. He may also have believed that a radical shake-up of their worship might bring them some much-needed luck. Israelites already regarded Yahweh as their special god. If they honoured him *even more*, and ignored all other gods, then, surely, he would protect them with greater power. So Hosea proposed the novel idea of a national contract between the Jews and a single supernatural being. It was an idea that would prove enduringly popular. But not yet.

Did the Jews of Israel take up Hosea's ideas? The answer, perhaps a little surprisingly, is *no*. A curiosity of the history of early Judaism is how determined most Jews were to resist worshipping only one god. As we will see, for several centuries the Jews clung doggedly to their polytheism, just as they resisted strict new religious laws. Hosea's proposals only succeeded thanks to a series of dramatic historical twists and turns, which worked in his favour.

The first of these occurred in the 720s BC. Around 725 the Assyrians, thoroughly fed up with Israelite disrespect, invaded the kingdom and, three years later, King Sargon II deported most of its population. Some ended up in the Assyrian army as chariot drivers, a role in which Israelites were famously skilful. Most ended up in southern Mesopotamia. Though the Israelites' fate was abundantly clear, remembrance of it soon became hazy, and they became immortalized as the Ten Lost Tribes of Israel, whose whereabouts became, two thousand years later, the subject of endless curiosity: Spanish explorers identified them as the indigenous peoples of the Americas, and in the later nineteenth century an eccentric British cult, the British Israelites, insisted they were the British themselves.

Hosea's grim warnings had been fulfilled. He had predicted that, if Israelites did not worship only Yahweh and obey his laws, their kingdom would be destroyed. Now, one would think, Jews in the surviving southern kingdom of Judah would take notice of Hosea's claims. Not at all. The Judaeans remained firm polytheists.

The next twist came precisely one century after the fall of the kingdom of Israel. In 622 BC, a curious event took place, which makes it clear that somebody, finally, had been won over to Hosea's ideas. The king of Judah, Josiah, sent his secretary, Shaphan, to the temple of Jerusalem, to deal with some minor payments and repairs. When he arrived, Shaphan had quite a surprise.

> And Hilkiah the high priest said to Shaphan the secretary, 'I have found the book of the law in the house of the Lord.' And Hilkiah gave the book to Shaphan, and he read it. And Shaphan the secretary came to the king, and reported to the king . . . 'Hilkiah the priest has given me a book' / And Shaphan read it before the king. And when the king heard the words of the book of the law, he rent his clothes. (2 Kings 22:8–11)

The book did not merely contain Yahweh's laws: they claimed to be Yahweh's Laws *as told directly to Moses.* And so the old Exodus story became merged with something quite new: the demand that Jews accept a single god and his laws. Unlike Hosea's earlier laws of God, which were lost, these laws have survived, with alterations, in a text that would become central to Judaism: Deuteronomy. As one might expect, they were on the stern side.

Jews were to abandon the worship of all gods but Yahweh, on pain of death. They were to make sacrifices to Yahweh only at his Jerusalem temple. They were to help the poor and needy. They were not to have sex before marriage, commit adultery or live dissolutely. They were also to destroy their false-believer neighbours in a kind of early jihad.

If the Jewish people obeyed these laws, the text found in the temple promised, then they would be blessed with great victories. If they broke the rules, Yahweh would inflict terrible punishment. This seemingly simple agreement concealed a sinister innovation. If *one* Jew broke the new laws, then Yahweh would punish *all* Jews. The text envisaged a system of collective responsibility whereby the sin of one endangered the whole nation. Jews had a duty not only to control their own behaviour, but also to snoop on their neighbours and lead a crowd against them if they broke the rules.

Where had this terrifying set of laws come from? It seems highly suspicious that they were suddenly 'found' in Jerusalem's temple. Some scholars have suggested the laws were invented at Judah's royal court, in a kind of religious *coup d'état* by King Josiah. The historian Robin Lane Fox believes that they were a version of Hosea's laws, which had been brought south by refugees fleeing the collapse of the kingdom of Israel, only to lie forgotten for a century, in the temple library. Wherever they came from, the laws fit perfectly with Hosea's grim warnings, amplifying his demands. Did the people of Judah heed them? The answer, again, is no. Within a few years even Judah's kings had slipped back to their comfortable old, polytheistic ways. Their minds would only be changed by a new disaster.

Though the Assyrian Empire had imploded by this time, it was quickly replaced by a southern Mesopotamian power, Babylonia, which, in terms of military ruthlessness, proved barely distinguishable from its predecessor. In 598 BC Judah was invaded by a Babylonian army under king Nebuchadnezzar. Judah's ruler was deported to Babylonia together with several thousand members of the ruling elite, where they doubtless encountered descendants of the Israelites deported over a century earlier. Eleven years later, in 587, after further Jewish resistance, the Babylonians invaded Judah a second time, deported yet more people, and, for good measure, destroyed Jerusalem's temple to Yahweh. As the kingdom of Israel had been struck, now was the kingdom of Judah, if on a less dramatic scale. This time only the elite was removed, and the poor majority was left alone.

How did the Judaean exiles react to this catastrophe? Did they angrily turn against their special god, Yahweh, for having failed to protect them? As we will see, throughout history people have often responded to poor treatment by their gods not with resentment, as one might expect, but rather with *increased devotion*. They have blamed themselves for not having pleased their gods and tried to do better. So it was with the Jewish exiles. Trapped in an unfamiliar land, they finally took up Hosea's radical ideas, which had never caught on at home. The laws of Moses found in the temple stated that Yahweh would protect the Jews if they worshipped him alone and did not break his rules. Clearly, the exiles decided, they *had* broken his rules. Like sin-fearing Mesopotamians, they concluded that the misfortune that had overwhelmed them must be entirely their own fault.

So, finally, a religious revolution began. Ancient texts, which the exiles had brought with them, were laboriously revised. Early Jewish history was rewritten, propaganda style, to fit with Hosea's one-god system. The heart of Jewish scriptures began to take form. It was around now that the Exodus story was expanded to include the Sinai episode, when Yahweh made his deal with Moses. The laws which had been mysteriously found in Yahweh's temple in Jerusalem, half a century earlier, and which claimed to have been given to Moses, now gained an exciting dramatic setting. Their key idea, though, remained the same as that preached by Hosea 150 years previously: Yahweh would protect the Jews if they worshipped only him and obeyed his laws.

Hosea's vision was finally winning the day. Still, it is doubtful that it would have triumphed had it not been for one final act in the drama. The Jewish exiles were relatively few in number and scattered throughout Mesopotamia. Those who had stayed behind in Judah were still happily worshipping their many gods. History needed to intervene once again.

By 559 BC a new power had emerged in the Middle East in the form of a previously obscure Iranian tribe, the Persians, whose king, Cyrus – almost certainly a convert to Zoroastrianism – defeated all who opposed him. Cyrus's rise probably inspired the prophesies of a Jewish exile named Ezekiel. Exiled in the ancient religious centre of Nippur – the same city where, 1600 years earlier, we saw the god Enlil dress for breakfast – Ezekiel declared that, through their sufferings in Babylonia, the Jews had now paid in full for their earlier sins. He predicted that they would soon return to their homeland and rebuild their destroyed temple.

As luck would have it, exactly such a thing happened. In 539, Cyrus captured Babylon, and Mesopotamian power was broken once and for all. The Persian king, who had a shrewd policy of religious tolerance towards subject peoples, allowed the joyful exiles to return home. The predictions of the prophets, from Hosea's warnings of doom to Ezekiel's optimistic vision, now seemed unassailable. In the past Jews had worshipped other gods and been punished. Now, in exile, they had respected Moses' laws and had triumphed.

The returnees set to work completing their religious revolution.

They rebuilt the destroyed temple to Yahweh, and converted those who had stayed behind from their polytheism. A new religious strictness prevailed to ensure that Yahweh would not grow annoyed again and inflict new disasters on his people. It is at this time that dietary restrictions against the eating of pork, shellfish and other foods, which had probably applied only to temple priests before this time, were now extended to all Jews, and were minutely set down in the text that became Leviticus 11. In the same text we have the first mention of a ban on homosexuality and on Jewish women marrying foreigners. Having felt themselves strangers in a foreign land, it seems that those returning from exile were determined to surround all Jews with a sense of their new religious national identity.

The returnees appear to have brought back much more than a radicalised Jewish religion, however. For all their intense Jewishness, they also seem to have adopted some very foreign notions, some stemming from King Cyrus's religion, Zoroastrianism. So Judaism adopted Zarathustra's idea of a perpetual struggle between good and evil, which were led by Yahweh and Satan. Judaism also absorbed Zarathustra's concept of history in three eras, in which people could hope to vanquish evil and bring a final, third age of perfection. Also borrowed from Zoroastrianism was the idea of the Messiah, who would lead men in a final victory against wickedness. Last but not least, the exiles seem to have had an eye for good stories: that of Noah and the flood was famously plagiarised from the already ancient Mesopotamian masterpiece, the *Epic of Gilgamesh*.

Two centuries late, Hosea had finally found success. A major sea-change in people's beliefs had begun. Until this time, people identified themselves as citizens of a city, inhabitants of a region, speakers of a language, or as a mix of all three. They saw their city or national gods as helpful, especially during war, but other people's gods could be useful, too. As Hosea's monotheism spread across the world – from Judaism to Christianity and Islam – people came to identify themselves, like the Jews, more by their religion. Their beliefs gave them a sense of being set apart, and more fortunate, even superior, to those who worshipped other gods. So the flip side of intense religious identity was new religious *intolerance*. It was a huge change. Whether it was a good change is quite another matter.

Monotheistic national religion was not the only creation of that astonishingly innovative people, the Jews. Another remarkable invention was on its way, one whose consequences would prove vastly destructive, not least for its unfortunate creators.

4

INVENTING THE END OF THE WORLD

Be Careful What You Prophesy

One day in 167 BC, almost certainly in Jerusalem, somebody about whom nothing is known, not even his name, set to work on a forgery. He – and there is little doubt it was a he – would have considered his deceit fully justified. His forgery was propaganda, designed to fire up Jews in a struggle against their Greek rulers, and also against some of their fellow Jews: a struggle in which the future of Judaism was at stake.

The forgery concerned a fictional character named Daniel, who until then had existed only as the hero of patriotic Jewish folk stories. Cunning Daniel, living in exile in Babylon, repeatedly outwitted the dull Babylonian king, saving his own life and keeping faithful to his Jewish religion. The unknown forger inscribed several of Daniel's existing adventures, including the famous lion's den story, but went on to add a wholly new section of text, which was quite out of kilter with the folk tales. Daniel was now a visionary rather than a trickster, and he had a dream. In this dream he foresaw events of the coming four centuries: up to, and just beyond, the forger's own time.

The dream not only predicted – apparently with uncanny accuracy – the rise and fall of earlier empires; it then looked ahead and foresaw the death of the Jews' Greek ruler, Antiochus IV, who, when the forger was writing, was still very much alive. Finally the dream looked further into the future, and told of how, after a period of non-violent Jewish resistance, angels would intervene, and deal with the Greeks once and for all. After this, a new golden age would begin, in which the world was ruled by an emissary of Yahweh. In the words – supposedly – of Daniel himself:

> I saw in the night visions, and behold, with the clouds of heaven there came one like a son of man, and he came to the Ancient of Days and was presented before him. And to him was given dominion and glory and kingdom, that all peoples, nations and languages should serve him; his dominion is an everlasting dominion, which shall not pass away, and his kingdom one that shall not be destroyed.

What the anonymous writer could not have suspected was that his effort would become one of the most enduring – and poisonously influential – pieces ever written. It would become the seminal text for a new strand of belief: belief in the imminent *end of the world*. If the author had only known what his forgery would bring, in the future, to the very people he was trying to help – the catastrophes it would lure them into, the centuries of cruelty it would inspire in their enemies – he would, one suspects, have quietly dropped it into the nearest fire.

We are still with the Jews. Surely, one might ask, their story is already told? As we saw in the last chapter, they had finally agreed to worship only Yahweh, and to obey Moses' laws, and they had been rewarded. The prophesies of Ezekiel, the optimistic exile, had been fulfilled. The Babylon deportees had come home and the temple to Yahweh had been rebuilt.

History, though, is poor at happy endings. Wait long enough and new trouble will generally come along. So it was with the Jews. Thanks to the efforts of Alexander the Great in the 330s and 320s BC, the Persian authorities who ruled Palestine were replaced by a Macedonian dynasty – the Seleucids – and under their rule something rather unexpected happened. A portion of the Jewish elite, which had been so devoted to Yahweh, began to show remarkable disloyalty. They fell in love with the Greek culture that the Macedonians had brought. In 175 BC a powerful Jewish family, the Tobiads, seized power in Jerusalem, and began the Greekification of the city. A Greek gymnasium was set up near Yahweh's temple, where Jews, including temple priests, took up the very un-Jewish practice of exercising naked. Some Jews were even said to have had undergone operations to reverse their circumcision.

Greekification, though, soon went badly wrong. When the Hellenizers split into two feuding factions, the Seleucid king, Antiochus IV, stepped in and pushed matters further than any but the most extreme Greekifier could have stomached. Antiochus made the Laws of Moses – which, as we saw, now lay at the very heart of Judaism – illegal. Circumcision and observation of the Sabbath were banned, and shrines to Greek gods were set up in Yahweh's temple. All the Jewish successes of the past four centuries were put in jeopardy and, hardly surprisingly, some Jews rose up in revolt. So began a long and highly confusing conflict.

The war eventually ushered in a century or so of full Jewish political independence. It also produced a theological spin-off that would be far more long-lasting: the notion of the end of the world. Our unknown forger wrote what was, in effect, the first known resistance literature: a text which promised patriotic Jews that their cause would triumph and their oppressors would be destroyed. It also promised that Jews who kept true to their old religion would be saved, while those who reneged would not. So the Book of Daniel introduced another novelty that would prove highly enduring: resurrection. As the forger wrote:

> And many of them that sleep in the dust of the earth shall awake, some to everlasting life, and some to shame and everlasting contempt. And they that shall be wise shall shine as the brightness of the firmament; and they that turn many to righteousness as the stars for ever and ever. (Daniel 12:2–3)

The Book of Daniel was not the only Jewish writing from this time that sought to wage war on Hellenism. Two like-minded texts, the Apocalypse of Weeks and the Book of Dreams, were also written in the 160s BC, only to vanish into obscurity, until they were eventually rediscovered in the Ethiopian version of the Bible., when it was translated into English in the 1820s. Who wrote these pieces? Daniel mentions how resistance to the Seleucids would be led by wise teachers, or *maskilim*, causing scholars to suspect that the author was just such a person: an educated Jerusalem scribe who decided to use the end of the world as propaganda .

Not that the concept was entirely new. As we have seen, a very simple version of it had been imagined by Zarathustra – a thousand or more years before our forger's time – with his notion of a future Third Age, when the forces of goodness would triumph over evil, and the world would be returned to lost perfection. The Jewish prophet Hosea had threatened Israelites with an end of their world if they failed to do as he urged, though he was probably thinking less of destructive angels than of Assyrian invasion. The later, and more optimistic, prophet Ezekiel, exiled in Babylonia, envisaged a kind of happy transformation, in which Jews would find their world improved for ever.

Likewise, forging scriptures was nothing new in the Jewish world. As we have seen, there was something distinctly suspicious about the fortuitous 'discovery' of Moses' laws in Yahweh's temple in 622 BC. Thereafter it became relatively common practice to tack new pages on to old texts, to give authority to one side in a religious dispute. Forgery was easy. There was no accepted Jewish religious canon at this time, but a large number of disparate scrolls, whose texts often varied slightly from copy to copy. So forgery was impossible to prove. Nor would it have been seen as much of a transgression as, after all, the words could be seen as having been inspired in the writer by God himself. Thus forgeries were added to earlier forgeries, so that, to this day, it can be hard to tell where one ends and another begins. The forgeries of the 160s BC, however, created something wholly new. If the end of the world had long existed as a background notion in this part of the world, it now came very much to the fore. Within a few generations, a stream of movements emerged whose members were convinced that the world was about to be violently transformed by supernatural forces.

The renowned sociologist of religion Max Weber observed that such movements usually followed a pattern. Their supporters were generally poor and uneducated. This should not surprise us. Those whose lives were tough, uncertain and spent in sight of others far more fortunate could be excused for hoping for a radical remaking of the world. The movements' leaders, by contrast, were usually charismatic individuals from the educated elite. The leader and his followers engaged in a kind of exchange.

The leader offered his followers a transformation of the world, and a new society, in which they would not only be saved while their enemies would perish, but where they would become great lords. It was the supernatural equivalent of winning the lottery. In return, the followers showed their leader loyal devotion, believed in his promises and helped him launch what was, in some cases, a wholly new religion.

Across the next two millennia, although other apocalyptic writings would join the fray, the leader of the pack would always be the Book of Daniel. This relatively short document would inspire innumerable movements, which were frequently disastrous for all involved, and to this day the text can have a hypnotic effect on readers. What made this piece of writing so enduring?

In some ways it was a rather unlikely success. Its forgery was clumsy. Having 'predicted' past events with perfect accuracy, it quickly ran into trouble when it tried to make a real prediction. This was in part because, unwisely, the forger chose not only to say *what* would happen, but *when*. Daniel prophesied that the hated king Antiochus IV would be killed by God after Jews had 'suffered three and a half' years of struggle with the Greeks. This meant he would be dead by 164 BC. When this year had come and gone, and the king was still very much alive, a new chapter (8) was hastily added, in which Daniel predicted that Antiochus would live for a *further* three and a half years. Unfortunately this time the prediction proved too long: Antiochus died unexpectedly of sickness only a year later. Hence yet another chapter (9) was added, in which the Angel Gabriel helpfully introduced a complex means of recalculating the king's death. This crude backtracking was easily spotted as forgery several centuries later by the pagan Roman critic Porphyry. Porphyry was unusual, however. Most of Daniel's readers, first Jewish and later Christian, did not question the text. After all, it told contemporaries what they wanted to hear – that the Greeks and their culture would soon be defeated – while to later eyes the text had the aura of being *mostly correct*. Though the forger slipped up on details, when it came to the big picture, luck was on his side. The Seleucids *were* defeated.

The book's lasting influence was also helped by its language. Jewish prophets had long written using strange imagery and metaphors, but the Book of Daniel excelled in this field, employing a symbolism that, to this day, has a strangely hypnotic quality. Thus, the empires whose rise and fall Daniel foresaw were represented by beasts, of which the empire of the Seleucids was:

> . . . a fourth beast, dreadful and terrible, and strong exceedingly;
> and it had great iron teeth: it devoured and brake in pieces,
> and stamped the residue with the feet of it: and it [was] diverse
> from all the beasts that [were] before it; and it had ten horns.
> (Daniel 7:7)

The beast had an extra horn, which had eyes and spoke, and which represented King Antiochus IV himself. Thus Daniel offered a series of symbolic puzzles to solve, which doubtless added to the text's power to persuade. Once readers had successfully decoded it, and had gained a sense of satisfaction at their own cleverness, they would be far less likely to question the book's predictions.

Symbolism also made the text *future-proof*. Had it been written with simple clarity, recounting the actual names of empires and events, the Book of Daniel would doubtless have faded from view, as people grew less interested in a distant struggle between Jews and their Seleucid rulers. Thanks to the book's strange symbolism, though, readers could continue to try and unlock its puzzles, long after their real context had been forgotten.

Throughout the centuries people have continued to apply the dream to their own day, enthralled by the thought that so ancient a text had predicted events happening around them, including, excitingly, the fall of people they particularly disliked. Thus, in England in the late 1640s, the Digger Gerrard Winstanley concluded that Daniel's four beasts were laws that favoured the rich, landlords, lawyers and Anglican clergymen.

Another factor in the Book of Daniel's favour was that it had some excellent support. In its early days it appears to have been energetically promoted by a kind of ancient Jewish *publicity team*. Most of what remains of this organisation is its library, which was hidden in several caves near the Dead Sea – probably in in the first century AD, in anticipation of an imminent assault by Roman forces – where it remained until it was rediscovered in the late 1940s. This collection is known as the Dead Sea Scrolls. The library belonged to a strange community – all-male, property-sharing, monkish and faintly military – which was based at nearby Qumran and was almost certainly part of a larger movement known as the Essenes.

What do the scrolls tell us about the people who wrote and read them? The movement's chief purpose was to urge the Jews to prepare for an imminent and violent supernatural remaking of the world. The Essenes were, in many ways, the Book of Daniel transformed into a whole organisation. Writings found at Qumran include not only Daniel's two apocalyptic rivals – the Apocalypse of Weeks and the Book of Dreams – but also no fewer than eight copies of the Book of Daniel itself. The earliest of these was inscribed barely forty years after the book was originally written.

Scholars of the scrolls have noticed that almost every text – if not every one of them – is in some way concerned with the end of the world. As well as copying old texts, the Qumran community wrote some new apocalyptic prophesies of their own. The War Scroll looks ahead to a final forty-year-long war between Jews and all their ancient neighbours, who would be led by the spirit of darkness, Belial. The text goes into precise detail as to what equipment and organisation the Jews should use, even down to banning soldiers with blemishes, as these might cause distress to the angels.

Yet keeping the angels sweet was becoming a little less of a concern. While Daniel had predicted that angels would do the real grunt work of the apocalypse, the Qumran communitarians expected to play an active role themselves. They foresaw a tough time of conflict and persecution, but all would be worthwhile in the end. When the forty-year war was finally over, and the Sons of Light triumphed over the Sons of Darkness, a Messiah figure would rule over a perfect age: a time of deliverance.

For all their monkish ways, the Essenes were not always inward-looking. They also sought to win new converts in the wider world. A text known as the Damascus Document refers to members of the movement who had families and day jobs, and formed small communal groups in towns and villages. They were the proselytisers of the and of the world. Some such people may have appeared in the historical record. In the early first century AD, when the sect was still highly active, and Jews had become subjugated by a new foreign oppressor, the Romans, a series of apocalyptic preachers appeared in Palestine. In the 40s a man named Theudas promised his followers that, like Moses, he would part the waters of the Jordan River, and probably also that he would free them from the Romans. (He failed on both counts and the Romans chopped off his head.) Another man, remembered only as 'the Egyptian', promised his many thousands of followers that he could cause the walls of Jerusalem to crumble, though he met with no more success than Theudas. Charismatics set up in the desert, warning all who would listen that Yahweh was about to wreak havoc on earth, and that nobody would be safe without their protection. The Romans dealt with these preachers, too.

But one apocalyptic movement, led by another charismatic, proved much more enduringly influential. This was the movement of Jesus of Nazareth.

Jesus the end-of-the-world man? Some may object that this is not the Jesus they know. What of the calm, wise Jesus, who preached a loving God and forgiveness of one's fellow man? Yet there is little doubt that Jesus *did* preach the end of the world. He emerges into history very clearly on the apocalyptic side of Jewishness. Jesus initially followed John the Baptist, another end-of-the-worlder, and it is highly likely that he was connected with, if not a member of, the apocalyptic Essene sect. Like the writers of the Dead Sea Scrolls, Jesus had an impressive knowledge of Jewish religious writings, and he had a quote ready for every occasion. He was also close to the Essenes in how he interpreted Jewish writings. In fact, a great deal of Jesus' teaching, which was once thought to be his own original thinking, has been found in the Dead Sea Scrolls, including, rather surprisingly, the idea of a loving, forgiving God. Here is just such a God, in a Qumran scroll that is believed to have been written a century or more before Jesus was born:

> Though my affliction break out, He shall draw my soul back from the pit, and firm my steps on the way. Through his love He has brought me near; by his loving kindness shall he provide my justification. By his righteous truth has He justified me; and through His exceeding goodness shall He atone for all my sins. By his righteousness shall He cleanse me of human defilement and the sin of mankind – to the end that I praise God for His

righteousness, the most High for His glory. (Rule of the Community, 1QS11.10– 15)³

There is also the evidence of what Jesus said. In the gospels he refers repeatedly to an approaching Kingdom of Heaven. Though the way he uses the phrase varies a little, it usually seems to have signified, as the historian E. P. Sanders describes it, 'a divine, restoring miracle' in which God would 'create an ideal world'.⁴ Under this kingdom the Jews would regain their lost greatness. The Ten Lost Tribes of Israel would be miraculously found and returned to their old lands. All of this seems very close to the conclusion of Daniel's Dream.

When was the Kingdom of Heaven to arrive? After Jesus' death, this became an increasingly awkward question, as time passed and nothing happened. There is every indication, however, that when Jesus was alive, his followers expected the end of the world to come very soon, certainly within their own lifetimes. Jesus told them so himself, in a nearly identical passage found in Mark, Matthew and Luke:

And he said unto them, Verily I say unto you, That there be some of them that stand here, which shall not taste death, till they have seen the kingdom of God come with power. (Mark 9.1)

At the Last Supper Jesus also told his followers what place they would have in the new order:

'And I appoint unto you a kingdom, as my father hath appointed unto me; That ye may eat and drink at my table in my kingdom, and sit on thrones judging the twelve tribes of Israel.' (Luke 22:29–30)

Jesus' chief disciples were to be judges – rulers – over the twelve tribes of Israel (including the ten tribes supposedly lost seven centuries earlier). Poor fishermen and hated tax collectors from remote Galilee who had become his followers were to be princes in Jesus' new Jewish state. This was truly a future to look forward to. If this were not already enough, there would also be the pleasure of seeing others – including those who considered themselves to be the great and good – being cast aside. Jesus made it clear that all who failed to follow him would be excluded from the new kingdom.

And how did Jesus see he himself in this future? In the gospels, he referred to himself on numerous occasions as 'the Son of Man'. Once again this was clearly a reference to the Book of Daniel, which, as we saw, predicted that 'one like the Son of Man' will descend on clouds and take eternal dominion. Did Jesus think of himself as the Messiah? Sanders believes that he regarded himself more as a kind of 'viceroy of God', who, with God's help, would rule over a revitalised, Rome-free Jewish kingdom. His supporters accepted this claim with enthusiasm. When Jesus rode into Jerusalem, days before his death, he did so on an ass, in a clear reference to a centuries-old prophesy by Zachariah, that a king would arrive in Zion, triumphant and victorious, riding humbly on a donkey. Jesus' supporters clearly understood the reference and hailed him as king and 'the Son of David'.

An educated, charismatic leading a band of poor, uneducated followers? Promises of an imminent end of the world? A movement in which the followers show their leader unquestioning loyalty in return for promises that their enemies will be destroyed and they themselves will be great figures in the new order? If all of this sounds familiar, so it should. It precisely follows Max Weber's analysis of apocalyptic movements.

Some may object that even if Jesus *was* an end-of-the-world man, his main interest was still love and forgiveness. Yet while there is no denying that love and forgiveness were close to his heart, these were almost certainly secondary interests. His chief concern was the coming apocalypse. This is made very clear if we look at Jesus' preaching career. And so, once again, we have the spectacle of a prophet struggling to make his way. Jesus first tried his luck in his hometown of Nazareth, but he did poorly there, and seems to have been discouraged even by his own family (Mark says they tried to seize him, claiming that he was 'beside himself', or deranged). Probably he was too well known. Prophets rarely did well on their home turf, where they would lack mystery, and both Zarathustra and Muhammad needed to wander before they found real success.

Like them, Jesus did much better when he took his preaching elsewhere. His success sprang, it seems, not from what he *said* so much as what he *did*. Jesus became renowned as a healer, and exorcist of demon spirits: two skills, which, at this time, would have been regarded as largely the same thing. We know that Jesus healed, and expunged demons, using his hands and his voice, while Mark reports that he also used more bizarre methods that were common at this time, from spitting to imitating the writhing of those possessed.

As telling as *how* Jesus won supporters was, arguably, *where* he won them. The four gospels recount that Jesus preached in the sleepy fishing villages around the Sea of Galilee. They make no mention of his preaching in larger towns, where he would have found educated people like himself, though there were several of these in the vicinity. One can only assume that he found that the poor and uneducated were the most receptive to his preaching. It is also highly likely that they helped *shape his preaching*. A preacher addressing a crowd has much in common with an actor performing in a theatre. Both are involved in a kind of dance with their audience, in which they lead, but their audience retains the ultimate power of judgement. A successful prophet would, one imagines, need to keep a sharp weather eye out for which parts of their message their listeners responded to. They would also need a little flexibility, and readiness to adjust their teaching. The process would have been a kind of *interactive theology*.

Jesus, famously, welcomed into his movement the poor and people from the margins of society: sinners who had broken Jewish religious laws, a former prostitute and even members of that most hated profession, tax collectors. He offered them forgiveness for their failings. This openness seems to have been of Jesus' devising and is something that, unusually, cannot be found in the Dead Sea Scrolls or in the teaching of Jesus' mentor, John the Baptist. What led Jesus to such a concept? While forgiveness was probably a notion close to his heart, it also made sound *tactical sense*. Poor Galilean fishermen, breakers of Jewish religious law, former prostitutes and tax collectors were just the kind of people who fitted Max Weber's analysis of apocalyptic movements. They were the ones who had little to lose and would have found a violent remaking of the world very appealing, especially if, as a consequence, they became raised up from the lowest level to the highest. Arguably, it made a good deal of sense for Jesus to preach against judging one's fellow man.

However, there was a condition to his acceptance of such people. On a number of occasions in the New Testament, Jesus tells his supporters that they are absolutely required to do one thing: they have to *follow him*. This demand was more radical than it may sound. Jesus makes it clear that this could mean casting aside everything else, including one's spouse, one's children or a dead relative awaiting burial. Even sex might have to go. Jesus expected total surrender to his mission.

Such an expectation may have been inspired, like so much else in Jesus' preaching, by the Essenes, whose leaders enforced strict control. Those found guilty of minor transgressions were required to do penance for days or weeks, while any who challenged authority were expelled from the sect, never to return. But even if Jesus was inspired by Essene rules, it is hard not to feel that he was also following the tug of his own personality. Remembering Jesus' repeated demand in the gospels that his supporters 'follow me', one wonders if, had he made an appearance in today's world, he would not have come across as a little monomaniacal. This egotism may have been key to his success. As we have seen, there were a good number of Jewish apocalyptic movements at this time, and all of these, with the exception of that founded by Jesus, quickly vanished into the sand. If Jesus had been less charismatic, intense and wilful, his movement would probably never have endured as it did.

Not that it endured for long, at least not under Jesus' leadership. Jesus' whole career as a prophet lasted, rather surprisingly, two years at most, and perhaps only one. What went wrong? In some ways we can see his movement as doomed from the start. End-of-the-world movements across the ages generally take on a kind of fatal momentum. Once their charismatic leader has promised his followers a cataclysmic remaking of the world, in which their enemies will be destroyed and they themselves will become great lords, something *has to happen*. If the leader continues to preach for too long, and nothing changes, his supporters' hopes will inevitably begin to turn stale and the movement will collapse.

Jesus' movement was no exception to this pattern. In the year or two that he preached by the Sea of Galilee he gathered, it seems, a few hundred enthusiastic supporters. What next? When cataclysm showed no sign of occurring, he appears to have decided to try and force matters. Like the unnamed Egyptian, he led his followers to Jerusalem, the Jewish religious centre. Better still, he did so at Passover, the greatest of Jewish religious holidays, when the city heaved with pilgrims, who had journeyed from every distant corner of the world to make sacrifices to Yahweh at his temple. Jesus and his followers evidently shared high expectations. Not only did Jesus enter the city riding on an ass to fulfill Zachariah's prophecy, but his supporters openly hailed him as Son of David and King. Now, surely, something *had* to occur.

In the event, it seems that Jesus *made it happen*. We know from the four gospels that he caused a scene in Yahweh's temple, knocking over the tables of the moneychangers and the seats of people selling pigeons. This was almost certainly *not* because he objected to these people's activities. The money changers offered, as Sanders phrases it, 'a mere convenience for pilgrims': a means, if they chose, of changing money into the currency used for temple fees. Likewise, the bird sellers sold pigeons to offer in the temple, if you wanted them, though you could bring your own. Jesus shows no interest in reforming temple practices elsewhere in the gospels. He viewed himself, almost certainly, as a traditional Jew. When he overturned the moneychangers' tables he was making a *symbolic point*. What point? Mark reports that during Jesus' trial some of his accusers claimed he threatened to 'destroy the temple' and that he promised to build another, in three days, 'not built with hands'. In other words, like the prophet Ezekiel, the author of Daniel's Dream and the members of the Dead Sea Scrolls sect, Jesus expected God to destroy the world, probably very soon, and to rebuild it in a better way. He overturned the moneychangers' tables to act out what he believed was about to happen: that everything around him would be destroyed.

If Jesus intended to provoke events, he succeeded, though probably not as he hoped. His behaviour was highly incendiary. Jerusalem at Passover was a tinderbox of vast, excitable crowds. Pilgrims who had travelled from far away to worship Yahweh and make sacrifices to him would hardly have welcomed the sight of someone knocking over tables and claiming that Yahweh's temple would soon be destroyed. Jerusalem was also a place where little patience was shown for any perceived troublemakers. The Romans had no tolerance for such behaviour. To be fair, they had little choice, as their empire was, in many ways, a surprisingly precarious arrangement. Aside from great armies at the frontiers, it was barely policed, and provincial cities were largely left to their own devices, so as long as they kept quiet and paid taxes. In Jerusalem it was up to the Jewish chief priest, Caiaphas, to keep the peace. Caiaphas knew that if he failed to do so, the Roman governor, Pilate – whom non-biblical sources describe as notoriously brutal – would step in with his small force of Roman soldiers and deliver a short and bloody shock.

Jesus himself seems to have realised what he had begun. During the Last Supper, we can sense, even through the prism of the gospels, that he was willing on the promised apocalypse. It was then that he promised his senior disciples that they would lead the Twelve Tribes of Israel. Raising a glass of wine, he told them:

> Verily I say unto you, I will drink no more of the fruit of the vine, until that day that I drink it new in the kingdom of God (Mark 14:25).

Caiaphas had him arrested that same evening. Jesus was clearly trouble. He had already caused an incident in the temple. He also had followers, perhaps several hundred, which made him even more dangerous. According to Mark, Caiaphas questioned Jesus about his title, asking if he were 'the son of the blessed'. The chief priest evidently knew of Jesus' claim that he was some form of king. What truly motivated Caiaphas, though, was almost certainly his concern that, if he did not remove Jesus and violence broke out, the Roman garrison would march out to show their authority, and the result would be slaughter.

Did ordinary Jews bay for Jesus' blood? Though this is possible, it seems very unlikely. The historian E. P. Sanders doubts that a Jewish crowd was present at Jesus' trial at all. The gospels, in which this claim is made, were written two and more generations after Jesus' death, when relations between Christians and Jews, which had never been good, were very bad indeed. Significantly, the Gospel of John, which is thought to have been written last, is the one that strives to put the Jews in the worst light. By John's time, Christians were intent on convincing the Roman authorities of their own respectability. It made sense, therefore, to make the Jews the villains in the story of Jesus' death. It also made sense to characterise the Roman governor, Pilate, despite what we now know about his brutality, as weak rather than evil.

The truth may have been rather more mundane. Jesus' trial and condemnation may not have been theatrical, but simply hurried. Rather than baying for Jesus' blood, most Jerusalemites and pilgrims may have barely noticed what was happening. They would, after all, have been fully occupied celebrating Passover. Jesus' arrest, trial and execution may have been little noticed at the time, except by his followers. For the new religion's founder to die like a common criminal, on a cross, was bad enough. That he died without attracting much notice would have been intolerable.

That same night, after his trial, Jesus endured the slow horror of crucifixion, with no sign that the end of the world was coming. Is there any evidence that Jesus may have shown disappointment at this outcome? One would hardly expect to find such a thing in the gospels, which were written by Christians who were still hoping that the end of the world would soon arrive. And yet there is a curious passage, found both in Mark (thought to be the earliest of the gospels) and Matthew:

> And at the ninth hour, Jesus cried out with a loud voice, 'Eloi, Eloi, lama sabachthani?' which is, being interpreted, 'My God, my God, why has thou forsaken me.' Mark (15:34)

Jesus' cry was a quotation from Psalm 22:2, a well-known Jewish text. According to Mark, bystanders recognised the verse and it made them realise Jesus' greatness. Their reaction, though, seems contrived: how would they recognise Jesus' status from a single brief quotation? The whole moment sits a little strangely in the narrative. One wonders if Mark is describing an occurrence that had caused unease at the time: Jesus' moment of visible doubt. An occurrence whose ghost still needed laying to rest?

Jesus' movement had been, in many ways, a sorry failure. A traditional Jew himself, his aim had been to win over other traditional Jews to his claim that the end of the world was fast approaching. He did poorly. During his short period of preaching, only a small number of Jews, most of them from the fringes of society, in remote Galilee, had accepted that he was a viceroy of Yahweh, who, after a violent cataclysm, would rule a remade world. Few Jews *ever did* accept his claims.

If Jews did not believe in Jesus, though, a great many of them believed in the end of the world. If anything, the idea appears to have gathered more support among them in the decades following Jesus' death. The consequences would be disastrous.

The Wrong End of the World

In the summer of AD 70, Roman forces fought their way, against furious Jewish resistance, through the burning city of Jerusalem towards the inner sanctuary of Yahweh's temple. The Jewish historian Josephus, who had fought with Jewish rebels but was captured and then joined the Romans, watched the terrible events unfold. The Roman commander, Titus, had given strict orders that the temple was to be preserved, out of respect for its antiquity. His orders, however, proved of little use:

> One of the soldiers, without waiting for orders, and without a qualm for the terrible consequences of his action, but urged on by some unseen force, snatched up a blazing piece of wood and climbing on another soldier's back, hurled the brand through a golden aperture giving access on the north side to the chambers built around the sanctuary. As the flames shot into the air the Jews sent up a cry that matched the calamity . . .'[5]

It was a disaster far worse than those of earlier centuries. Not only had Yahweh's temple been destroyed, but the whole city of Jerusalem. Worse, by order of the Romans, Jerusalem ceased to be a Jewish city. It became transformed into the barracks of the Roman 10th legion. Loss of life during the struggle seems, in terms of numbers, depressingly modern. Titus had begun his siege of the city during the same Passover ceremony that had drawn Jesus and his followers three decades earlier: a time when Jerusalem was packed with pilgrims. For several months Titus softened up the city with starvation, until its inhabitants were reduced to corpse-like figures, and dead bodies were thrown from the walls by the thousands. When, growing impatient in the summer heat, Titus finally attacked, he was forced to fight his way through the city, street by street. Josephus claimed that, by the end of the struggle, no fewer than 1.1 *million* Jews had died, while another 97,000 were taken as slaves, many of them to die, too, in the Empire's mines and arenas. Aware that such numbers might seem exaggerated, Josephus took care to justify them, and, though they may still be questioned, the death toll was clearly huge.

The fall of Jerusalem was not only a political but also a religious disaster. The national triumphs of earlier centuries, which the Jews believed had been won because they had rejected all gods but Yahweh, and accepted of his laws, were now lost. The one temple where Jews could sacrifice to Yahweh, which had been rebuilt after such great trials, had again been lost. Worse, the war would spark a new and insidious belief, which has endured ever since. This was the idea that the Jews were a conspiratorial, malevolent nation secretly at war with everyone else. Anti-Semitism was born.

A little surprisingly, perhaps, this poisonous notion seems to have begun as Roman state policy. As the historian Martin Goodman recounts, in AD 69, the Flavians – the family of Jerusalem's conqueror, Titus – became Rome's new ruling dynasty. Having no other victories to celebrate aside from their defeat of the Jews, they made the most of this, which became a centrepiece of Imperial propaganda. The Flavians' victory commemorations went beyond the usual processional triumph through Rome, with Jewish booty and prisoners, and the building of triumphal arches in the city. The new dynasty also introduced a highly dubious innovation: a head tax, payable by Jews, and only Jews, all across the Empire. To add to the humiliation, the tax was used to pay for the rebuilding of Rome's pagan temple to Jupiter, which had been burned down during the Flavians' struggle for power. The new tax was brutally implemented. The Roman historian Suetonius describes how an elderly man was forced to strip naked in a crowded courtroom, as he had been accused of having been circumcised, but had not paid. State prejudice encouraged private prejudice, as in this passage by another Roman historian, Tacitus. Written three decades after the Jewish War of AD 70, it has disquietingly modern overtones and would not have been out of place in 1930s Germany:

> The other practices of the Jews are sinister and revolting, and have entrenched themselves by their very wickedness. Wretches of the most abandoned kind who have no use for the religion of their fathers took to contributing dues and free-will offerings to swell the Jewish exchequer, and other reasons for their increasing wealth may be found in their stubborn loyalty and ready benevolence towards brother Jews. But the rest of the world they confront with a hatred reserved for enemies. They will not feed or intermarry with gentiles. Though a most lascivious people, the Jews avoid sexual intercourse with people of alien races. Among themselves nothing is barred. They have introduced the practice of circumcision to show that they are different from others. Proselytes to Jewry adopt the same practices, and the very first lesson they learn is to spite the gods, shed all feelings of patriotism, and consider parents, children and brothers as readily expendable. However, the Jews see to it that their numbers increase.[6]

What had brought this great calamity upon the Jews? In many ways it was begun by the very combination of events that had been feared by Jerusalem's high priest, Caiaphas, when he had Jesus arrested. Three decades later, in AD 66, tensions between Jerusalemites and the city's Roman authorities, which had been growing for some time, boiled over. On the orders of the governor at the time Gessius Florus – who was every bit as brutal as Pontius Pilate – the Roman garrison embarked on a senseless massacre of the city's inhabitants in which, Josephus claims, several thousand were killed. After a brief Jewish civil war, between those who wanted to fight the Romans and those who did not, which was won by the war party, Jerusalem's Roman garrison was massacred in turn. What really led the Jews to disaster, however, was an unlikely victory. An incompetently led legion sent against them was annihilated by Jewish guerrilla forces. In Roman eyes, such a humiliation had to be answered with a show of revenge that would impress subject peoples across the Empire and so discourage trouble elsewhere. Titus' campaign provided just such a spectacle.

How, we might wonder, could the Jews have been so foolish as to imagine they would defeat a vast empire, which stretched from Scotland to Sudan, and was at the very height of its power? Josephus offers an answer:

> [The Jews'] chief inducement to go to war was an equivocal oracle, also found in their sacred writings, announcing that at that time a man from their country would become monarch of the whole world. This they took to mean the triumph of their own race . . . The Jews interpreted some of the prophesies to suit themselves and laughed the others off, till by the fall of their city and their own destruction their folly stood revealed.[7]

A 'man from their country who would become monarch of the whole world'? The quote sounds all too familiar. What can it refer to except the Book of Daniel? For a short time Jews seem to have believed the prophesy of a revitalised, remade Jewish state had finally come true. Their belief would have been strengthened by events. For three years the Jewish rebels were left alone by the Romans, who were distracted by struggles for the Imperial throne. An independent Jewish state existed, briefly, issuing coins with Jewish symbols and patriotic slogans written in Hebrew, which had been dead for centuries except as a religious language. There was even a new calendar, beginning, as in many later revolutionary states, from Year One. The new state gave itself an old name: Israel.

This short-lived triumph only deepened the disaster that followed. Josephus describes how, during the siege of Jerusalem, Titus repeatedly tried to convince the defenders to surrender. He marched his huge army around the city to show its strength, and had Josephus go up to the walls and urge the Jews to give up. Titus' efforts were ignored. Jerusalem's defenders fought tenaciously, as if, though they were besieged and outnumbered, and had no allies to come to their aid, they still had hopes to the very end of victory. In all likelihood they *did* have hopes. Though nothing is known of the city leaders' thinking at this time, as no trace of them has survived, it is probable that they were waiting for God's intervention. They would have believed that if they impressed Yahweh with their devotion, he would intervene to save them. He would destroy the Romans and raise the Jews up to a world power, just as Daniel's Dream had promised.

It was not to be. Did the disaster of the Jewish war cure Jews of hopes of an end of the world? Rather surprisingly, it did not. In AD 116, forty-six years after the fall of Jerusalem, rebellions broke out in three separate Jewish diaspora communities within the Roman Empire, in Cyprus, Egypt and Cyrenia (modern eastern Libya). It cannot be proved that these uprisings were motivated by apocalyptic hopes, yet their intensity, brutality and, most of all, *hopelessness*– the diaspora Jews formed only a minority in these lands – suggest that this was the case. Cassius

Dio, writing a century later, claims that deaths reached hundreds of thousands, and the revolts left such bitterness that, even in his own time, Jews were still banned from the island of Cyprus on pain of death.

No uncertainty surrounds the third and final Jewish rebellion against Rome in AD 132–5. This was, unquestionably, an *apocalyptic war*. Again details are sketchy, this time because the conflict was so terrible, and so inglorious for both sides, that neither Romans nor Jews wanted to record for posterity what had happened. It seems to have been Rome's *Vietnam War*. Roman legions in the countryside around Jerusalem struggled for three years against resolute and elusive bands of Jewish guerillas, who launched attacks from maze-like complexes of tunnels. Although the Romans finally won, this was, tellingly, the only Roman victory that was never commemorated in any way. The Jewish leader, Simon Bar Kokhba, was accepted by Jews and their religious leaders as the Messiah. Bar Kobha, in other words, succeeded where Jesus had failed. He convinced his countrymen that he had been sent by Yahweh to transform their world. He did not, needless to say, deliver on his promise, and later Jewish references to him were bitter with disappointment.

By the war's end a wide area around Jerusalem was reduced to an empty wilderness, and the few Jews who remained there were obliged to hide their religion to stay alive. The Romans removed even the very name of Judaea from the region, replacing it with the old Greek title, Syria Palaestrina. Out of the wreckage of their disastrous struggles with the Romans there emerged, by necessity, a new and headless Jewish religion that no longer revolved around the great temple to Yahweh. Put simply, Jews began to follow something that was recognisably like modern Judaism. It was a religion of autonomous local communities, each with its own religious leader, the rabbi. It concentrated on interpreting the old Jewish scriptures and ensuring that Jews lived their lives according to Yahweh's laws. Though they mourned the loss of Jerusalem and their temple, the dwindling Jewish population of the Levant showed little interest in trying their luck as a fighting advance guard, to help bring forth God's remaking of the world.

But the torch of the apocalypse had not gone out. It had simply been passed on to others.

Daniel's Dream: The Sequels

In the year AD 95, a woman named Domitilla began a sea journey to Pandataria, a small, bleak island about twenty-five miles from the Italian coast, to begin a life of exile. Little is known of Domitilla. She is reported by Roman historian Cassius Dio to have been exiled because she had 'drifted into Jewish ways'. Early Romans, though, often got Judaism and Christianity mixed up. It was an understandable mistake to make, seeing as the two were so closely entwined. Domitilla was claimed by Christians as one their early martyrs, and her name was recorded in some of Rome's earliest Christian catacombs just a few decades after her exile, so it seems altogether more likely that she had drifted into *Christian ways*. What makes Domitilla of interest, though, is not so much her religion as her family. She was niece to the reigning emperor, Domitian, and as Domitian was childless her two sons were the Flavian dynasty's heirs, designated to be the next rulers of the Empire.

As we will see in the next chapter, early Christians, in spite of their avowed love for the meek, had rather a weakness for the rich and famous. They saw, no doubt, that it was only through such people that they could achieve real success. In the year 95 it seems that they hit the jackpot: they converted the mother of the Roman Empire's next emperor. Two centuries later, another imperial conversion would give Christianity its great breakthrough, which would put it on the road to becoming the state religion of the Empire. In 95, though, things went badly wrong for the Christians. Domitian had no wish to see his empire, or his relatives, fall under the sway of a new, foreign and – worst of all – poor man's religion. He exiled his niece and launched a general persecution of Christians. He also, unknowingly, inspired Christianity's first apocalyptic text. On the island of Patmos, a man called John, about whom nothing is known, except that, like Domitilla, he may have been living in exile, wrote what was, in effect, *Daniel II*. It was the Book of Revelation.

Why, we might ask, did the Christians feel a need for a new end-of-the-world text? Surely the Book of Daniel was enough? The simple answer is that new end-of-the-world writings were needed to predict the bloody demise of *new enemies*. The Book of Revelation was the first of three new prophetic accounts would that would appear during the ensuing centuries, all of them written to reassure and rally beleaguered Christians by foretelling the destruction of adversaries. These texts, like Daniel's Dream, would soon find their original context largely forgotten. All three were forgeries, claiming to be older than they actually were. All three would add new and lurid details to their predecessors. So the apocalypse became a kind of serialised work of fantasy fiction, written by four separate authors across eight centuries, each providing new plot lines and details. These texts would become medieval and Renaissance Europe's greatest bestsellers, endlessly copied and recopied, and, later on, printed.

What was new in these sequels to Daniel's Dream? First, the Book of Revelation, which managed to sneak its way into the Bible through a mistaken belief that its author, John, was the same

John who wrote one of the gospels. Copying the bizarre imagery of Daniel's Dream, Revelation portrayed a Roman emperor – almost certainly Domitilla's uncle, Domitian – as a ten-horned beast. It prophesied a gory end to the city of Rome and its empire, in scenes worthy of a special-effects scene from a fantasy film. Again following on from Daniel, it described a great resurrection and last judgement, when those whose names were not written in the Book of Life were consigned to a Lake of Fire. Revelation introduced the term Antichrist, although, for the moment, this seems to have been more of an idea than a living, villainous character. It also told of something else that Daniel had omitted, though the idea had appeared in other, earlier Jewish texts: that a New Jerusalem would descend from the sky and the saved – or saints – would live within its jewel-encrusted gates. In addition, Revelation introduced the Seven Seals and the Four Horsemen of the Apocalypse, and finally the idea that Jesus would return to rule the world for a thousand years:

> [An angel] laid hold on the dragon, that old serpent, which is the Devil, and Satan, and bound him a thousand years . . . After that he must be loosed a little season. Then I saw thrones, and they sat upon them, and judgment was given unto them: and I saw the souls of them that were beheaded for the witness of Jesus, and for the word of God, and which had not worshipped the beast, neither his image, neither had received his mark upon their foreheads, or in their hands; and they lived and reigned with Christ a thousand years. (Revelation 20:3–7)

The infamous *millennium* had arrived. Why infamous? Because later Christians would conclude that it wasn't enough simply to wait for this age to arrive. They needed to take action, to prepare for its arrival. As we will see, these preparations would be bad news for non-Christians.

The next apocalyptic sequel, Tiburtina, appeared some 250 years later, around the 340s, though, as usual, it pretended to be much older. It sought to bolster Christians against a popular new Christian heresy, *Arianism*, which questioned how divine Jesus had been. Tiburtina's chief novelty was a new saviour figure. This was a Greek emperor named Constans, who, Tiburtina foretold, would unite the Roman world in a golden age lasting for more than a century. During this time Constans would deal with all Christians who had denied their lord (notably the Arians), kill all pagans and convert all Jews. Once he had done this, he would make way, rather puzzlingly, for the evil Antichrist, who was now very much a character rather than a notion. An Antichrist was probably a dramatic necessity. After Clemens's golden century, matters had to grow worse again, in advance of Jesus' triumphal return to earth to begin his glorious millennium. If all had already been glorious, his return would be rather an anticlimax.

Finally a third apocalyptic sequel – Daniel's Dream Part IV – known as Pseudo-Methodius, appeared in late seventh-century Syria, this time to bolster Christians' faith in the face of Muslim conquest. Its main innovation was to embellish the story of the saviour emperor, who now became something of a fantasy fiction hero, waking from sleep after he had long been thought dead, to crush the Ishmaelites (Muslim Arabs) from India to Egypt.

With Pseudo-Methodius the plotline of the end of the world was largely complete. Details, though, would continue to be added. The most important innovator was a Calabrian hermit named Joachim of Fiore, who, in the 1190s, gave the apocalypse new chronological precision. Joachim believed he could see clues, especially in the Book of Revelation, which allowed him to comprehend time as nobody had done before. He saw three ages. First came a time a time of slavery and fear the Age of the Father; next a time of faith, the present Age of the Son; and finally The fast-approaching the Age of the Spirit; This would be a joyous time, when men would finally come to know God, and would be able to rest, in a kind of never-ending Sabbath. Before this could happen, though, a new order of monks would arise, which would convert all Jews to Christianity, and whose leader, the *Novus Dux*– a version of Emperor Constans – would lead mankind towards the coming golden age. Joachim's ingenious calculations left him in no doubt that the Age of the Spirit would begin between 1200 and 1260.

Did these bizarre texts have any practical effect on Christians? Sadly they did. Only sixty years after the Book of Revelation was written, it inspired its first movement. In the year 156, in a bleak area of western Turkey called Phrygia, a man called Montanus announced that he was the Holy Ghost and claimed that the Book of Revelation's New Jerusalem in the sky was about to descend to earth – in Phrygia, naturally – where it would provide a new home for the saved, while everyone else perished in the Lake of Fire. Most Christian bishops refused to accept that Montanus was the Holy Ghost, but as Christianity was, at this time, an underground religion within the Roman Empire, it proved hard to eradicate his movement, which lingered for several centuries after Montanus' death.

Already Church leaders had begun to realise that the apocalypse could be a threat to their authority. So a radical transformation took place. When Christianity finally became the favoured religion of the Roman Empire, in the fourth century, and Church leaders tasted real power, they sidelined the idea that had been at the very centre of Jesus' movement. Henceforth the end of the world was replaced by *paradise*, which, as we will see in more detail in the next chapter, was an altogether less threatening prospect.

Their efforts bore fruit, at least for a time. Though, as the end of the world faded from view in Europe, it thrived elsewhere. By the sixth century, Daniel's Dream found plentiful supporters in the Middle East, where it inspired numerous end-of-the-world preachers, seeking followers and fame. These included a man called Muysalima in Mecca and a young Jewish boy in nearby Madina. Neither achieved much of a following, and we only know of them because they were both encountered by another apocalyptic preacher: Muhammad. Yes, the founder of Islam was another end-of-the-worlder, urging his listeners to repent before it was too late. The success of his new religion encouraged apocalyptic expectations still further. As Arab armies swept across the Middle East and beyond, destroying old orders from Persia to North Africa, many began to wonder if the world really was approaching its end and apocalyptic movements sprang up like mushrooms after rain: some Christian, some Muslim, some Jewish and some, to the alarm of many, of all three mixed together.

In Western Europe, a very different pattern emerged. Having largely lost interest in the end of the world, European Christians rediscovered it when, after centuries of destabilising invasions, their world grew calmer and less poor, and when the Church enjoyed unchallenged power. Why? The end of the world's return seems to have been inspired precisely *because* of the Church's hegemony. By the eleventh century, the Church of Rome had become Western Europe's largest single landowner and also its largest tax-gatherer. Those whose lives were independent yet precarious – small-town artisans and clothmakers or rural shepherds – were increasingly resentful of the comfortable lives of churchmen. Such people now joined end-of-the-world movements led by educated charismatics who were often ex-monks, ex-hermits or both.

End-of-the-world movements of educated charismatics leading followers from the fringe of society? We are back with Max Weber. The supporters of these movements were powerfully drawn to Jesus' original preaching, which is not at all surprising, as he had been preaching to *people just like them*. Like Jesus' first supporters, they had ambitions hopes. The Galilean fishermen had believed that the end of the world would raise them high while the rich would be cast aside and Roman power would be broken. Medieval apocalypticists likewise hoped to see themselves raised up, while their rich neighbours and their taxman – the Church – would be broken.

That said, one of the first great apocalyptic outbreaks did not consider the Church its enemy, though the Church may have had different views. This movement was inspired by a dubious papal invention when, in the 1090s, Pope Urban II called what would become known as the First Crusade. Urban's wish was less to conquer Palestine for Christianity, and mostly to help the ailing Byzantine Empire against advancing Turks, but he soon found his plans overtaken. As we saw, the Book of Revelation, Tiburtina and Pseudo-Methodius all prophesied that Jesus' kingdom could only come into being *after* the Antichrist had reigned in Jerusalem. Some Christians concluded that it was vital to gain control of the city, so they could despatch the Antichrist the very moment he appeared. They argued Muslims could never be entrusted with such work, as they were on the Antichrist's side.

A charismatic known as Peter the Hermit began preaching that the Crusade should concentrate on Jerusalem. Peter impressed crowds by telling them he had already been to the city, and that while he was there Jesus had appeared to him there and given him a holy letter instructing him what to do. Armed with this holy missive, Peter inspired large numbers of poor artisans and farmers to join his 'People's Crusade' that set out to capture Jerusalem and usher in a new age. Like other apocalyptic preachers before him, Peter assured his followers that they were an elite, chosen by God. Some of them were sure that if they looked carefully enough at the sky, they could see their future home, the Book of Revelation's supernatural Jerusalem, glimmering there, ready to descend.

So began one of Europe's greatest and most enduring horrors. As we have seen, the apocalyptic texts prophesied that Jesus could only return after the world *had been prepared,* by the conversion of all Jews to Christianity and the extermination of all other non-believers. Although the texts implied that these tasks would be carried out by God, Peter the Hermit and his followers decided that it was their sacred duty to lend a hand. So, as the Crusader armies began making their way south-east across Europe, they were accompanied by bands of Peter the Hermit's People's Crusaders, who gave Europe its first experience of anti-Semitic mob murder. People's Crusaders invaded the Jewish quarters of Mainz, Trier, Metz, Cologne and other cities, demanding that Jews accept baptism and killing all who refused. Though local churchmen and aristocrats tried to defend them, thousands of Jews were killed, in what soon became a terrible tradition that was repeated whenever a crusade was called. The People's Crusaders then took their murderousness with them to the Holy Land. Although most of them died before reaching the Levant, a terrible rump survived, known as the Tafurs, which was feared even by the Crusader knights. When Jerusalem fell, in 1099, it was the Tafurs who were said to be largely responsible for the massacre of the city's Muslims and Jews.

Thereafter, end-of-the-world movements made regular and usually violent appearances. They took numerous different forms. In 1260 there emerged a kind of *masochist apocalypticism.*

Self-flagellation, which had occupied monks in the Italian monasteries of Camaldi and Fontre Avellana for two centuries, now became the activity of choice for a new Italian movement, the Joachimites. As admirers of Joachim of Fiore, who, as we saw, had given the apocalypse a new timetable, the Joachimites determined to prepare the world for the Age of the Spirit, which Joachim had said would begin before the end of 1260. In the autumn of that year bands of Joachimites marched northwards across Italy, punishing themselves as they went, so humankind might be forgiven its sins. Despite the fact that the Age of the Spirit had by then missed its deadline, the movement re-emerged a year later, now north of the Alps. Reappearing intermittently, the flagellants' great days came a century later, from late 1348, at the height of the Black Death. Groups of enthusiasts marched from city to city across Europe, beating themselves three times daily until their bodies were swollen blue flesh, to try and persuade God to keep the plague away. Claiming to be an army of saints sent by God, they prepared for Jesus' coming kingdom (due, they believed in thirty-three and a half years' time, as this was thought to be Jesus' lifetime.) by inciting massacres of the clergy, the rich and, most of all, the Jews. Until the Church had had enough and in 1349 excommunicated them all.

Even after their demise, the flagellants continued to captivate minds, and two decades after their fall from favour a new movement emerged that was a kind of *apocalyptic cult of blood*. It was founded in German Thuringia and led by a man named Konrad Schmid. Schmid's version of the end of the world was quite unique. As well as claiming that he was the rightful king of Thuringia, he also insisted that he was senior to Jesus, and that with God's help he would, in 1369, create his own kingdom on earth. Like most apocalyptic leaders, he promised his little band of followers that they would be great lords or saints in the new arrangements. Unusually, though, Schmid's apocalyptic vision was based on bloodletting. As others baptised with water, Schmid baptised with blood. He claimed that the scriptures' account of how Jesus had been lashed as he carried his cross had in fact been a foretelling of how Schmid and his little band of followers would beat themselves to glory. His disciples could look forward to becoming princes in his coming kingdom only if they obeyed him, confessed to him and, most of all, were beaten by him. Though Schmid himself was caught and burned by the Inquisition in 1368, and so missed his own apocalypse, his movement endured: secretive, blood-obsessed, and even instituting its own gruesome form of infant baptism, in which newborn babies were lightly beaten till they bled. As we will see, his arrangements would probably have seemed rather familiar to blood-obsessed Mayans and Aztecs.

Next came a kind of *communist apocalypse.* Leaders of England's 1381 Peasants' Revolt, such as John Ball, urged on their supporters with slogans that Lenin would have admired, including 'When Adam ploughed and Eve span, who was then the gentleman?' A generation later, in Bohemia, members of a like-minded movement, the Taborites, abolished all taxes and burned down their own farms, so they would be free of property and might bring Jesus' kingdom closer. So began what would grows into an enduring feature of European politics.

The Protestant Reformation did nothing to dampen enthusiasm for the end of the world. To many, including Martin Luther, the uncertainties of the age seemed clear proof that it was about to arrive. The end of days proved particularly alluring to some of the array of fringe groups that formed the radical left of the Reformation and were termed Anabaptists by their enemies. In 1534 one such group gained control of the city of Münster in northern Germany, and established a kind of *apocalyptic state,* declaring that the end of the world would take place the following Easter (and when it failed to materialize, the Easter after that). Only the chosen, in Münster, would be saved. When a failed actor named Jan Bockelson took the movement's lead, his supporters declared that God would make him king, not only of Münster, but of the whole world. In preparation, Bockelson imposed the death penalty for the smallest infraction, executed a good number of townspeople, had all books except the Bible burned and ordered his followers to be entirely celibate – even if married – only to then have a change of mind and order them to be polygamous. (As leader of the saved, he himself took fifteen wives, including, naturally, the town's greatest beauties.)

Like those of so many others before him, Bockelson's promised apocalypse ended in disappointment. Having united Catholics and Protestants against him – a rare achievement at this time – he was captured and extensively tortured, and his body suspended in a cage from Münster's cathedral spire, as a warning to all, while his activities were long remembered and brought radical Protestantism into disrepute for many years. Yet the apocalypse lived on. It next found fertile ground in The Seventeenth century in revolutionary England, where the tenth horn of Daniel's beast was now identified, by the latest generation of its decoders, as King Charles I. The tailors, clothiers and shopkeepers of the *Fifth Monarchy* movement – named after Jesus' coming kingdom – happily anticipated a time when the country's great dukes would be toppled for ever and replaced by a new aristocracy: themselves.

The apocalypse of the *Diggers'* movement, by contrast, included no aristocracy at all. Diggers looked forward to a remade world of communally shared property. Their leader, Gerard Winstanley, claimed that humankind had been led down the wrong road because, after the Fall, Adam had come to rule men, leading them to desire property. When Jesus returned he would remove Adam from men's hearts, and a new age of reason would begin, in which, as Winstanley wrote, 'none shall say, this is mine, but everyone shall preserve each other in love.' To help matters along, Winstanley urged a great redistribution of land. To start the process, in 1649 he set up a kind of early kibbutz on St George's Hill in Surrey, which endured for a few months before being abandoned, both because of the poorness of the land and the hostility of their neighbours.

As Europe calmed down after the religious upheavals of the Reformation, was the apocalypse finally laid to rest? No, it simply went into abeyance. It returned to life in nineteenth-century America, through the efforts of William Miller who, in 1833, after a careful decoding of the apocalyptic scriptures, declared that the end of days would take place in 1843, and then, again, the following year. Despite the *Great Disappointment* of 22 October 1844, Miller's movement did not die, but fractured into sub-movements, and sub-sub-movements.

One such movement evolved into the most successful and enduring apocalyptic sect ever seen. This was the Bible Student Movement, later renamed the *Jehovah's Witnesses*. Much of its success can be ascribed to the energy – often highly controlling energy – of its leaders and to the relative flexibility of its notions. The movement's founder, the son of a Pittsburgh clothier named Charles Taze Russell, asserted that Jesus had returned to earth in 1874, but *invisibly*. It was a claim that was hard to disprove. Though the end of the world was repeatedly predicted for 1878, 1881, 1910, 1914, 1918, 1925 and beyond, these were 'marked years', when the end of the world was likely, rather than certain. When disappointment struck, and struck again, Witnesses were encouraged with the news that 'the wrong thing had happened at the right time.' The march towards apocalypse, which had begun with

Jesus' invisible return, was proceeding, if not quite as promptly as had first been hoped.

All the while the movement's leaders, first Russell and then, from 1917, the moody and controlling Joseph Franklin Rutherford, created a well-organised and tightly disciplined worldwide movement, using every modern means, from its journal, the *Watch Tower*, to its radio stations, to gain converts. Yet, for all their apparent modernity, the Witnesses closely resembled end-of-the-world groups from past centuries. Though at first Russell declared that *all* Protestant Christians were eligible for saving when Christ returned, he then changed his mind and decided that only his own followers stood a chance. Russell's writings were raised in status to just below that of the Bible, and he prohibited his supporters from attending any other churches' study groups. So gradually the Witnesses became something of a *society within a society*, estranged from the wider world, just like earlier apocalyptic groups such as the Anabaptists and, for that matter, the early Christians.

Yet the Jehovah's Witnesses had no monopoly of the end of the world. Among many minor groups to emerge from the wreckage of the Millerites, one evolved into the Branch Davidians, who came to a famously terrible end in 1993, during the Waco Siege in Texas. A more recent and altogether milder outbreak of apocalypticism occurred in 2010, when a retired Californian civil engineer named Harold Camping predicted that the world would begin its demise on Friday, the 21st of May 2010. On this day, Camping claimed, some two million of the saved would be 'raptured', or taken up, via a kind of express lift, to paradise, thus avoiding the months of earthquakes, plague and destruction that would despatch the remaining billions of sinners. Camping's predictions, which he publicised through radio broadcasts, inspired an innovative entrepreneurial response. Bart Centre, a

New Hampshire atheist, offered pet insurance for those who expected to be raptured. Self-proclaimed non-believers, who thus had no chance themselves of being raptured, agreed to collect, feed and walk the raptureds' pets after they had been taken up. By 19 May 2010 Bart Centre had sold insurance to 250 clients. His policies offered no refunds.

Why would middle-class Americans come to believe in the end of the world? Camping's supporters were not poor artisans, shepherds or fishermen, struggling on the margins of society. They were stolid, conservative citizens, who do not fit Max Weber's analysis in the slightest. For an answer we should look perhaps to one particular aspect of apocalyptic movements. The apocalypse did not only offer a violent remaking of the world. It also offered supporters the tempting prospect of being a new elite of survivors, picked out by God, while the great mass would be cast aside. Feeling you are one of the elect appears to be as alluring today as it ever was.

But it is time to step back a little, as we are getting ahead of ourselves. We have seen how the apocalypse, although it was one of Jesus' chief concerns – if not his *chief* concern – became sidelined within Christianity. If the heart of Jesus' preaching had been removed, then, we might ask, what exactly is *Christianity*? And how on earth did it manage to become such a thing?

5

INVENTING HUMBLE HEAVEN

Jumping Hurdles

In the autumn of the year 312 a ruthless career soldier named Constantine, who had fought his way to become ruler of the western half of the Roman Empire, was enjoying a little relaxation time in Rome. Among his activities in the city, he commissioned a huge statue to be made of himself, which he then had set up in the city's newest public hall, the vast Basilica Nova. There was nothing very unusual in this behaviour: it was the classic action of a successful emperor showing his power. There was, however, something very unusual about this particular statue.

It held a silk military banner, embellished with a symbol that would never have been seen in a Roman public place before this time: a Christian cross. Constantine, who had been converted to Christianity only a few weeks earlier, on the eve of the battle at the Milvian Bridge, which had won him Rome, was making it clear that his was to be a Christian empire.

As an exercise in public relations, however, the banner went badly wrong. Constantine had it soon taken down, after protests from Rome's aristocratic elite. They considered themselves inheritors of a long and triumphant pagan past and few of them had time for a newfangled religion that was strongly associated with, of all people, the illiterate poor. Most of Rome's aristocracy probably assumed that the emperor's new religious project was doomed to failure, and one can understand why. Though it is hard to estimate numbers, in 312 Christians probably made up no more than 10 per cent of the Empire's population, and perhaps considerably less. And while they had a fairly strong presence in the Empire's big cities, and in certain areas such as Egypt, many provinces were hardly touched by Christianity. Most important of all, Constantine's own power base, the Roman army, remained solidly pagan.

Yet Christianity had luck on its side. When he conquered the eastern half of the Empire, Constantine, despairing of the pagan Romans, set up a new capital, Constantinople, where Christianity could spread more freely through the Imperial power structure. He and his three sons proved highly adept at keeping hold of power. They also proved long-lived, at least when compared with their pagan predecessors. Between them, they were able to promote Christianity for an unbroken half-century – long enough to change power allegiances permanently. Disaster completed their work. As barbarian peoples swept across the Empire, and, in 410, Rome itself fell to the Visigoths – a humiliation not seen in eight centuries – Roman patriotic self-belief began to die. Christianity filled the vacuum. In the year 400 one still finds numerous references to high-ranking, educated pagans. By 500 these have all but vanished. The Mediterranean, which had been the world's most religiously diverse region, had become its most monochrome: a Christian sea with a sprinkling of Judaism.

It was a signally unlikely triumph. If one had taken a brief tour of the world just after Jesus' crucifixion, around AD 35, and tried to pick a religious movement that would one day monopolise a large part of the globe, that founded by Jesus would, one suspects, have come at the very bottom of the list. It had been brief, lasting only a year or two; it had been small, probably gathering only a few hundred followers; and it had ended disastrously. Its leader's promises of a world transformed had come to nothing and now he was dead. His followers were demoralised and dispersed. Obscurity beckoned. How did Jesus' movement emerge from defeat to become such an extraordinary success? Put simply, it did so by leaping a series of hurdles. With each jump, Christianity found new followers and its beliefs changed. Until, like Mahayana Buddhism, it emerged as something that Jesus himself would have found entirely unrecognisable.

The first, and probably the greatest, hurdle to be overcome was Jesus' own death. The sudden loss of their leader was enough to extinguish most other end-of-the-world movements. Though Christians would later decide that Jesus' death had been divinely intended and had therefore taken place for good reasons, it is clear from the gospels themselves that there was no such perception at the time. Jesus' followers, having been filled with excitement at the prospect of their leading roles in the coming new order, were stunned by what had happened. Jesus, who had claimed that he had the power of God behind him and promised that the world would be utterly transformed, had died without anything being transformed after all. Every one of his claims must have looked shaky, to say the least. Some of his followers, like Peter, panicked and briefly renounced the movement. Others fled home to Galilee. Jesus' mission, it seemed, was finished.

What restarted it? In short it was a new belief, that Jesus had done something special after all. He had returned from the grave.

And if he had managed one feat that was beyond ordinary humans, then there was hope that he might fulfil his other promises, too. His followers might yet become great lords of a renewed Jewish kingdom. As we saw earlier, the idea of the resurrection can be found in the Book of Daniel. Members of the Qumran sect were much taken by the idea, and had added further details. Yet there is of course a great difference between regarding something as possible, and believing that it has *actually happened*. How did Jesus' followers come to believe that he had returned to life? Was it, as some sceptics have suggested, nothing more than deliberate fabrication?

The simple answer is almost certainly no. Jesus' resurrection became central to Christianity so quickly that it makes little sense as a mere invention. Why lie? The lifeblood of Jesus' movement was its belief that the end of the world was coming. If, with his death, this belief had collapsed, one would expect his followers to walk away, rather than try to revive their belief with false claims. Also, one would expect a lie, once made, to be retold always as precisely the same story. Instead the scriptures are highly contradictory. The earliest account of Jesus' resurrection, in Paul's first letter to the Corinthians, lists numerous people who saw Jesus, including a group of no fewer than 500. Intriguingly, Paul reports that they saw Jesus not in a *bodily* but in a *spiritual* form. According to Matthew and Mark, the first to see him were Mary Magdalen and his mother Mary, in Jerusalem, though he was later seen by the eleven apostles, who had returned to Galilee. Luke, too, says that Jesus was seen by the apostles, though this time not in Galilee but in Jerusalem, where the apostles did not at first recognise Jesus, but they then all ate a meal together. According to Acts Jesus visited his disciples over a period of forty days, coming and going as he chose.

What could really have happened? It is surely significant that the very earliest account, in Paul's letter to the Corinthians, states that Jesus' followers saw him in a *spiritual* form. It is not unusual for people suffering great loss to believe that they feel the presence of, and even *see*, the person who has died. Jesus had clearly been highly charismatic. He would have filled the lives of his Galilean followers in a way they would never have experienced before. It seems highly plausible that they might have dreamed of Jesus, or even believed that they briefly saw him. One claim could have inspired others, until followers *expected* to sense Jesus. As years passed, accounts may have changed, as stories usually do with re-telling, until the Jesus they had dreamed of, or sensed, became a Jesus tangibly brought to life, talking and enjoying meals with his disciples. Intriguingly, one group of early Christians maintained that something like this happened. In the second century, the *Gnostic Christians,* who will be examined more closely later, believed that Jesus had not been physically brought back to life, but had appeared only in his followers' visions.

What really mattered, though, was not *how* such a belief had occurred, but *that* it had done so at all. Whatever one may think about whether Jesus was resurrected, his movement certainly was. Jesus had recruited followers of greater determination, and inspired in them greater passion, than other charismatic Jewish religious leaders of this era, such as the anonymous Egyptian. Filled now with missionary zeal, Jesus' followers began speaking in synagogues, and in the Temple of Jerusalem, trying to persuade their fellow Jews that their leader would soon return *again*, this time transforming the world as he had promised.

Jesus' movement had leaped its first and, arguably, its greatest hurdle. Overcoming this crisis, though, had caused it to change. Already, within a few months of Jesus' death, it had begun its slow evolution towards being a different religion. The belief that

Jesus had returned to life was now placed at its very core, and it was marked by a new – and some would say bizarre – ritual. Within a few years after Jesus' crucifixion, his followers were celebrating mass. They showed their acceptance that Jesus had come back to life by magically bringing him back to life *again*, in the form of blessed bread and wine, which they then ate and drank, believing it to be his flesh and blood. This ritual which later critics would attack as cannibalistic, may, like so many Christian practices, have had originated with the Essenes. The Dead Sea scroll, Rule of the Community, mentions a grand, military-style banquet that would occur when 'the Messiah has been revealed', while a ritual of blessing wine and bread was performed at every meal at which more than ten communitarians were gathered.

For first-century Christians, though, the ceremony clearly had a new purpose. It was to show allegiance to the belief that had restarted their movement: that Jesus had been resurrected. By celebrating Mass Christians were required to regularly and publicly acknowledge that Jesus had come back to life. As such, Mass seems suspiciously like an invention intended to crush any lingering unease among Christians on the matter. If so, it was not entirely successful. As I have mentioned, the Gnostic Christians did not accept that Jesus had been physically resurrected.

Another important development of this early time was the attempt to answer the question of *why Jesus had died*. Within four years of his crucifixion, Paul wrote that Jesus had died 'for our sins'. He had died to save others, although not yet all of mankind. That would come later. So the shocking pointlessness of Jesus' death was now made good. It had been intended by God that he would die. In this way it was decided that his movement had, despite all appearances, *succeeded*. During his year or two of preaching, Jesus had told his followers that he *would be special*, as a ruler of the coming kingdom. After his death his followers proclaimed *that he had already been special* before he died. In fact he had been the anointed one, The Messiah or Christ. His crucifixion was not shameful, but confirmed his special status.

So Jesus enjoyed his first posthumous promotion. Although he appears to have held a very high view of himself, as a future king and viceroy of God, he had never, it seems, claimed to be a Messiah. In the first decades after his death, Jesus still appears to have been regarded by his followers – including Paul – as thoroughly human and not a god. But he was on his way up.

Already the fledgling Christian Church was beginning to take a few steps from the strict single God of the Jews. Like Buddha – and far more speedily – Jesus had become *supermundane*. But this was not the only faint blurring of monotheism to occur at this time. A third force began to take shape in minds of early Christians: the Holy Spirit, In the earliest years of the religion, some of Jesus' followers fell into an ecstatic state, speaking an unintelligible language. Their opponents accused them of drunkenness. Yet ecstatic outpourings and 'speaking in tongues' were hardly new. Arguably they were descended from one of the very oldest religious phenomena: entering a trance to reach spirits. Whatever their origins, though, these events now became accepted as God manifesting himself. When people ranted incomprehensibly, they were seen as *God's mouthpieces*. The Holy Spirit would be a cause of constant unease for church authorities over later centuries. If people could have a direct, lightning rod connection with God, did they need a large and expensive organisation of well-fed priests? Yet like that other destabilising element, the end of the world, its place close to the heart of Christianity would mean it could never be expunged.

Another great change in the Jesus movement sprang directly from his execution. As Jesus' followers looked to follow the example of their cult's founder, Christianity became a *cult of death*. So we enter the age of the Christian martyr. This was a new departure. Jews had had martyrs during their conflict with the Greeks, when the Book of Daniel was written, but these were warriors who had died in the battle. The Jesus of the gospels had shown little interest in martyrdom, at least until it was about to overtake him. He had been interested in life: in eating and drinking, in debating Jewish scripture and religious rules, in gathering a band of loyal followers and in looking ahead to becoming the *living* ruler of a powerful, restored Jewish kingdom.

After Jesus' death, though, martyrdom became the great dream of zealous Christians. In this they were helped by their religion's outcast status. Though persecutions were, for the most part, relatively few and far between, and were much exaggerated by later Christian propaganda, Christians undeniably were persecuted – firstly, and on a small scale, by the Jewish authorities and later by the Romans. Yet when it came to martyrdom, it took two to tango. Members of other illegal sects, such as the Gnostic Christians and the atheist Epicureans refused to die for their beliefs, preferring to publicly deny their religion (which was all that the Roman authorities asked of them) so that they could quietly return to it afterwards. By contrast, a zealous minority of Christians was *eager* to be martyred. Such as Perpetua, a 22-year-old new mother who, as she awaited execution in a Carthage jail in the year 203, had the foresight to keep a diary:

> My father returned from the city spent with weariness; and he came up to me to cast down my faith, saying: 'Have pity, daughter, on my grey hairs; have pity on thy father, if I am worthy to be

called father by thee; if with these hands I have brought thee unto this flower of youth – and I have preferred thee before all thy brothers; give me not over to the reproach of men. Look upon thy brothers; look upon thy mother and mother's sister; look upon thy son, who will not endure to live after thee. Forbear thy resolution; destroy us not all together; for none of us will speak openly against men again if thou sufferest aught.' This he said fatherwise in his love, kissing my hands and grovelling at my feet; and with tears he named me, not daughter, but lady. And I was grieved for my father's case because he would not rejoice at my passion . . .[8]

Needless to say, Perpetua ignored her father's pleadings. She did the same to those of the judge at her trial, telling him, when he urged her to think of her newborn child, 'I am a Christian', before going 'cheerfully' down to the dungeon. She died in the arena shortly afterwards at the hands of a gladiator who, according to the anonymous contemporary editor of her diary, was shocked when she guided his sword to her throat.

Her fellow martyr Felicity showed even greater determination. She was eight months pregnant and, according to Roman rules, a woman who was with child could not be executed (by no means the only instance when Roman authorities seemed rather more humane than the Christians they persecuted). Felicity became anxious that she might miss out on her martyrdom, but, after intense prayers with other Christian prisoners, she managed to give birth prematurely and so attained her wish.

Why were Perpetua and Felicity so determined to abandon their babies and die? Loyalty to their religion, and to their fellow Christians, was no doubt hugely important, just as Perpetua reported in her diary. There were also, though, sound selfish reasons to be a martyr. By the time of Perpetua's execution, martyrdom was seen as a kind of *express lift to salvation*. Martyrs, regardless of any black sins they had committed, were guaranteed a place at the highest level of paradise, close to God himself. To the disquiet of Bishop Cyprian of Carthage, in the third century AD, some martyrs-to-be, awaiting execution in jail, feasted, drank and fornicated freely with visiting Christian women, knowing that their actions could not prevent their ascent to Heaven.

Martyrs also enjoyed great status on earth. Uniquely, they were considered to be even more virtuous in the eyes of God than that other highly prized group, virgins. Much like dead pharaohs a couple of thousand years earlier, they were thought to have God's ear. As they awaited death, martyrs were frequently visited by Christian sinners hoping for prayers on their behalf. They were even sought out by bishops, to decide thorny issues of Christian dogma. No wonder martyrdom was so popular. It soon became so desired that matters threatened to get out of hand. Early Christian writers, such as Clement and Origen, insisted that Christians should not voluntarily hand themselves in to the Roman authorities. Instead, they had to wait patiently in the hope of arrest.

Martyrdom produced, as a spin-off, another new and strange element of Christianity: bone collection. If martyrs were close to God, then, arguably, so were their bones. Christians came to believe that these bones had a kind of magical power: to cure diseases, bring luck, avert drought and even, later on, win battles. As early as the second century, martyrs' bones – along with any bones that could be claimed as Christian – began to vanish from graves. It was a radical new departure. In Judaism, dead bodies had always been considered as unclean and had to be buried as quickly as possible. By contrast, Christians revered martyrs' remains, storing them in their churches and carrying them in processions. When persecution ceased, and the supply of martyr bones dried up, bone hunting became increasingly intense, and by the high Middle Ages whole military campaigns were fought over prestigious – and probably fake – relics.

All of these many changes had followed on from the first great hurdle Christianity needed to leap: the death of its founder. Another hurdle, hardly less great, though, lay just around the corner.

Jesus for Gentiles

In the year 47 or 48, at a Roman military settlement at Pisidia Antioch, in today's central Turkey, a man called Paul found himself preaching to a very troublesome group of listeners.

> And the next Sabbath day came almost the whole city together to hear the word of God. But when the Jews saw the multitudes, they were filled with envy, and spake against those things which were spoken by Paul, contradicting and blaspheming, (Acts 13:44–5).

Paul, as we will see, grew impatient. One can understand his frustration. Having survived the disaster of Jesus' death, Christianity had struck another great problem.

As we saw, Jesus' followers, fired up by the belief that he had come back to them, then tried to convert their fellow Jews to his message, preaching in synagogues and the temple in Jerusalem. Yet they had little success. Though their movement seems to have expanded in the years after Jesus's death, it was still supported by only a tiny minority, and most Jews remained obstinately unconvinced by its claims. During his lifetime they had not believed that Jesus had been sent as a viceroy of God, and now they did not believe that he had been the Messiah. Though it had survived the death of its founder, Christianity was on the road to becoming a small, outcast sect, destined to gradually dwindle away. Among Jews this would, in fact, be its exact fate.

How was Christianity's next hurdle overcome? In effect by moving to another target group: non-Jews. This idea, though it may seem simple enough, involved a vast shift. It quickly became apparent to Paul that non-Jews, or Gentiles, would only become Christians if they were exempted from Jewish law: from having to follow Jewish food restrictions and, if male, from having to be circumcised. This was a radical step for a Jewish religious movement. These laws, we should remember, were accepted by Jews as God's laws, which had been given by him to Moses. They were obeyed as the price for Yahweh's protection of his people. They were the very core of the Jewish religion. However unsuccessful the Jesus movement had been with Jews, it saw itself as being a part of Judaism, if not the *truest* part, which was closest to God. According to Paul, however, Jewish laws, rituals and beliefs could now be ignored. The gulf between Jesusism and Judaism, which was discernible even when Jesus led his followers to Jerusalem, now yawned wide indeed.

Would Jesus, had he lived, have countenanced these changes? Would he, for that matter, have wanted non-Jews in his movement? It seems highly unlikely. Jesus was a traditional Jew, highly learned in, and carefully observant of, Jewish law. Nor does he seem to have had any great love of Gentiles. According to Mark when Jesus is approached by a Greek woman who wants him to exorcise her daughter, he tells her, memorably, 'Let the children [of Israel] first be filled: for it is not meet to take the children's bread, and to cast it unto the dogs.' (Mark 7:27) (When the woman answered, 'Yes, Lord: yet the dogs under the table eat of the children's crumb', he relents and exorcizes her daughter after all). Mark's gospel was written almost two generations after Jesus' death, when his movement was already becoming dominated by Gentiles. One wonders what else he may have said that was quietly, and diplomatically, forgotten.

It took an outsider to change the fledgling movement's direction, and there was no greater outsider than Paul. Though Jewish, he was not from Galilee, or even from Judaea, but from Tarsus, in modern south-east Turkey. He was an expat, a part of the Jewish diaspora. Also unusually for a Jew, he was a Roman citizen. He had not been part of the original movement, but joined only a year after Jesus' death. Worst of all, he had been *on the other side*. Before his famous conversion on the road to Damascus, after which he changed his name to Paul, he had been Saul, the 'pharisee of Pharisees': a determined persecutor of Christians who had organised the stoning to death of Christianity's very first martyr, Stephen.

With such a disadvantageous background, Paul, who clearly had ambitions within his adopted movement, could hardly hope to compete with the Christian old guard in Jerusalem, who had all known Jesus personally. Shrewdly, he took Jesus' claims elsewhere. After returning to Tarsus for a few years – probably to wait for the end of the world – he began travelling, preaching Jesus' message of love and the apocalypse to Jewish diaspora communities in Asia Minor and Greece, only to find that Jesus the Messiah was no more acceptable here than he had been in Jerusalem.

I suggested earlier that a preacher seeking converts is much like an actor in a theatre, interacting with their audience. This *may* have been the case with Jesus. There is no question that it *was* the case with Paul. We know this, because his eulogistic biographer, the author of Acts, describes it happening. Rebuffed at Pisidia Antioch by his fellow Jewish expatriates, Paul told them:

Then Paul and Barnabas waxed bold, and said, 'It was necessary that the word of God should first have been spoken to you: but seeing ye put it from you, and judge yourselves unworthy of everlasting life, lo, we turn to the Gentiles.' (Acts 13:46).

Paul had become a kind of rogue preacher, reinventing Christianity as he saw fit. One would expect such a figure to strike trouble when he returned to base, and this is precisely what seems to have happened when, a year or two later, Paul finally came back to Jerusalem and faced the old guard, led by Jesus' surviving brother, James. Exactly what happened is hard to assess, as this was history written by its victors: Paul and his supporters. The author of Acts paints Paul as a heroic, dynamic figure, making converts and firing off letters to tell Christians how they should behave. By contrast, the Jerusalem old guard – Jesus' true inheritors, The apostles – appear only in a few short and puzzling lines. They endorse Paul's exemption of Gentile Christians from Jewish religious law. But they also warn him that he is getting himself into danger, as Jews in Jerusalem think he is leading the Jewish diaspora astray:

'Thou seest, brother, how many thousands of Jews there are which believe; and they are all zealous of the law: And they are informed of thee, that thou teachest all the Jews which are among the Gentiles to forsake Moses, saying that they ought not to circumcise their children, neither to walk after the customs. What is it therefore? The multitude must needs come together: for they will hear that thou art come . . .' (Acts 21:20–22)

Was the old guard not warning Paul but berating him? One senses the shadow of an old squabble, and it is hard not to wonder if the old guard really did endorse Paul's radical changes. Old rancour is also suggested by what happened next. The old guard ordered Paul to show his adherence to traditional Judaism by undergoing seven days of purification, together with four other Jewish Christians. When, having done this, Paul then took his four companions into the temple, he was accused by a mob of bringing Gentiles into the sacred place – a religious crime – and he was beaten and arrested. It is quite possible that Paul did indeed take Gentiles into Yahweh's temple. Certainly it would explain The anger directed against him. The account in Acts certainly seems awkward, and faintly accusatory, implying that the Jerusalem old guard was in some way responsible for Paul's fate.

In the bigger picture, though, Paul had won. His Jewish-law-lite version of Christianity became a hit with non-Jews across the eastern Mediterranean, and soon in Rome itself. But although Paul dropped various rules on food and circumcision, other restrictions remained: notably, the ban on adultery and homo-sexuality. This ban brought something quite new to the Greek and Roman worlds. Though both these activities had had their detractors in Rome and Athens, they had not been connected with religion. Now, for the first time, Gentiles began to see them as a bar to salvation.

Why did Jesus' movement succeed with Gentiles but not with Jews? One can only speculate, but an important factor is likely to have been *cultural distance*. Jews were familiar with ideas of the end of the world, and would have been well aware of failed movements led by self-appointed saviours. To Gentiles these ideas were untainted by previous failures. Paul was doing what Zarathustra and Jesus had done, and Muhammad would do almost Six centuries later. He took fledgling Christianity into exile, where it found more open listeners.

To Gentiles Paul offered a religion that was both little known and exotically ancient. Though Jews had had a strong presence across the eastern Mediterranean for centuries, there is no evidence that they attempted to convert Gentiles to their beliefs. Judaism was a national religion, not something to be pushed to outsiders. Now, for the first time, a group of Jews was preaching to non-Jews. Gentiles came into contact with such exciting ideas as a single and all-powerful yet also forgiving and loving God. They felt the pull of ancient prophesy. And, most of all, they learned of the imminent transformation of the world, in which they could become part of a new elite. Better still, they could enjoy all of these novelties while continuing to eat their favourite pork and shellfish dishes and, if male, without undergoing a minor but painful operation. No wonder the mix was popular.

Thanks to Paul, Christianity had leapt its second hurdle. It had found a new and enlarged audience. Little clusters of Christians, most of them gentile, could soon be found in all the major cities of the Roman Empire, especially in the eastern Mediterranean. As with the first hurdle, though, the movement hit the ground changed. This was not only a matter of abandoning Jewish law. In effect, Paul reinvented Christianity. Preaching to people who had little knowledge of Judaism, let alone Jesus' version of it, he took the opportunity to remake Jesus' religion as he chose, The Christianity that grew out of Paul's preaching was radically different from the ideas of Jesus, so much so that it can almost be regarded as a new religion: *Paulism*.

What was new in Paulism? Most of all, it was a good deal more puritanical than Jesusism. Jesus seems to have been little interested in demanding that people repent their sins. Monomaniacal yet forgiving, the only sin for which he showed zero tolerance was failure to follow him. Paul, by contrast, railed against every kind of trespassing, while his expectations of virtue were high, to say the least. Even joining Paul's church was tough.

Would-be Christians had to endure a three-year apprenticeship as catechumens, an arrangement that precisely mirrored entry to the Qumran sect. During this time they were tested on their knowledge of Christian teaching, they were regularly required to confess past sins before the congregation, they were exorcised and, of course, they were carefully watched for any sign of lapsing into sin.

What were the new sins of Paul's church? High on the list was ostentation. This was something quite new. Jesus had praised poverty and ordinariness – perhaps because most of his followers were poor and ordinary – but not *plainness*. The gospels report that he was frequently eating and drinking, not only with his disciples but with tax collectors and sinners: in short, with anyone who would follow him. He was even criticised for eating and drinking too freely. By contrast, Paul's church was a *cult of the plain*. Early Christians wore plain clothes, behaved in a modest, plain way and ate plain food, if they ate at all, that is, and were not fasting.

By making plainness a virtue, Paul's Christianity offered its followers the mesmerising vision of a world in which *status was turned upside down*. A poor Christian washerwoman in Rome or Antioch could delight in the secret knowledge that she was actually better off than the ostentatious rich whose dirty clothes she cleaned. In a world where the gap between the poor and the rich was steadily widening, and where ostentation ruled, Christianity, uniquely, gave the poor a sense that they were winning the class war. They could consider themselves both more virtuous and possessing a brighter future. When Jesus returned and transformed the world, they would be saved, while rich pagans would die. At early church services, rich Christians (and congregations often had one or two) had to follow the lead of the poor, casting aside their fineries and behaving meekly.

The issue on which Paul's church was plainest of all was, of course, sex. Paul was probably not wholly to blame for this state of affairs. In family-centric Judaism, adultery had been forbidden, along with homosexuality, from at least the sixth century BC. The Qumran sect was all-male, and so, we must assume, at least aspired to celibacy. According to the gospels, Jesus regarded the Kingdom of Heaven as a place where there would be no marriage and so, one supposes, no sex.

Paul, though, took matters altogether further. He urged that sexual abstinence was the perfect state for Christians, which would take them closest to God and salvation. In the early Church even *married* Christians sometimes took vows of celibacy, to live (or try to live) like brothers and sisters. Best of all, though, was *never to have indulged at all*. So there appeared in Christian communities a curious new phenomenon: little groups of venerated – and often rather conceited – virgins. Virgins, as I mentioned earlier, were supposedly viewed by God as being second only to martyrs. Fed and clothed by their fellow Christians, and often living in the local bishop's home, virgins came in all shapes and forms. They could be female or male, teenaged or middle-aged.

Why this obsession with abstinence? Some have suggested that Paul had *a thing about sex*. If he did, he was far from alone. The Corinthian Christians to whom he wrote appear to have been just as keen to exclude sex from their lives as was Paul. When Paul urged abstinence he seems to have hit a chord, at least among his more zealous readers. One has to remember, of course, that most early Christians were poor and female. Perhaps the sort of sex on offer to them was none too desirable. Yet for some early Christians celibacy seems to have had a magnetic appeal in its own right. It offered an internalised battleground in which to prove one's own virtue. As the historian Robin Lane

Fox memorably observed, 'those who wished for an obvious contest, where merit and failure were clearly marked, could now find it in a battle against their own instincts. The ideal had the simple merit of being difficult, but self-centred.'[9]

What of those who failed the test? Paul's church, unlike Jesus', was unforgiving. Deadly sins were beyond all absolution. It was *one strike and you're out*. Lesser sins could be pardoned, but only after communal shaming. The sinner was ostracised and forced to do penance, waiting outside the door of the House of God (often an apartment, or house provided by a rich member of the congregation) to beg the virtuous to pray on their behalf. Only after several weeks of such humiliation, coupled with public confession and exorcism, would the sinner be readmitted. Yet the Goody Two Shoes did not have everything their own way. As early Christians became ever more finely attuned to each others' failings, sin was found in those who thought themselves most virtuous, through the sin of pride. The most plain-living, celibate Christians could be guilty of arrogantly thinking themselves better than others. Ambitious Christians (and there were many) had to be constantly vigilant, criticising themselves before others did so, and analysing their every feeling for the minutest hint of conceit, or selfishness.

So, though early Christians scorned the ostentation of their rich pagan neighbours, they were not immune to one-upmanship. They simply competed *by other means*. As Robin Lane Fox describes, early churches were intense fishbowl-like worlds, in which members constantly watched one another for failings – from pride to eating tasty food to wearing smart clothes to sexual pleasure. As with much else in Paul's church, this fascination with self-denial had not existed in Jesus' movement. For that matter it was new to the ancient world. Among both Pagans and Jews it had been quite enough simply to obey religious rules.

Christians, by contrast, strove to obey the rules even better, so one might impress God *even more*.

The intensity of their world was doubtless enhanced by another Christian preoccupation: fasting. Christians, to keep themselves in a constant state of starved religious intensity, added extra fast days to their religious calendar. Hunger, of course, was also helpful in the struggle for celibacy. There was nothing like a diet of plain, stodgy food, and not much of it, to keep sex off the menu.

Something else that was very much off the menu in Paul's church was *women with power*. Jesus seems to have had no problems here, and women held prominent places in his movement, including even the reformed prostitute Mary Magdalen. Soon after Jesus' death, though, women appear to have become sidelined, and the old guard in Jerusalem was all-male. under Paul's, guidance women, though they appear to have made up a large majority of his followers, were relegated to a distinctly second-class role. Paul himself made it quite clear how they should behave.

'Let your women keep silence in the churches: for it is not permitted unto them to speak; but they are commanded to be under obedience, as also saith the law' (1 Corinthians 14.34)

The innovation of Paul's church that was, arguably, most doubtful was its hunger for absolute *ideological control*. Paul and his successors showed no tolerance for divergent beliefs, both within the church and without. This thinking was wholly alien to pagan religions, which were quite used to rubbing along beside one another. Judaism, of course, was far less open-minded. The laws of Moses required uniformity of belief in only one God, and even called for a kind of *jihad* against heathen neighbours.

Yet the Jews were too powerless and too schismatic to carry uniformity very far. Conquered rather than conquering, the Jews, instead of obliterating their neighbours, had to put up with other religions on their doorstep. By Jesus' time they had split into three separate sects – Pharisees, Saducees and Essenes – each with profoundly different ideas, and although they showed little liking for one another, they displayed no interest in controlling or destroying each other. As for Jesus, though he clearly expected complete dedication from his followers, it is hard to see his movement as ideologically controlling.

Early Christian authorities, by contrast, refused to acknowledge other religions in any way, seeing them as the work of the devil. They also sought to impose a single supernatural vision on all members of the Church. This intolerance was all the more remarkable because it was so impractical. Christians existed in tiny, dispersed, undergound worlds across the Roman Empire: an arrangement that seemed designed to defy uniformity. Yet uniformity was attempted. Total control lay in the hands of that classically Christian figure, the bishop. Bishops were absolute monarchs over their flocks. They made and enforced the law. They were their congregations' exchequers, and they administered the rituals surrounding births, marriages and deaths. They had the power to ostracise, and, most terrifying of all, as intermediaries between their flock and God, they had the power to deny their subjects' hope of salvation, through excommunication. There could be no appeal against their judgement.

When do bishops emerge? The first one to step clearly into the light is Bishop Clement, who ruled the Christians of Rome two generations after Jesus' death, in the 90s, and was not averse to lecturing other churches, too. Here he his thundering at schismatic Corinthians,

We have been somewhat tardy in giving heed to the matters of dispute that have arisen among you, dearly beloved, and to the detestable and unholy sedition, so alien and strange to the elect of God, which a few headstrong and self-willed persons have kindled to such a pitch of madness that your name, once revered and renowned and lovely in the sight of all men, hath been greatly reviled . . .[10]

The template of the Christian bishop, though, may have been created a generation earlier, in none other than Paul himself. Certainly his growls and roars seem very bishop-like. Here he is, denouncing already schismatic Corinthians, some four decades before Clement of Rome.

But instead, one brother goes to law against another – and this in front of unbelievers! The very fact that you have lawsuits among you means you have been completely defeated already. Why not rather be wronged? Why not rather be cheated? Instead, you yourselves cheat and do wrong, and you do this to your brothers Do you not know that the wicked will not inherit the kingdom of God? (1 Corinthians 6:6–10)

Among the first victims of bishop power were *visionaries*. These individuals had been in vogue in very early Christianity, where, like virgins and martyrs, they enjoyed high status within this intensely competitive new movement. Like prophets, including Jesus himself, they would often take themselves away to a remote spot, where they would starve themselves until they felt the presence of the supernatural. The trouble with visionaries, though, at least as far as bishops were concerned, was that they lacked any sense of self-restraint. Once they had come to believe that they had seen angels, or Jesus himself, and that they had a hotline to the supernatural world, they frequently saw themselves as *above the Church*. They claimed that they had been instructed by God to berate the Church for its failure to follow the rules more zealously. Visionaries were loose cannons. Worse, they threatened the authority of bishops. Naturally this was not something bishops tolerated. From the end of the first century, visionaries became increasingly ostracised as heretics.

Not that visionaries were the only ones who found themselves on the wrong side of Church power. As Christianity grew, an increasing number of groups emerged that did not fit with Paul's prescriptions. As would be the case across the coming millennia, these were often reactions against aspects of the main church that some Christians found objectionable. Unsurprisingly, one area of tension was Paul's sidelining of women. One of the first Christian heretic movements, which we encountered briefly in the last chapter, was led by the preacher Montanus. Montanus' apocalyptic Sect could hardly have been more female-friendly. It was based on the visions of a prophetess, who claimed to have been spoken to by Jesus *dressed as a woman*. The movement proved highly popular, so much so that Church authorities had to go through the convoluted process of having Montanus denounced by martyrs awaiting execution in Lyons, though even then his cult continued to find followers for several centuries. Another early Christian, Marcion, set up his own church organisation, complete with women priests and bishops, before he, too, was sidelined as a heretic.

The most remarkable of the anti-Paulists, though, were the Gnostic Christians. Little would be known of this group if a collection of its scriptures had not escaped official Church destruction, by being buried in a large pot at Nag Hammadi in Egypt, and then rediscovered in 1945. The texts included gospels by – supposedly – Thomas, Mary Magdalen, Philip, Jesus' brother James and many more besides, while the picture that emerges from them is one of deliberate resistance to Paul's church.

Gnostic Christians had no autocratic bishops. In fact, they had no hierarchy at all, selecting a new leader at each meeting by lot. Gnostic Christians did not aspire to other-worldly salvation or to a place in an apocalyptically transformed world. Rather they sought a kind of divine self-knowledge.

As to women, Gnostic Christians did not merely give them a greater role in their church. They wrote them into the very heart of their theology. Like Zoroastrians, Gnostics believed that there was not one god, but two: one good and one bad (predictably, they claimed that the main church was worshipping the bad one). They believed that the good god was both male and female. Gnostics even had their own account of the Garden of Eden, in which a *good, wise serpent* encourages Adam and Eve to eat the forbidden fruit, which, in turn, allows them to find enlightenment.

Paul's church responded with propaganda of its own. In the 160s the Bishop of Lyons, Irenaeus, wrote a denunciation of the Gnostics that ran to several volumes. The main defence of Paul's church, though, was a kind of *institutional line of succession.* Christian clergy claimed that only they had legitimacy because they were the latest in a continuous series of appointments – made through the ritual of a bishop laying hands on a new bishop – which could be traced back to Jesus himself, who, in turn, had been appointed by God.

This idea was already being promoted by the end of the first century when the last of the four gospel writers, John, claimed that, after his resurrection, Jesus had anointed Peter as his successor. Around this same time claims first appear that Peter came to Rome and became the city's first bishop, anointing his successor and so beginning the Papal line,. Yet there is no early evidence that Peter ever reached Rome. In the scriptures he fades from view soon after Jesus' death. All in all it seems quite possible that his presence in Rome was a deliberate invention, to link the original Jesus movement with the church founded by Paul. At a time when the anti-hierarchical, female-friendly Gnostic Christians were on the rise, a little forgery could have been seen as well justified. If this was what occurred, it certainly succeeded. The main Church grew while Gnostic Christianity shrank away.

Mainstream Christianity, having leaped over its second hurdle – its failure to win over the Jews – had triumphed. Other hurdles, however, remained. The next concerned a matter that had been at the very heart of Jesus' teaching, but which became increasingly problematic with the passing years. As we have seen, Jesus had promised his followers that the world would soon be apocalyptically transformed. At the last supper he had told his disciples that they would see this happen with their own eyes. Yet years passed, the disciples died, and nothing happened. A crisis loomed as Christianity, in effect, approached its sell-by date.

This crisis was overcome with a new invention. In one of the last texts to be included in the New Testament, the Second Epistle of Peter, it was claimed that God had a different system for calculating time from humans: 'With the Lord a day is like a thousand years, and a thousand years are like a day.' This playing around with time was nothing new. As we saw, the anonymous author of the Book of Daniel had used a similar device to adjust his prophesies until he hit the correct date of Antiochus IV's death. Thanks to Peter II, the end of the world was postponed and, after further calculations, postponed again. By AD 200, most Christians believed that the kingdom of God would not appear for several centuries.

This may seem a simple change. The consequences, though, would be great. By moving the end of the world from the imminent present to the distant future, Christianity became, in effect, a different religion, which even Paul might have found difficult to recognise.

It was not merely that Christians no longer expected to experience the end of the world. Salvation, in effect, had *moved location*. Jesus' followers had expected to be saved on earth, in Jesus' transforming kingdom. Now salvation had been relocated to God's celestial heaven. Christianity, belatedly, had found paradise.

It was a rather Egyptian arrangement. Then again, this is probably not surprising. The Egyptian cult of Osiris, which we last saw inspiring the tomb builder Kha to fill his own last resting place with every possible possession that he might need, had, by Jesus' time, begun to spread across the Roman Empire, where it would be one of Christianity's greatest rivals. It seems highly possible that the Christians may have borrowed some ideas from Osiris' worshippers, and not only in the matter of paradise. Osiris worship had become something of a family cult, with a trio of divinities: Osiris, his wife Isis (who was also, a little awkwardly, his sister) and their son Horus, ruler of the living world. By the end of the second century, a similar trio had also emerged in Christianity in the form of God the father, Jesus the son, and his mother Mary. Just as temples to Osiris had featured images of Isis breastfeeding baby Horus, Christian images of Mary breastfeeding baby Jesus became increasingly common.

This new, family-group Christianity entailed some major changes. Jesus had never considered himself a god. Even Paul does not seem to have thought him one. The earlier gospels, Mark and Matthew, written a couple of generations after the crucifixion, still portray Jesus as human, and take the trouble to produce a faked genealogical line, from ancient Israel's hero King David directly down to Jesus' father Joseph. By the early second century, though, Jesus had become fully supernatural. A new story emerged, that he had been God's actual child, conceived by Mary through divine impregnation, making poor Joseph the cuckold he has been ever since.

It is not hard to see where this idea had sprung from. Similar stories had long been in circulation elsewhere. Zoroastrianism's Messiah, as we saw, was expected to be conceived when Zarathustra's magically preserved sperm impregnated a virgin in a lake. Perhaps more puzzling is *why* Jesus was promoted to a full god. Other religions' founders, from Zarathustra to Muhammad, remained human. In all likelihood Jesus' promotion was a response to anti-Christian attacks. Status-conscious Romans would have been unimpressed by a prophet who had been executed as a common criminal. In an era when even emperors were thought to be semi-divine, it may have seemed that nothing less would do for Jesus.

The new story of divine impregnation also entailed a big promotion for Mary. She now became that most exalted of early Christian figures, a *perennial virgin*. Mary's rise no doubt proved very useful, filling a yawning gap in Paul's church: the absence of a feminine presence. Women and men now had a supernatural mother to appeal to. Mary the virgin proved an immediate hit, especially in the eastern Mediterranean, where the Osiris family trio had been so well established. In fact, she soon grew so popular that Muhammad – whose grasp of Christian theology seems to have been patchy – mistakenly took the Trinity to be Jesus, his divine father and his mother Mary. It was an understandable mistake, as by Muhammad's time Mary was a goddess in all but name to eastern Christians. Later she would captivate Western Europeans, too, becoming almost as popular as Jesus himself. Her Lady Chapels can be found in countless medieval churches and cathedrals.

Mary's promotion to Mother of God was relatively painless. Jesus' promotion, however, brought countless problems. If Jesus was a god, *and* the son of God, did that mean there was more than one God? Such a thing would contradict the heart of Jewish scriptures, which insisted very clearly that there was only one.

From around AD 200 Christian thinkers began to try to answer this dilemma, although, as we will see, in many ways this only made matters worse. The idea of the Trinity was born. Three gods in one: the Father, the Son and the Holy Spirit. The more closely Christians examined the concept, though, and especially the idea of a supernatural Jesus, the more questions were raised. Was Jesus born divine, or did he only become divine when he died? If he had been a god when alive on earth, and he and his father were the same supernatural entity, was any deity left in heaven? Who was minding the shop? And how could Jesus have cried out to God on the cross, if he and God were the same being? Had he appealed to help from himself?

Such questions began to trouble Christianity as it leaped the final two hurdles that threatened to hold it back from dominating the Mediterranean world. The first of these was that it was still a religion designed for small clusters of self-denying zealots, not for mass membership. This deficiency became painfully evident in the year 250, when the Roman emperor Decius, no doubt alarmed by Christianity's rising popularity, made the first serious attempt to quash it through persecution. Though his effort was a dismal failure and abandoned within months, it caused Christianity considerable problems. It turned out that, though a zealous minority yearned for martydom, the majority of Christians had no wish to follow Perpetua's example. A large number of those who were caught by the authorities simply did as they were asked, and renounced their religion to save themselves. Previously such behaviour had been seen as beyond forgiveness within Christianity. In 250, though, so many Christians lapsed, and then begged to be readmitted to the Church, that Bishop Cyprian in Carthage proposed that the Church should relent. Although a hardline elder of his church, Novatian, insisted otherwise, Cyprian won the day.

This was not Cyprian's only novel concession. He also declared that adulterers could be saved, if they followed a suitably severe ritual of fasting and humiliating public confession. A major change had begun. The 'one strike and you're out' system advocated by Paul was being quietly dismantled. The watering down of Paul's Church would prove a long and enduring process. One by one, sins that had been beyond all forgiveness became forgivable after all. Loopholes were found so that the foibles of the majority would not exclude them from hope of salvation. Although diehard celibacy, plainness and self-starvation did not disappear, they became increasingly the preserve of specialists: hermits, monks and nuns.

As centuries passed, the Church made constant adjustments to its rules to suit its congregations, especially their richer members. Yet the strictness of Paul's Christianity did not vanish away. Instead Christianity became a religion of reaction and counter-reaction, torn between severity and laxity, one giving rise to the other, each, in extreme form, inspiring revulsion. A pinnacle of laxity was reached in 1517, when the cash-strapped Pope Leo X authorised an agent, Johann Tetzel, to sell forgiveness for sins *not yet committed*.

But we are jumping far ahead. Christianity still had one last hurdle to leap before it could hope to dominate a sizeable part of the earth: Roman power. Yet why, we may wonder, were the Romans so against Christianity? Why did they persecute Christians, if irresolutely, for close to three centuries, while the Jews, who were no less unbending about their beliefs and, like Christians, refused to worship emperors, were left in peace, at least when it came to their religion? It seems that Judaism was tolerated because of the Romans' respect for antiquity. Christianity, a new, upstart religion, fared less well. And yet the squabble between Christians and Romans was about more than just religion. The

Romans recognised, quite correctly, that Christians were utterly opposed to *everything* they held dear. In fact, one can hardly imagine two cultures more at odds with each other.

Romans idealised themselves as austere, tough fighters. One of their greatest fears was that they might grow soft and lose their power. They took their children to watch gladiator fights in the arena, to be toughened (though their parents also enjoyed placing a wager on who would win). Christians, by contrast, who had an understandable prejudice against the arena, preached non-violence and forgiveness. Romans admired wealth, status and fine living. Christians admired meekness, plainness, humility and dreary food. Romans lived in a class world and were intensely aware of their social status. Early Christians – rich, poor, even slaves – mixed almost as equals. Worse, Christians inverted the class system, venerating poverty. Roman thinkers, as admirers of Greek rationalism, argued with logic, while Christians – whose claims could look very fragile under a logical spotlight – insisted that faith answered all questions.

Yet, intriguingly, there was a moment when the two reached a kind of accommodation. After a second ineffectual attempt at general persecution, by Emperor Valerian in the late 250s, both sides recognised that they had reached a stalemate. The Romans saw that Christians were far too entrenched in the Mediterranean world to be defeated. In turn Christians realised that they could not force their beliefs on Roman authorities. From 260, the Empire came to an intriguingly modern arrangement, under which Roman authorities accepted Christianity as one of the empire's many religions. Intolerant Christians adapted surprisingly well to the new arrangement, and in 272 one finds the curious spectacle of Christian bishops appealing to a pagan Roman emperor, Aurelian, in their dispute with a rogue bishop, Paul of Antioch. The historian Robin Lane Fox even suggests that without persecution, Christians began to slip into complacency and were at risk of being outflanked by the new and more austere religious movement, Manichaeanism, that had lately been founded by the Mesopotamian preacher Mani. Renewed persecution, by Emperor Diocletian in 303, though it was no more successful than previous efforts, may have put new life into Christianity. Then, just nine years later, Christians made their great breakthrough by winning the support of the rising imperial star, Constantine.

The ploy of trying to win over the great and the good had preoccupied Christians almost from the beginning. It is a curious fact that leaders of a religion supposedly devoted to the meek were intensely interested in reaching people with money and power. Though Jesus seems to have been immune to this impulse, Paul certainly was not. His early converts included a Corinthian judge and city steward, several very wealthy women and the Roman governor of Cyprus. As we saw earlier, it seems that Christians nearly hit the jackpot in the early 90s when they converted Domitilla. In 312 they finally succeeded.

How did Christians respond to having, as they increasingly would do, the armed might of the Empire at their disposal? *Badly*. Squabbles over ideological uniformity now turned murderous. By the sixth century the chief battleground between Christians was the vexed question of how divine Jesus had been. In the early fourth century, Arius, the Christian presbyter in Alexandria suggested, with some logic, that Jesus had not been divine after all, inspiring a large movement: Arianism. A century later the Monophysites argued that Jesus had been entirely divine, while the Duophysites insisted that he had two natures, divine and human. Both groups disdained the rival Nestorians, who said that these Jesuses had two natures that were barely connected. The gulfs between these groups can seem, to modern eyes, hair-splitting in the extreme. Often they were more a matter of loyalty to phrases – and to the regions of the Empire where they thrived – rather than any clearly distinguishable ideas. Yet these divisions would prove increasingly lethal. So a new phenomenon occurred: the persecution of Christians *by other Christians*.

For a time the Monophysites held sway in the East, persecuting Duophysite clergy. In the sixth century, under Emperor Justinian, the pendulum swung back and the Duophysites gained the upper hand. Monophysite bishops were dismissed or exiled, their monasteries emptied, Monophsysite hermits were dragged from their pillars, and a few diehard Monophysites were imprisoned in leper hospitals until they changed their tune. Nestorians, scorned by both sides, fled the Empire, finding converts in Iran and later in China. Some took refuge in southern India, where they found peace, at least until, a thousand years later, Portuguese colonists arrived and began persecuting them afresh.

History is not often a place to look for justice, but Justinian's brutality towards his fellow Christians offers an exception. Though he survived unscathed, his successors would pay a high price for their persecution. A new faith was about to appear, whose success would spring, in part, from Christians' violent need for visionary control.

6

INVENTING A RELIGION, INVENTING A NATION

In the year 632, a woman named Aisha tried to give comfort to her sick husband.

A man of the family of Abu Bakr happened to enter with a fresh toothpick in his hand and the apostle of Allah looked at it in such a way that I knew he wanted it. I asked, 'Shall I give thee this toothpick?' and he replied, 'Yes'. So I took it and chewed it until it became soft and gave it to him. He rubbed it against his teeth, more sharply than I had ever seen him do, and then he laid it down again. Then I found that he was becoming heavy in my lap, and looked at him and saw that his eyes were turned upwards; and he said, 'Nay! Rather the companion in paradise!' I had often heard the apostle say, 'Allah takes no prophet away without giving him a choice', and when he died his last words were, 'Rather the companion in paradise'. Then I thought, 'He has not chosen our companionship. And I said to him, "The choice was thine, and I swear by Him who sent thee that thou hast chosen what is right." Then the apostle of Allah died, at noon on Monday.'[11]

For Muhammad to die peacefully in his wife's arms might not seem unusual. If one glances at the fates of other religious founders, though, his end seems very much so. Zarathustra was murdered by a priest. Siddartha is said to have been killed by a poisoned mushroom dropped into his begging bowl. The founder of Manicheanism, Mani, died in a Persian jail. Jesus was executed. Prophesy was a dangerous profession.

It was not only in his death that Muhammad can be seen as exceptional. No other prophet was so successful during their lifetime. When they died, both Zarathustra and Jesus left small, struggling movements. When Muhammad died, by contrast, he had already converted most of Arabia to his cause. Twenty years after the deaths of Zarathustra and Jesus, the religions they had founded were still relatively small and obscure. Twenty years after Muhammad's death, his successors had simultaneously defeated both of the region's great powers – the Byzantine and Persian empires – and were creating a vast new empire of their own, which already stretched from Yemen to Egypt to Iran.

What was the secret of Muhammad's success? Islam was probably a little less novel in Arabia than one might suppose, as something faintly like it already existed. When Muhammad was born, most Arabs worshipped a pantheon of gods, the most senior of whom was *Allah*. Christians and Jews had gained a strong presence in the area, and some Arabs were attracted to their beliefs, but were put off by their foreignness. Out of this religious mix emerged a group called the *Hanufa*, who were Arabian monotheists and believed they were descendants of Abraham, but rejected Christianity and Judaism. Muhammad preached this same combination of notions. So it seems that Muhammad, like Jesus, gave voice to ideas that were already in the air.

What precisely were Muhammad's ideas? As is so often the

case with new religious movements, a clear answer is elusive. Although the Arabs shot into the historical record with remarkable rapidity, no Islamic writings were set down until after Muhammad's death, and most were recorded only two or more generations later. Still, it is possible to have an approximate idea of Muhammad's claims. The heart of his preaching was that there was only one god, Allah, and that people should submit wholly to him. They should also repent of their sins, in preparation for the imminent end of the world.

Neither of these ideas was, needless to say, at all original. At the time of Muhammad's birth Arabia was virtually encircled by monotheism, while, as has been seen, the notion of the end of the world had been around for eight centuries. During Muhammad's lifetime the apocalypse inspired excitable movements right across the Middle East, and Muhammad encountered at least two rival end-of-the-world prophets: Muysalima of the Banu Hanifa tribe and an unnamed Jewish boy in Madina who, like Muhammad himself, as the historian Jonathan Berkey describes, 'uttered incantations in a trance-like state, and claimed to be an apostle of God.'[12]

In fact few if any of Muhammad's ideas can be seen as new. Like Mani, the founder of the Manichaeans – a curious, puritanical sect which saw wickedness in sex, eating meat and even growing crops, and encouraged a diet of melon – Muhammad saw himself as the last in a line of prophets which included Abraham, Moses and Jesus. Like Zarathustra, Muhammad required his followers to pray five times per day. As in apocalyptic Christianity, Muhammad's end of the world would be announced by a trumpet blast, and would be followed by a day of judgement, when the dead would be resurrected. Like heaven-seeking Christians, Muhammad also offered a paradise, which, like the paradise of Nestorian Christians, was lush and green. Most of all, though,

Muhammad borrowed from Judaism. Like the Jews, Muhammad opposed all worship of idols.

But Islam clearly offered something new which these existing religions had not, or it would not have succeeded as it did. Arguably, this was, in large part, Muhammad himself. So we have a further chance to study a prophet as he set out his stall of ideas, tried to win followers, and adjusted his preaching to what found favour with his audience. Muhammad, though, had to adjust his stall *considerably*, not so much in terms of what he said as *what he did*. This process of adjustment would, in fact, lead him down a new and wholly unexpected career path.

Muhammad's religious journey began around 610 when he was about forty years old: the classic age for new prophets. A merchant in Mecca, he started spending time in the desert hills outside the town, where he said he was contacted by the angel Gabriel. From this experience came the early verses of the Qu'ran. Though Muslims regard the Qu'ran as the word of God himself, dictated directly to Muhammad, more sceptical minds may see it rather as Muhammad's own thoughts, albeit a little altered and edited, as the book was set down in writing only after his death.

For some ten years Muhammad preached his message to his fellow Meccans. In some ways he was fairly successful. As we have seen, prophesy in one's hometown is generally doomed to failure, probably because the prophet is too well known to be taken seriously. Muhammad failed to win most Meccans to his cause. He also made enemies for his attacks on idols in the town's shrine, the cube-shaped *Ka'ba*, so that, in 622, he was forced to leave the town. Yet he did not leave alone. In contrast to Zarathustra, who went into exile having converted only one cousin, and to Jesus, who left Nazareth with few, if any, followers, Muhammad had won a sizeable group of supporters. In another place, where he would have a greater aura of mystery, his movement would surely flourish?

Instead it stalled. Why? It may have been because Muhammad tried to win over the *wrong people*. He and his followers left Mecca for the town of Yathrib – later renamed Madina – some 300 kilometres to the north. , where he had been invited to negotiate between two feuding Arab tribes. However, Madina was not populated only by Arabs. At this time a Jewish minority existed across Arabia, many of whom were probably refugees from their earlier disasters at the hands of the Romans. Madina was home to a particularly large Jewish population, consisting of three separate tribes, and Muhammad set his hopes on converting them. His decision had a good deal of logic. The Jews' numbers meant that they were *worth* converting. At the same time, Muhammad may also have believed that Jews would come round to his message more easily than his Meccan neighbours had done. They were already monotheists, after all. In an effort to win over Madina's Jews, Muhammad angled his preaching towards them. He instructed his followers to observe uniquely Jewish practices such as celebrating Yom Kippur and praying towards Jerusalem and to follow Jewish dietary laws (hence the Muslim ban on eating pork).

His efforts failed, however. Arabian Jews did not accept that God had sent Muhammad as his chosen prophet, any more than Judaean Jews had accepted that Jesus had been sent by God as their future king. After a year or so Muhammad gave up his efforts. He replaced Yom Kippur with a new celebration, *Ramadan*, and redirected his followers' prayers from Jerusalem to Mecca. Thereafter Muhammad concentrated his efforts on Madina's Arabs. Even here, though, he seems to have had little success. By early 624 his career must have looked highly doubtful. He was now in his mid-fifties and, after fourteen years of preaching, had won over only a small group of Meccan exiles. Although he had an informal authority in Madina as the leader of this group, and through his role as a successful negotiator, his movement was bogged down. Yet, a mere six years later, Islam would be accepted across much of Arabia. What caused this huge transformation?

Put simply, Muhammad took on a new career. In March 624 he led a force of Madinese in an attack on a Meccan camel train at the town of Badr. Raiding was a well-established practice in Arabia at this time, and Muhammad was taking up a familiar role: that of a tribal chief seeking to bring his people the spoils of war. He had, in effect, extended his role as a conflict negotiator and reinvented himself as a political and military leader. This change of direction is reflected in the Qur'an itself. As the historian Bernard Lewis has pointed out, the book's early sections, which originated when Muhammad was still in Mecca, are chiefly concerned with religion, while the later ones, which had their origins in Madina, look at social rules, politics and war. They include a whole chapter on how booty from raids should be divided.

Muhammad's new role seems to have suited him rather better than preaching. His raid was a resounding success from which the Madinese came home rich with booty. Treasure appears to have succeeded where words had not. Madina's Arabs now accepted both Muhammad's leadership and his religion. Muhammad had promised them that if they worshipped his single god, and repented their sins, then they would be rewarded. And so they had been.

Muhammad continued to bring victory to the Madinese. The Badr raid sparked a six-year-long war with Mecca, during which Muhammad repeatedly defeated forces that well outnumbered his own. When Madina's three Jewish tribes sided with the

Meccans, Muhammad dealt with them with ruthless effectiveness, exiling first one tribe, then a second, and finally killing and enslaving members of the third. Muhammad's successes caused a kind of chain reaction, with ever more Arabian tribes accepting his leadership and his religion. When, in 630, he raised what was by the standards of seventh-century Arabia a huge army, Mecca capitulated.

Muhammad had achieved something that had never been done before. The struggling religious preacher had tamed a previously untameable land of feuding tribes, and united it as, in effect, Arabia's *first king*. As we have seen, most major religions, from Zoroastrianism to Buddhism and Christianity, achieved a breakthrough when they converted the leader of a powerful state. Muhammad went about things rather differently. He himself became a powerful ruler. He had *invented* the Arabs as a unified nation, just as he invented their first unifying religion: Islam.

A raid had transformed Muhammad's movement, and it was through raiding that it made its next great leap. Muhammad clearly recognised that, if the momentum of his movement were not kept up through further attacks beyond Arabia, and the capture of more treasure, his kingdom's fragile unity might collapse. In the last few days of his life, he assembled a large army to strike northwards. Though this campaign was abandoned because of his death, it was relaunched four years later, in 636, by Muhammad's next but one successor, Caliph Umar. Umar's timing could not have been better. The lands north of Arabia were in a state of ruin and exhaustion, after an epically destructive struggle between the Byzantine and Sassanid Persian empires. The Arabs, united for the first time in their history, found themselves to be a formidable force. The raids, probably to Caliph Umar's surprise, quickly evolved into conquests.

It was not only their neighbour's exhaustion, though, that favoured the Arabs. They were also helped by Christianity, and specifically by its hunger for ideological control. From Syria to Egypt, Byzantine subjects were happy to submit to the armies that appeared mysteriously from the desert, whoever they might be – and in the beginning many were indeed unsure who they were – as anybody seemed preferable to their existing rulers. Jews, Manichaeans, and Monophysite and Nestorian Christians had all suffered persecution at the hands of the Byzantine Empire. When Arab armies invaded Egypt at the end of 639, they found it on the brink of civil war, as Monophysite Christians – now an underground church – were terrorised by the Orthodox patriarch Cyrus, who had Monophysites seized and mutilated. Unsurprisingly, many Egyptians declined to help the Byzantine defence, or even took the Arabs' side.

Yet political submission was a very different thing from religious conversion. By the 650s, Arab Muslims formed a tiny minority ruling over a sea of peoples who were neither Arabs nor Muslims. Six centuries later, though, the majority of Arab subjects from Morocco to Central Asia followed Islam, while many of them spoke and wrote in Arabic, and thought of themselves as Arabs. How did this happen? Ironically, part of Islam's appeal almost certainly stemmed from the fact that the Arab conquerors did not seek to convert their new subjects, at least not at first. In the early days Arabs saw Islam as their *national religion*, much as Jews viewed Judaism. It was not something for foreigners. Indeed, rather than encouraging their new subjects to join, Arab conquerors put obstacles in their way. Would-be converts were required, in effect, to *become Arabs*, taking an Arab name and joining an Arabian tribe, which was no easy task.

Religious persecution frequently has the opposite effect to that intended. Rather than winning converts, it strengthens the resolve of the persecuted. Religious toleration can be a much more persuasive force. So it was in the Arab Empire. Rather than being driven to resist their Muslim rulers, non-Muslims found themselves largely left in peace. They soon came to see the advantages of converting to Islam. For a start, Islam offered a considerable tax break. This does not seem to have been a device deliberately established to win converts. It originated with Muhammad himself, who devised it as a kind of extension to war booty. When he conquered a Jewish oasis fortress at Khaybar he decreed that its inhabitants could stay – unlike the Jews of Madina – so long as they paid a special tax, from which Muslims would be exempt. Later, when non-Muslims were conquered in vast numbers, the same tax was levied on them, too. As centuries passed, not paying it proved increasingly alluring.

Eventually Muslim rulers came to actively discourage religions other than Islam, though their methods were not brutal so much as humiliating. Non-Muslims were forbidden to carry weapons, ride a horse or wear green. A non-Muslim man could not marry a Muslim woman, although the reverse was allowed. Non-Muslims could not build or repair their places of worship without permission. All the while it became increasingly hard for non-Muslims to rise high in government. Degradation succeeded where force would probably have failed and, little by little, Christians, Zoroastrians, Manichaeans and Jews, weary of their status as second-class citizens, joined Islam.

Besides, even with the original obstacles, Islam was fairly easy to join. It required no painful or complex initiation, unlike Judaism (circumcision for male converts) or early Christianity (creed-learning, self criticism and exorcism). The actions required of Muslims – the *Five Pillars* – were simplicity itself. Muslims were, and are, required to acknowledge Allah as the one true god; they were to pray five times a day; they were to give a portion of their income to the poor; they were to fast during Ramadan; and, at least once in their lives, they should make a pilgrimage to Mecca. These simple tasks gave Islam another attraction: Muslims had a strong feeling of belonging. As the historian Albert Hourani commented, 'Muslims went on pilgrimage at the same time, fasted throughout the same month, and united in regular prayer.'[13] As Islam grew, those remaining outside it felt increasingly excluded.

Islam changed the peoples of its empire, but they in turn changed Islam. Despite the claims of their founders, religions never emerge into the light of day fully formed. They take centuries to develop their essential characters, and never cease to evolve. When Muhammad died he had created little more than a bare outline of what his religion would become. Islam, like Judaism, was not just a route to paradise, but a set of life rules, and it soon began to absorb the customs of the peoples it had conquered. Although it had been born in small-town western Arabia, it grew up in big-city Iran, Iraq, Syria and Egypt.

This cultural mixing led the Arabs to some surprising places. In the 750s, Caliph al-Mansur began one of the greatest projects of cultural importation ever seen: the systematic translation of classic Greek texts into Arabic, known as the Translation Movement. At a moment when these texts were being *lost* in the Byzantine Empire, in the chaos of the iconoclasm controversy (a violent dispute over Christian images) they were being *preserved* further east. This same fascination with Greek learning led to one of the more curious episodes of early Islam. In the eighth century a religious group emerged who became known as the *Mu'tazalis* (those who stand apart). Influenced by Greek logic, the Mu'tazilis argued that, since the Qu'ran stated that Allah had no human features, Allah could not have *dictated* its verses to Muhammad, and the Qu'ran must have been created in another way. One of Islam's fundamental beliefs – that the Qu'ran was God's word – was under attack.

Surprisingly, rather than discourage this subversive thinking, the ninth-century Islamic leader, Caliph al-Ma'mun, gave his backing to the Mu'tazilis and persecuted their opponents. It was the only serious attempt by Muslim rulers to impose Christian-style ideological uniformity over all Muslims. Needless to say, it failed. The Mu'tazilis' chief opponent, the theologian Ahmad ibn Hanbal, had popular belief on his side. His view offered certainty and reassurance – the bedrock of all religious belief – while the Mu'tazilis offered argument and uncertainty. Eventually abandoned by the authorities, the Mu'tazilis fell into obscurity.

Other divisions proved more enduring. That they occurred was probably inevitable, as it is the fate of any large religion to break up into rival factions. What came to divide Muslims, though, was in many ways rather surprising. While early Christian fault lines followed theological differences – notably the thorny question of how divine Jesus had been – Muslims had no such problems. They were unanimously agreed that Muhammad had been human, not divine. Likewise, Islam's God posed no difficulty. Allah was one deity, in marked contrast with the baffling Christian notion of the Trinity. All Muslims accepted their religion's basic requirements, the Five Pillars. Though they might disagree over interpretation, they all accepted Muhammad's rules on life. Even Islam's writings were largely a source for unity. While Christianity's scriptures – written by numerous authors with wholly diverse agendas over the course of a thousand years – were endlessly contradictory, Islam had one, relatively short holy book, which, as the work of one individual, was comparatively contradiction-free.

What, then, *did* Muslims come to blows over? The answer, in effect, was *genealogy*. Though it is perhaps truer to say that the tremors showed themselves as genealogy. The true fault beneath was Islam's unique blending of religion and politics, which grew out of Muhammad's own career. That such a thing became a battleground was, in large part, Muhammad's own doing. By taking on roles as both God's prophet and as ruler of a new nation, and by being seen as a model of perfection in both, he had created a dangerous precedent. Much was expected of his political inheritors. If a Muslim caliph, or successor, was unsatisfactory (always possible in a political leader) then it could only mean that the *wrong person* had gained power. The rightful candidate, who had God's approval, must have been pushed aside.

How would one know the rightful candidate? Arabians had long been fascinated by genealogy, and those who found fault with their rulers looked to Muhammad's family tree. As the prophet had left no direct male heir, it was his cousin and son-in-law, 'Ali, who was widely accepted to be his successor. 'Ali, though, had had a chequered career. Having been passed over as caliph for Abu Bakr, and then twice more for his two successors, 'Ali finally became Islam's fourth ruler in 656, only to be deposed five years later by his predecessor's nephew, who founded a new dynasty, the *Umayyads*. Yet to all who found Ummayad rule unsatisfactory, 'Ali remained God's true choice. After 'Ali's death, his descendants were considered to be his divinely chosen successors, or *Imams*. So began the division between Shi'a and Sunni Islam. The Shi'i supported the claims of 'Ali's family and the Sunni supported the succession that began with Abu Bakr.

Islam's genealogical splits, though, had only just begun. 'Ali's descendants endured through many generations, with a large number of supporters. When the eleventh in the line, who was kept under house arrest by nervous authorities, died apparently without an heir, in 873, his followers decided he must have had a secret son, who was soon expected to return – just like Jesus – at the end of days, as a *Madhi*('guide'), to usher in a new age of justice. From this point onwards the main strand of 'Ali supporters were known as the *Twelver Shi'a*, named after the twelve successors to Muhammad.

Not all 'Ali's supporters, though, accepted the same genealogical choices. The *Zaydis* opposed their candidate for the fifth descendant of 'Ali, preferring his brother Zayd. The *Isma'ilis* rejected 'Ali's seventh descendant, instead supporting his brother Isma'il. Later, the Isma'ilis broke into rival sects. One Isma'ili, Ubayd Allah, claimed that he was himself the true Imam, and established a new dynasty, the *Fatimids*, that ruled over Egypt with great success for two centuries. When one of Ubayd Allah's descendants, al-Hakim, vanished in 1021, his disappearance inspired the emergence of yet another sect, the *Druze*, who looked forward to al-Hakim's messianic return.

These divisions were not only the result of disagreements concerning Muhammad's extended family tree. They often also reflected political antagonisms or ancient rivalries between different peoples within the Empire. The longer such schisms continued, the deeper they became, as each side produced evidence to support its claims. Sunni Muslims presented a series of supposedly contemporary quotations recording what Muhammad had said and done (*hadiths*) which for them were second in authority only to the Qu'ran itself. Undaunted, Twelver Shi'is produced their own *hadiths*. Sunnis and Shi'i celebrated rival festivals to mark the days when they claimed that Muhammad had appointed his successor – 'Ali for the Shi'is and Abu Bakr for the Sunnis.

Sometimes these divisions brought violence. In the main, though, different sects of Muslims were far more willing to accept one another's existence than early Christians. Likewise, as we have seen, Muslims were relatively tolerant of their Jewish and Christian subjects, who as 'Peoples of the Book' were recognised as following movements connected with Islam and enjoy greater status than other religions. Eventually, however, Muslim patience with other religions became more brittle. Why? Part of the cause was probably a matter of numbers. As Muslims found themselves in the majority in the lands they ruled, their respect for members of other religions thinned. The main cause of Muslim intolerance, though, was altogether more brutal. Muslims became intolerant as a reaction to violent intolerance against themselves.

The first such attack was the Crusades, whose many atrocities included, as we have seen, the massacre of Jerusalem's Muslims and Jews in 1099, by the apocalyptic military mob, the Tafurs. Just over a century later, a far more dangerous threat appeared, from a non-Muslim people from faraway Central Asia: the Mongols. In the early 1220s the Mongols destroyed almost every city in today's Iran, Afghanistan and Pakistan, slaughtering their inhabitants. They then returned three decades later, and in 1258 they captured the Islamic world's political heart, Baghdad, burning its great monuments and killing as many as a quarter of a million of its inhabitants. The Mongols also extinguished Sunni claims of an unbroken line of succession. The 'Abbasid Caliph Mutasin, who was the closest Islam had to a unifying leader at the time and who claimed – if rather dubiously – to be a direct descendant of Muhammad's family, was rolled up in a carpet and kicked to death by horses.

The Mongol leader, Hügelü, followed the standard Mongolian policy of divide and rule, excluding Muslims from his government in favour of Christians, Jews and Buddhists from the eastern part of the Mongolian Empire. Though Muslims were not actively persecuted, other religions were favoured over them. Churches appeared across Iran, along with, more surprisingly, Buddhist stupas. Ultimately, though, it was non-Muslims who would suffer. When, in 1295, Iran's Mongol ruler, Ghazan, converted to Islam, his Muslim subjects took their revenge. Buddhist stupas were destroyed and, in a display of intolerance that finally matched that seen in Christian Europe, churches and synagogues were attacked, and Christians and Jews were persecuted and forced to wear humiliating identifying clothing. So, with infidel help, Islam finally discovered intolerance.

Until now this book has concentrated very much on beliefs invented in the Middle East and the Mediterranean. I make no apologies for this fact, as this region was the seedbed for a remarkable number of key religious beliefs. Yet it was far from being the only source of innovation. What of religion in different parts of the world, where traditions were quite different? Did people in other lands come up with wholly different imaginings of the supernatural? This question leads to a wider one: How original are we? Would people, if they were isolated from the example of others, devise visions of the world uniquely their own?

7

INVENTING ELSEWHERE

Ecstasy in Sober China

Around 1150 BC, near Anyang, capital of China's very first historical state (the Shang kingdom) someone put a turtle shell in a very hot fire. We know little about this moment – what building it happened in or who was present – as all that has remained of it is the turtle shell itself, but we do know *why*. The gods were being asked a question. The Chinese sought their gods' advice on all kinds of matters at this time, from how to treat someone who was sick, or whether to launch a military campaign, to what the quality of the next harvest would be. The process was simple. Two different outcomes were written on opposite sides of the turtle shell, and after this had been baked in a fire, a careful inspection was made of cracks caused by the heat, which were thought to indicate which outcome the gods had chosen. For future reference their choice was then written on the shell.

Chinese writing, medicine, language, philosophy and food all followed a radically different road from elsewhere in Eurasia. What of Chinese religion? Did it, too, develop on wholly novel lines? In 1150 BC, when Chinese religion first begins to emerge into the light, the answer appears to be a very clear *no*. Nothing about the ritual at Anyang was remotely original, aside perhaps from the use of a turtle shell. By 1150 BC the Mesopotamians had been trying to gain inside information about the future for at least 2,000 years. Even the gods the Chinese consulted were familiar. The senior Chinese deity, Di, was a controller of weather, like Enlil in southern Mesopotamia. The pantheon of gods beneath Di – gods of the sun, of mountains, of crops, of the Yellow River – closely resembled that of other peoples.

These similarities, though, are a little deceptive. Even in 1150 BC, the seeds can be found of a distinctively Chinese view of the world. The Chinese already believed that another class of supernatural beings existed beneath their gods: their *ancestors*. In the decades after our turtle shell was baked, something rather surprising happened: China's rulers lost interest in their gods. Turtle-shell questions became addressed not to deities, but to ancestors. China, uniquely among farming societies, became a land without gods, at least for a time. As well as ancestors, the Chinese also believed in spirits – a direct inheritance from hunter-gatherer shaman religions – who, like spirits in Mesopotamia and other lands, were more troublesome than helpful and required constant placation, as otherwise one's stove might not light and one's crops might not ripen. This dismissal of gods was a shift that, arguably, helped point China in a very different and more *practical* direction from lands further west.

Even China's afterlife had an aura of practicality. In early China, ancestors were not thought to be dwelling in a dismal underworld or in paradise, but in a world much like that of the living, where they had human-like concerns. The Chinese underworld had its own bureaucracy of titled officials, from the Director of Life Spans, and the Commune Chief of the Tomb Gate, to the Earl of the Tomb. As the historian David N. Keightley commented, this human-sized view of the supernatural world 'may help account for the characteristic this-worldliness, not only of Shang religion itself, but of subsequent Chinese philosophy'.[14]

It is well known that a rational revolution occurred in Greece from the sixth century BC, as Greek thinkers developed a new view of the world in which religious beliefs were tested with logic. It is less well known that the same change began in China *a century earlier*. In 639 BC, the ruler of the state of Lu, Zang Wenzhong, produced the first known instance of transparently rational political thinking, when he forbade the punishment of shamans who failed to deliver promised rain, arguing that the state should instead provide relief to those who suffered from the ensuing drought. A century later the great Chinese philosopher Confucius argued that religious belief should be kept quite apart from the practicalities of life, remarking that 'respecting the ghosts and spirits while keeping them at a distance – this might be called wisdom'. [15]

China's pragmatic approach to the supernatural world could also take another, rather more disturbing, form: the desire by Chinese authorities for complete state control of religion. This trait became apparent in 221 BC, when China, which had long been divided between rival states, became reunified under the first Qin emperor. To honour the new leader, China's old gods, which had been abandoned for eight centuries, were brought out of their mothballs, but they were now very much an imperial monopoly. Only the Chinese emperor, as the Son of Heaven, could worship Heaven, the country's most senior god. The rest of the population could merely look on and hope that the emperor had worshipped correctly. If he had worshipped wrongly, or behaved badly, it was they who would pay the price, when Heaven showed his displeasure by mean of earthquakes, droughts and famine.

And yet, as the pharaohs of Egypt had discovered more than a thousand years earlier, it was not easy to keep control of religious imagination. Deprived of direct access to the state-approved gods, ordinary Chinese looked for gods of their own to give them reassurance, and they soon found them. So two new religions emerged in China, which the imperial authorities found themselves powerless to resist and which set the country on a new and highly emotional road.

The first was that most bewildering movement, Daoism. Though Daoism's ideas are hard to pin down – being a strange amalgam of folklore, morality, god worship and ideas on healthy living – close to its heart lay the hope of achieving eternal life, or, at the very least, a long life. At times it seems to be not so much a religion as a system of alternative medicine.

Though Daoism's roots may have been far more ancient, it emerges clearly into the light around 100 BC, with the first mention of the Queen Mother of the West. Living far beyond the western horizon, the Queen Mother was believed to have the power to make people immortal and to provide her worshippers with children and wealth. Best of all, ordinary people could bypass the emperor and appeal to her directly. This possibility became especially attractive when the emperor failed in his duty to keep China in good health, and it was at just such a moment, when northern China was struck by an intense drought in 3 BC, that the Queen Mother of the West came into her own. A huge movement of her followers marched across the parched countryside, carrying straw tokens to show their belief, which they imagined would save them from starvation. They expected the

Queen Mother to appear at any moment to end the disaster. In the end she did not need to. When autumn came, the rain fell and her followers dispersed. Yet something of Daoism was already discernible. The Queen Mother's movement was popular and emotional, and, in keeping with Chinese tradition, offered its followers something intensely practical: a way to seek the *avoidance of death*.

Two centuries later, Daoism came into sharper focus through another popular movement, this time roused by the slow collapse of the Han dynasty. In AD 184 a religiously inspired uprising broke out, whose followers worshipped *two* deities: the Queen Mother of the West and Laozi: a supernatural figure who would become the key Daoist deity and who may have begun his existence as an anonymous medical text that described ways to gain immortality. The rebellion marked a Daoist high point. One strand of the revolt, the Five Pecks of Grain movement, evolved into a brief but fully fledged Daoist state in Sichuan Province. Intriguingly, this Daoist theocracy was, like Judaism and Christianity, much concerned with sin and penance. In Sichuan, as in earliest Mesopotamia, sickness was regarded, rather unkindly, as proof of sin. Fortunately, numerous forms of penance were available to remove both sin and disease. Daoists could cleanse themselves by performing good deeds or by publicly confessing before other Daoists; they could withdraw to 'houses of quiet' to reflect on their errors or, more unusually, they could take part in road-building work, Sichuan being at this time a wild and roadless part of China.

The rebellion of 184 also marked the appearance in China of a religious phenomenon we have seen elsewhere. The Daoist rebels were firm believers in the imminent end of the world. The apocalypse had taken root in China. How it found its way there is hard to say. As we have seen, the notion had existed further west for several centuries, so it could have made its way east along the Silk Road. It is also possible, of course, that the Chinese came up with the notion quite independently. In a land prone to drought and famine, it is easy to imagine that people's thoughts might have strayed in this direction.

One might suppose that a religion which emerged from peasant uprisings would have little appeal for the rich and powerful, but no: before long some members of China's elite became drawn to Daoism and its promised end of the world. Followers of the Daoist Maoshan School, which grew up in southern China from the fourth century, believed that they alone – the 'seed people' – would survive the coming cataclysm. Highly cultured and educated, they looked forward to a new age of fine manners, elegant conversation and literary good taste, with no commoners to spoil their apocalypse.

Under the Tang dynasty (618–907) some emperors proved as susceptible to the promise of eternal life as hungry peasants had been. Though their enthusiasm sometimes proved unwise. Daoism offered various means of bringing about eternal life, from worship and physical exercises to special potions that Daoists believed would rid the body of the impure substances which caused death. Emperors, naturally, could afford the very best ingredients. Pure, un-rusting gold was a favourite, as was red cinnabar (an ore of mercury). As may be imagined, neither of these is particularly beneficial to one's health. Across the centuries a good number of Chinese emperors who died suddenly and unexpectedly are believed to have succumbed to their own immortality potions.

Daoism, though, was not the only new, popular religion to sweep across China at this time. There was also a second movement, this time not Chinese in origin, but a foreign import: Mahayana Buddhism. Having, as have seen, evolved rather unexpectedly from a philosophy of life to a full paradise religion, Buddhism now managed a second transformation. Just as it was falling into terminal decline in India, it began a remarkable rebirth further east. So it was that the idea of heaven, having sneaked its way into Siddartha's philosophy, infiltrated China.

Buddhism, which is first mentioned in China in the year AD 65, was probably brought by merchants travelling the Silk Road. For a brief time the religion was simply added to Daoism, and Siddartha the philosopher found himself a surprising bedfellow of the Queen Mother of the West and Laozi. However, as Buddhist sutras were translated into Chinese and the movement became better understood, Buddhism and Daoism split apart into friendly – and sometimes unfriendly – rivals. Each shamelessly stole the ideas of the other. Chinese Buddhism stole Daoism's belief in the imminent end of the world. Daoism stole reincarnation and copied Buddhism's structure of temples and monasteries. Yet key differences remained. Most of all, while practical Daoists looked forward to *extending* their bodily existence into immortality, Buddhists looked forward to *escaping* bodily existence altogether, in nirvana paradise.

Intriguingly, Daoism and Buddhism each seem to have accidently inspired one of China's great technological breakthroughs. Mahayana Buddhists believed that to make a copy of a sacred text counted as a good work, which would advance one along the road to nirvana. The more copies one made, naturally, the more one would benefit. This notion seems to have set minds to work. A set of Buddhist scrolls found in Polguk-Sa temple in Korea, dating from the early seventh century, form the very earliest known printed texts. It appears that the development of printing was inspired by Buddhist beliefs. By the tenth century, China had embarked on the world's first printing revolution, in which books became widely available and affordable. It was a breakthrough that would not occur in Europe for another five centuries.

What world-changing technology did Daoism bring? As we have seen, two key ingredients of Daoist immortality potions were gold and red cinnabar. Red cinnabar, however, was often hard to come by. When it was unavailable, another mixture was used in its place, comprising mercury, saltpetre and sulphur. As it happens, these are also the ingredients for something very different, which is known to have first appeared in China around the year 850. This was *gunpowder*. One can only suppose that some unremembered Daoist alchemist, preparing a batch of immortality potion near a naked flame, had a great surprise.

Between Daoist eternal life and Buddhist paradise, which was the greater crowd pleaser? Despite its foreignness, which was no small handicap in patriotic China, the answer was Buddhism, which became much far popular than Daoism, and included among its followers a good number of emperors. One can understand why. Mahayana Buddhism appealed to rich and powerful Chinese for the same reasons that it had appealed to the rich and powerful Indians. They could look forward to guaranteed salvation, and could enjoy the kudos of being worshipped, even during their lifetimes, as bodhisattvas. In the later sixth century the ruler of the northern Chinese kingdom of Wei went a step further and declared that he was himself the Buddha, reincarnated. So this new, foreign religion could be as serviceable as the old cult of Heaven in marking imperial prestige.

With time Mahayana Buddhism transformed China's very landscape. The countryside became dotted with Buddhist stupas, Buddhist shrines, Buddhist retreats and, most of all, Buddhist monasteries. China's cities became crowded with Buddhist pagodas, and temples decorated with paintings of multilayered heaven and hell. Buddhist processions marched through the streets, led by highly valued and almost certainly fake religious relics – such as Buddha's supposed finger-bone – as devotees burned and cut themselves, to prove that they felt no pain and so were immune to suffering.

With its great monasteries, its relics and processions, its promises of paradise and threats of hell, Chinese Mayahana Buddhism may sound rather familiar, and with good reason. It has often been compared with Christianity. One of the major differences between the two, however, was in their attitudes towards other creeds. Chinese Buddhism was never intolerant of other religions. Despite their movement's popularity, Chinese Buddhists never tried to gain a monopoly over the country's supernatural beliefs. So the golden age of Chinese Buddhism, which occurred between the seventh and ninth centuries, under the T'ang dynasty, was also a golden age of religious diversity. China's capital, Chang'an, contained mosques, Nestorian Christian churches and Buddhist, Daoist, Zoroastrian and Manichean temples. Alongside the cold, bureaucratic afterlife of earlier beliefs, the Chinese now had numerous exciting futures to look forward to, from Daoist immortality to Buddhist nirvana and Christian paradise.

With time, though, Buddhism became something of a victim of its own success. Chinese traditionalists had long regarded foreign religions with suspicion, while Buddhism was criticised for its un-Chinese emotionalism and the bizarre scenes it inspired, when, in extreme cases, followers would harm themselves, and even cut off parts of their bodies. Buddhism became even more vulnerable because of its wealth. As ever more Chinese converted, they donated property to Buddhist temples and monasteries, which became great landowners. In the year 845, the Daoist T'ang emperor Wu-Tsung launched an assault on Buddhism. China's era of religious diversity was on the wane. Of many thousands of Buddhist monasteries and temples, only a few dozen were permitted to continue functioning. As many as a million monks and nuns were flung out, some injured or killed. Nestorian Christians and Manicheans, too, came under attack as worshippers of foreign gods.

Four hundred years later, distrust of the foreign was further inflamed, this time through foreign invasion. In the thirteenth century, China was conquered by the same Mongol Empire that had sacked Baghdad and had come within a whisker of devastating Western Europe. China's Mongol ruler, Kublai Khan, determined to keep a distance from those he had subjugated, filled his government with Central Asian Muslims and European Christians such as Marco Polo. He also actively supported foreign religions, and Beijing became home to numerous Christian churches. As in Mongol Iran, when Mongolian rule finally collapsed, the Chinese were left with a sharpened suspicion of foreigners and their beliefs.

Where did all these upheavals leave Chinese religion? When the dust settled, the country returned to its roots. Religion once again became subject to rigid state control, as a new balance was decreed by China's rulers: Buddhism and Daoism became state-sanctioned religions. So, too, rather surprisingly, did Confucianism, which had never claimed to be religion at all, but rather a philosophy of life, politics and statecraft. Under the Ming dynasty (1368–1644) Confucianism became remade as something more like a religion. In imitation of Buddhism, it took on a more emotional side, advocating meditation, respect for life and concern for the poor. Across China appeared Confucian temples where followers could venerate the philosopher and which included a vast temple in Confucius' home of Qufu in Shandong Province.

So Confucianism, Daoism and Buddhism, three movements with different roots and strongly contradictory ideas, became China's 'Three Doctrines': state-approved and declared to be not only equal, but wholly compatible. The state authorities permitted, even encouraged, the Chinese people to follow all three. Much later, under Mao Zhedong's rule, state-sanctioned versions of Protestant and Catholic Christianity would be added to the list; though maintaining government control would never be easy. In times of hardship and political weakness, religious uprisings continued to break out and threaten the state. To this day China's rulers continue to clamp down on independent religious movements, from Christian groups to the Buddhist Falun Gong organisation.

So, to return to our earlier question: was Chinese religion radically different from religion elsewhere? Mostly it was not. Although Chinese religion had, at times, a more this-worldly and pragmatic, approach towards the supernatural, most of the key ideas that appeared in western lands also appeared in China, and in roughly the same order, progressing from shamanistic spirit worship to paradise and the end of the world. Then again, perhaps it is a mistake to expect that the Chinese might have broken the mould of religions elsewhere. They had, after all, had regular contact with Indians, Iranians, Egyptians and Europeans, so probably it is not wholly surprising that they came up with similar beliefs.

If only there were a land that had remained isolated from the rest of the world, for thousands of years. Then, surely, we might find an entirely different approach to religion. As luck would have it, there was just such a place.

Blood, Calendars and the Ball Game

On 26 October, AD 709, the ruler of the Mayan city of Yaxchilán – on today's Mexican frontier with Guatemala – held up a flaming torch, as his wife, Lady Xoc, did something decidedly gruesome.

She pulled a piece of string spliced with thorns through her tongue. Blood spattered out and fell on to pieces of bark paper that had been carefully placed in a basket below and was later burned as a sacrifice. To achieve what? The ruler, whose name was Itzam Balam, meaning Shield Jaguar, had recently become father of a baby son, and the sacrifice was to encourage the gods to look favourably on his new heir; rather unfairly, though, the newborn was not Lady Xoc's, but the child of another of Shield Jaguar's wives.

In AD 709 people in the Americas had been isolated from those in Africa and Eurasia for around 10,000 years. Separately, Mesoamericans had developed their own farming, their own art and their own architecture. As early as 500 BC Mesoamericans – though not South Americans – had their own writing. Early Americans built their own great cities, one of which, Teotihuacán, was, in AD 300, one of the largest on earth, with a population estimated at around 150,000–250,000 people. What beliefs did they devise?

The cultures whose religion we know most about are those of central Mexico, and, even more so, the Mayans of the Yucatán, both of whom had writing. During their greatest age, between AD 300 and 900, the Mayans had an intriguing way of foretelling the future. With the help of their remarkable numerical system, the Mayans employed a fiendishly complex system for recording time that involved not one but *three* calendars: one based on the solar year; one based on a sacred year of 260 days; and a third that simply counted each day from the creation of the earth, which they believed had occurred on 13 August, 3114 BC. The Mayans took the idea that history repeated itself to extreme lengths, and precisely recorded past dates because they were convinced these could unlock the future. Combining the solar and sacred calendars, Mayans created long units of time, spanning almost twenty years, that were grouped in batches of thirteen, totalling 256 years. They believed that the events of each epoch would reoccur exactly 256 years later.

In the right hands, this notion could be a powerful *political weapon*. In the seventh century the city of Tikal, which had once been one of the most powerful in the region, was in a bad way, repeatedly defeated in battle by its great rival, Calakmul, and its many allies. In AD 679 Tikal suffered one of its greatest humiliations, when its ruler was captured by Calakmul's rulers and sacrificed. His son, Hasw Chan Ka'wil, should rightfully have acceded to the throne, and continued the struggle, but instead he did something altogether more cunning. He *delayed*. He finally became ruler of Tikal three years later, in 682. This date was precisely 256 years after the accession of one of Tikal's most successful warrior rulers, Stormy Sky. Hasw Chan Ka'wil's decision helped bring a decisive shift in Tikal's fortunes. Though precise details of what happened are lacking, Tikal's demoralised inhabitants appear to have been rallied, while neighouring states came over to Tikal's side, and it was her enemies that became fearful. In 695, thirteen years after he formally came to power, Hasw Chan Ka'wil launched a devastating attack on Calakmul, and triumphantly brought back its king and his entourage as captives to be sacrificed.

The Mayans, like early farming societies all over the world, believed in a dismal underworld, yet they had an unusual idea as to where this could be discovered. They supposed spirits and gods lurked beneath the very centres of their cities and, most of all, beneath their ball courts. So we come to another distinctive feature of Mesoamerican culture: the ball game. This seems to have had very early origins, going back to the region's first culture, of the Olmecs, which grew up from 1800 BC, in a rainy area of Mexico's east coast that was plentiful with rubber trees, from whose rubber the balls were made. The game required great skill, and players had to keep the ball from touching the ground using only their thighs, hips and upper arms, but never their hands or feet.

Yet the ball game was much more than a mere sports event. For the Mayans it was close to the heart of their religion. It even featured in the Mayan creation story, in which the 'Hero Twins', Hunahpu and Xbalanque, gain immortality after playing, and beating, the lords of the underworld: the equivalent of Adam and Eve beating Satan in a game of football. The ball game was full of religious symbolism. The ball had to be kept from touching the ground because this was the realm of the spirits. Though some games were played purely as sport, the stakes could be altogether higher, with losers being killed as sacrifices to the gods. If a Mayan city defeated a rival in war, crowds might watch enemy captives, even a captured king, as they were forced to play and lose (the game would be rigged) before being sacrificed.

So we come to the most striking feature of early American religion; blood sacrifice. Unusually, this practice was prevalent in both American continents, among peoples who would have had no knowledge of one another's existence. From Mexico and the Yucatán to Peru, and across a thousand years and more, one finds grimly similar stone reliefs, depicting the stacked skulls of sacrifice victims. This ubiquity suggests very early origins What was the thinking behind such practices? The Mayans believed that living beings – and some non-living things, too, such as special stones – possessed a kind of *spiritual potency*, which, in humans and animals, was located primarily in their blood. To keep the gods amenable, the Mayans reasoned, the only currency they were sure to accept was this potency: blood.

Most blood sacrifice, like that of Lady Xoc, was performed

on a small scale, and quite voluntarily. These days it would probably be considered self-harm. To Mayans it was regarded as a sensible means of keeping supernatural powers well disposed towards them. Mayans of all ages and classes, from kings to the lowliest corn farmers, were habitually cutting at themselves to make blood offerings to their gods. There is evidence that a young person's first blood sacrifice was marked by a special ceremony that was the Mayan equivalent of Christian confirmation or a Jewish bar mitzvah.

Blood sacrifice, though, was not always voluntary. Numerous early-American societies, from the Tupanimbá of Brazil to the Iroquois of North America, sought to capture enemy warriors to give as a sacrifice. Mayans, during their greatest age, from the fifth to the ninth centuries AD, believed that the more exalted a victim, the more pleased the gods would be. So human sacrifice became a kind of *war aim*. Mayan cities fought each other regularly, not to destroy their enemies, but to make off with some of their inhabitants – ideally their great lords and rulers – so their blood might be presented to the gods.

In the fifteenth century, 500 years after the greatest age of the Mayans had ended in a catastrophe of overpopulation and ecological collapse, lands to north-west, in Mexico, became dominated by a new culture, which was little less than fixated with blood sacrifice: the Aztecs. The Aztecs fought perpetual wars in which they and their ally, Texcoco, battled against two rival states, to harvest enemy hearts. These were then presented to the sun god Huitzilopochtli, to bribe him to continue to rise up each morning from the underworld, and not abandon the earth to darkness.

Whatever the religious reasoning behind human sacrifice, it is hard not to find the enthusiasm with which it was performed by both Mayans and Aztecs rather disturbing. The Mayans, eager to shed as much aristocratic blood as they could to please their gods, sometimes tortured their captives extensively before killing them. Captives could be kept alive for long periods. The unfortunate ruler of the city of Palenque, K'an Hoy Chitam II, was kept for ten years by his Mayan captors, so that he might be bled on special occasions. When their final moment came, high-ranking captives faced a number of grim scenarios, from being decapitated, burned alive or disembowelled to having their hearts cut out from their chests, and from being tied to a wooden frame and riddled with arrows to being bound tightly into a ball and thrown down the steep steps of a temple.

The Aztecs sacrificed on an almost industrial scale. The stairways that led to the summit of the great temple to the gods Huitzilopochtli and Tlaloc, in the centre of the Aztec capital, Tenochtitlán, were caked in human blood. Though it is impossible to be precise as to numbers, it is thought that several hundred captives were dispatched each year, if not several thousands. Purpose-built skull racks found by archaeologists close to the temple site could display thousands of heads. Sacrifice even had a role to play in a distinctively Aztec ritual of penance. Anyone who felt a need to atone could purge themselves by wearing the skin of a flayed sacrifice victim for twenty days. By the end of this time, penitents could be smelled from far away.

Most disturbing of all, though, to modern eyes, was the sacrifice of children. In times of drought the Aztecs killed children on mountaintops to try and persuade the god Tlaloc to bring rain. Children were also sacrificed, albeit in small numbers, in another empire, 5,000 kilometres to the south, which grew up at about the same time as that of the Aztecs, in the fifteenth century: the empire of the Incas. The Incas picked the most beautiful children on the grounds that these would be most pleasing to the gods, and it was considered a great honour for parents to have their child selected. Still, it is hard to believe that all welcomed the privilege.

The Incas, though, also practised an altogether gentler form of sacrifice: walking. Though Inca beliefs are less well understood than those of the Aztecs, not least because the Incas possessed no known writing, their *zeq* system appears to have been a vast network of sacred paths. Some straight, some zigzag, these spread out from the Incas' most venerated temples in Cuzco, reaching to shrines all across the Inca heartland. Different paths were allotted to different social groups, as the Incas endeavoured to keep the goodwill of their gods through the efforts of something resembling *supernatural rambling clubs*. While some of these ritual pathways were short, others extended for hundreds, even thousands of kilometres, to the very frontiers of the Empire. One of them finally comes to an end at what is now the world's highest archaeological site, on the peak of Llullaillaco in Argentina, at the remarkable altitude of 6,739 metres. Here, above an ancient Inca base camp, archaeologists have found a platform and a number of sacrificial objects, from feathers and gold to figurines and silver llamas, placed there by a long-forgotten group of religious mountaineers.

These practices seem very different from anything we have seen previously. And yet were they? So we return to the question asked earlier: were early-American beliefs radically unlike any that grew up in the eastern hemisphere? The simple answer is *no*. In fact, early American beliefs are remarkable for their similarity to those elsewhere.

In early times this is not surprising. It was only natural that the first Americans believed in hunter-gatherer shamanism, as they would have brought the religion with them when they first arrived in the Americas from Asia more than 10,000 years ago.

Yet even after Americans became entirely separate from people in Eurasia and Africa, they developed very much the same beliefs. As farmers, Mesoamericans came up with similar gods to those that had been imagined on the Euphrates, the Ganges and the Nile: there were weather gods, planet gods, gods of the crops, and animal spirits promoted to gods. Mayan gods were intriguingly contradictory – at once good and evil, both male and female – like Hindu gods. The Mayans watched the skies for signs sent by they gods, in the hope that these would foretell future events, like the Mesopotamians and the Chinese, among others. The Mayans sought supernatural advice as to which days were lucky or unlucky for an important undertaking, as had Egyptians and Romans. And, like early farming peoples across the world, early Americans feared they would suffer disaster if they did not continuously placate their gods with rituals, bribes and labour-intensive projects.

Mesoamericans even came up with their own version of a happy afterlife. Brave Mayan and Aztec warriors looked forward to escaping the fate of the majority, who would end up in a dark underworld filled with the stench of rotting corpses, as they would instead be raised up to paradise. Such an afterlife was also promised, intriguingly, to warriors who were caught by their enemies and sacrificed. And, perhaps more surprisingly, to women who died in childbirth and anyone who died from drowning. Early-American paradise seems to have been based on a mixture of compassion and admiration for bravery. Yet, in contrast with paradise in Eurasia and Africa, the early-American happy afterlife never underwent a popular revolution. For more than a thousand years it remained available only to a select elite, while most had to endure the prospect of the dark and miserable underworld. Then again, paradise for all took many centuries to evolve in Eurasia and Africa. It is quite possible that indigenous

Americans would have come up with a popular heaven if they had been left alone for longer.

Even early Americans' fascination with blood sacrifice can hardly be seen as original. As we saw earlier, organised human sacrifice was almost certainly practised at Çayönü in today's Turkey from 8000 BC, and probably also in many other places, from Jericho to Çatalhöyük. Even in historical times, human sacrifice continued, though it was relatively rare. It was usually employed to provide a great lord with helpers in the afterworld, and victims have been discovered in tombs in early Egypt and early China and in Viking burials. In a moment of desperation even the rational Greeks resorted to the practice, killing three captured Persians before the battle of Salamis in 480 BC. The early Americans simply took blood sacrifice rather further than others had.

Likewise, the Mesoamerican ball game has echoes in gladiatorial fights, a practice first devised by the Etruscans to mark a great man's funeral. Although under the Romans such fights became a form of entertainment, and also national toughening, the atmosphere in a Roman arena was probably not unlike that around a Mayan ball court: an intoxicating mix of gore and gambling, as spectators cheered on their chosen side, in the hope of making a little profit.

Dividing time into different eras, as the Mayans did, was common in numerous other religions, from Hinduism to Christianity, while trying to predict the future was an almost universal preoccupation. Even the Inca *zeq* system cannot claim to be truly novel. Parties of devout travellers could be found all over the world, from Hindus and Sikhs visiting their holy places, to Muslims journeying to Mecca for the Haj, to Christians walking to pilgrimage sites, such as at Santiago de Compostela. Even early-American religious architecture resembled that found elsewhere. The pyramids of Teotihuacán in Mexico, in the Mayan city of Tikal, or at Chan Chan in Peru are easily recognisable as cousins of the pyramids of Egypt or the ziggurats of Mesopotamia.

So, to conclude, this glance at beliefs in China and the Americas indicates what remarkably *unoriginal* creatures we are. Put people in a certain situation, with particular ways of feeding – themselves and trying to stay alive, and they will have the broadly the same fears and will seek to reassure themselves by inventing similar beliefs. All of which seems to confirm the notion that religion is a kind of mirror, reflecting the things about which we are most anxious.

We have looked at how and why we may have first invented gods. We have followed the rise of most of the religions that dominate belief today, including Buddhism, Christianity, Judaism and Islam. Is there anything more to tell? Human imagination is restless. New inventions were on their way that would go on to inspire some of the most destructive events of recent times. Intriguingly, they emerged in the very part of the world where religious imagination was banned.

8

INVENTIONS FROM THE UNDERGROUND

Laughing All the Way to the Pyre

In the year 1022, a knight named Aréfast travelled to the French city of Orléans together with his clerk, Heribert, ostensibly so he could learn new religious wisdom. There was, though, nothing straightforward about Aréfast's visit. The people he was seeking out, who included a former confessor to the queen of France, formed a little clandestine circle that rejected key beliefs of the Catholic Church.

The group refused to accept that Jesus had come to life again after his death, or that he was brought to life during mass. They denied that the Church was the only way for people to reach God. They believed they could reach him directly, through *inner illumination*, and that they could even cleanse one another of sin, through a ceremony they had devised of laying on hands. In effect, the group had robbed the Church of its most essential role: of being God's representative on earth. In the eyes of eleventh-century Europeans such notions were a clear case of *heresy*.

If the Orléans circle had secrets, however, so did Aréfast. His clerk, Heribert, who had already been won over to the dissidents' views, believed he had succeeded in converting his master. Aréfast, though, was playing a double game. He had secretly contacted the king of France, Robert the Pious, and the Church authorities at Chartres. With their approval Aréfast was going undercover, to root out these enemies of the Church.

In Orléans, the knight won the heretics' trust until they explained their beliefs to him. Then Aréfast sprung his trap. At his request several bishops travelled secretly to Orléans. So, too, did the French king and his queen, Constance, doubtless because they feared they might be themselves endangered by the stain of heresy. The circle's leader, Stephen, had, after all, been Constance's confessor. The day after the royal couple arrived, the whole group, numbering about twenty people, was arrested by royal officials, in a house they frequented, and brought in chains to a local church for trial. The royal couple watched as they at first denied the charges against them and then, when Aréfast broke cover and denounced them, defiantly admitted all. The clerics among them were stripped of their vestments and punishment beckoned. For Queen Constance, there would also be personal *revenge*.

> At the king's command, Queen Constance stood before the doors of the Church, to stop the common people killing them inside the Church, and they were expelled from the bosom of the Church. As they were being driven out, the queen struck out the eye of Stephen with the staff she carried in her hand. They were taken outside the walls of the city, a large fire was lit in a certain cottage, and they were all burned . . . except one clerk and a nun, who had repented by the will of God.[16]

It was almost the first instance of heretics being executed in Western Europe. There had been only one other, 700 years earlier: a Spanish bishop, Priscillian, who was accused of Manicheanism. The Orléans executions marked the beginning of a dubious new trend, and many more burnings would follow. Why, it might be asked, would anyone choose to risk being accused of heresy? Why provoke the power of the Church and the state? Why place oneself on the wrong side of Christianity's obsession with belief control? Stranger still, why stick to one's beliefs, and suffer a gruesome death, when you could save yourself by repenting? One account reports that the Orléans circle laughed as they were tied to the pyre, meeting their fate with joy.

Contemporary sources are rarely very illuminating as to why heretics acted as they did. It was not a question that they considered important. The main source on Aréfast's denunciation of the Orléans group – Paul of Sant Pere de Chartres – simply states that they had been 'ensnared by diabolical heresy'. His concern was not to understand heretics, but to show that they had been won over to wickedness by the devil. No further analysis was required. Nowadays we can do a little better. The reasons why people risked the pyre varied greatly, depending on the beliefs they took up. None of these groups, needless to say, would have considered themselves heretics, a label given to them by the Church. A more suitable name, from today's vantage point, would be *religious dissidents*. They considered their way of worshipping God was the true one, and that it would win them places in paradise, while those who followed the official Church were doomed.

One group risked the pyre because they thought of themselves as *divine*. They believed they could reach God by entering trances, and that they were as close to him as Jesus had been. These beliefs lay at the heart of the phenomenon that was denounced by the

Church as the 'heresy of the free spirit'. The name first appears in the early thirteenth century, when it was given to a group of fourteen clerics in Paris, who, aside from three who recanted, were burnt in 1209. The circle's beliefs, though, were far, far older than this.

In many ways they can be seen as direct descendants of the very earliest religion, when shamans contacted animal spirits by entering a trance. This intense losing of oneself in worship, known as *mysticism*, went on to have a presence in numerous religions, including Christianity in its early days when it showed itself as 'speaking in tongues': as we have seen, people ranted incomprehensibly in the belief that they were filled with the Holy Spirit. The Church had no difficulty with such behaviour. This changed, though, when enthusiasts took matters altogether further, and supposed they were themselves divine. Such thinking challenged the Church in every way. Who needed bishops to mediate between you and God if you had him within you? The idea of self-divinity was also very ancient. Egyptian pharaohs had considered themselves divine, Greek philosophers, notably Plato, proposed that people had divinity within them, and Gnostic Christians assumed they were godlike. The unfortunate circle in Orléans seem to have had similar ideas.

The Subtle of Spirit, as people of this belief called themselves, proved extremely hard for the Church to deal with. Despite the Paris burnings, the movement endured for several centuries, as tiny, intense circles, dispersed across Europe: an arrangement that made them difficult to unearth. These groups were usually comprised of a charismatic, who was considered to be divine, and devotees, who endured a long and degrading apprenticeship of absolute obedience in the hope of becoming so.

Why did people risk their lives to join such groups? A key motive may have been *frustration* with the narrowly conservative world in which they lived. Unusually for groups deemed heretical, the Subtle of Spirit were often educated and wealthy. They were people who expected something of their lives, rather than simply surviving from day to day. Their beliefs allowed them to *feel free*. Being divine, and therefore perfect, they felt superior to saints, angels and sometimes even Jesus. They also *could not sin*. In fact the Subtle of Spirit considered that they had a *duty to commit sin*, as obedience to Christian rules was a sign of the devil. This notion meant in particular that they could, and should, have sex with anybody they chose. Their groups indulged in a kind of medieval free love.

They should also *take* anything they liked. The Subtle of Spirit reasoned that as God had created all things, and they were themselves God, all things belonged to them. The ex-monk Martin of Mainz, who was burned in 1393, believed that he had every right to lie, to steal, to eat in a tavern without paying, and to beat or kill anyone who disagreed. So this phenomenon, which encouraged individuals to discover their true potential, and resist the pressures of the herd, can be seen as the precursor of two worldviews that continue to capture minds today: anarchism and romanticism.

Most of those branded as heretics by the Church had a rather simpler worldview. They refused to accept the Church's authority – the definition of heresy – because it was an institution they detested. Their resentment was generally inspired by matters of money, power and sex. By the eleventh century, when heresy burnings began, the Church had become Western Europe's greatest landowner and tax collector. Many clerics lived in great comfort, which was paid for by the tithe taxes paid by non-Church people. Priests lived openly with their mistresses and their illegitimate children. Some people found it impossible to believe that a Church they despised had God's approval. So, to them, the Church failed to deliver the most essential product of any religion: reassurance. But if the Church did not have God on its side, then how could it get one into heaven? The result was a kind of *paradise panic*.

Curiously enough, such thinking was first inspired by the Church itself. When the Church cleansed itself, heretical movements died away. When Church leaders turned a blind eye to corruption, dissidence flourished. So for 500 years the Church and its opponents engaged in a kind of *tango for two*. This dance began around 1050, after the papacy had disgraced itself by a series of spectacularly depraved popes in Rome, culminating in a murderous teenager, Benedict IX, who sold his office, then changed his mind and seized it back. Reaction followed, when a group of idealistic ex-monks gained control of the papacy and began a great cleansing, known as the Gregorian Reforms. They banned the practice – never legitimised, but quietly accepted for centuries – of priests living with mistresses. They attacked Church wealth and corruption. Most curiously, they encouraged attacks on rich clergy by their poorer colleagues and even by non-churchmen. The Church was purged from below and from without, in a kind of Catholic *Maoist Cultural Revolution*.

There was next to no religious dissidence during the purge. Trouble came when it flagged. Having been encouraged to demand poverty and chastity of their clerics, some Christians found it impossible to stay quiet when, from 1100, the Church returned to more slovenly ways. Heretical movements sprang to life. One of the most notorious of these began in 1112 in the Low Countries, where people flocked to hear an eloquent wandering preacher named Tanchelm, who denounced a priest in Antwerp for living with his mistress. When Tanchelm widened his attacks to the whole Church, telling people not to go to mass or pay their tithe taxes (always a popular proposal), he became a king-like figure in the Utrecht area, travelling with a armed escort carrying his banner. As his power grew, so did his self-estimation and, like the Subtle of Spirit, he decided that he was divine and on a par with Jesus. To illustrate his claim he even conducted a ceremony in which he was betrothed to a wooden statue of the Virgin Mary. His followers saw nothing wrong in such behaviour, and, a little disturbingly, sought bottles of his bathwater to drink as holy water. In their eyes Tanchelm, who claimed his was the only true Church, offered a far more convincing road to paradise than the Church. Even after he met a violent end, killed by a priest, and was officially disgraced, he continued to be revered for some years.

Tanchelm soothed paradise panic by persuading people that he was as close to God as Jesus. There were, though, many other forms of balm on offer. Some, as we have seen in an earlier chapter, offered their followers a complete alternative to paradise, in the form of the imminent end of the world, which would take place without any help from the Church. Some took a more learned approach and claimed to have a direct connection with God *through his words:* the Bible. Gaining access to God's words was not easy at this time. Most medieval Europeans could not read, while the Bible was only available in Latin. It was a situation that suited churchmen rather well, as it put them firmly in control of all things theological. They could practise a kind of *pick and mix* of the scriptures, ignoring parts that were troublesome or contradictory, as was inevitable in a book that had been compiled by dozens of authors over many centuries.

The first medieval European to make a concerted attempt to try and hack into the Bible was a devout but uneducated Lyons businessman named Peter Waldo. In the 1170s he exchanged his wealth for poverty, began preaching on the streets of Lyons and, in order to understand his religion better, commissioned scholars to translate the Bible into the local French-Provençal language. A little learning proved a dangerous thing. To his poorly educated followers, The Waldensians, their excitement at finding they could interpret the Bible themselves soon led them to criticise the Church for its corruption. The movement was declared heretical, and though it continued to exist for another three centuries, its members became increasingly preoccupied – understandably enough – with Church attempts to unearth and burn them. So it eventually evolved into a kind of secret society: a collection of hunted, underground Bible-reading groups, mostly hidden away in the Carpathian Mountains, whose members assassinated anyone they suspected of planning to play traitor.

Another group that emerged at this same time had an altogether more ambitious approach. They sought to *replace the Church with another*. So we come to what was surely the strangest of medieval heretical movements: the Cathars. The Cathars were the Western European branch of a movement that had first emerged in tenth-century Bulgaria, the Bogomils, who although they considered themselves Christian were barely recognisable as such. Radical Bogomils, shocked that their world was so filled with evil, concluded – like Zoroastrians, Manichaeans and Gnostic Christians before them – that it had been created not by one, but by *two* gods: one good and one bad. For good measure they also believed that there were *two* creations, *two* heavens, *two* earths, *two* eternal worlds and *two* kinds of angel.

In Languedoc and northern Italy, Catharism became, in the late eleventh century, a rival church, with its own structure, complete with bishops. What made it so attractive? Part of its appeal no doubt lay in the fact that it was *not the Church*. For all who were disgusted by the clerical worldliness, and doubted the Church's claim that it could help one into heaven, Catharism offered the allure of *extreme virtue*. Cathars had an elite, suitably named the Perfect, whose self-denial outdid even that of Paul's early Christians. Perfects were prohibited from sex of any kind.

If married, they had either to leave their spouses or live with them in strictest celibacy. Constantly fasting – they were famous for their thinness and pallor – Perfects were not permitted to eat food that had been produced, even indirectly, through sex, which ruled out meat, eggs and cheese (though, thanks to a poor understanding of reproduction, Perfects *were* allowed to eat fish, which they believed had been created sexlessly, by water). Their austerity won recruits, who considered that anybody who could follow such an impressively dismal lifestyle must have God's blessing.

Wisely, Catharism also offered a second and less demanding regime for those who were not so puritanically minded. Non-Perfect Cathars could have sex and eat meat whenever they liked, and yet still reach Cathar paradise, so long as they became Perfects on their deathbed, through a ceremony known as *consolamentum*. Even if something went wrong and they died without being initiated, there was still hope, as the Cathars believed in reincarnation. Another chance beckoned in the next life.

Yet in some ways Catharism was a puzzlingly *unreassuring* religion. That it became popular was probably down to its secrecy. Only Perfects were informed of its full range of doctrines, which were discouraging to say the least. Even a fully abstemious Perfect was not guaranteed a place in paradise. The reason for this sprang from the Cathars' curious version of the creation story. According to this account, of which there were a number of variations, soon after creation the bad god, Satan, had invaded heaven and imprisoned previously genderless angels in sexual, human bodies. Cathars believed that when they received consolamentum, they escaped their human bodies and returned to their original, angel state. Unfortunately they could not be sure they had been one of the angels tampered with by Satan. They might not have been an angel at all, but a devil, made by Satan in his wicked creation. If they had been an angel created by the good god they would proceed, after death, to Cathar paradise. If, though, they had been a devil, they would spend eternity in hell.

This was not the only fear to trouble Perfects' sleep. They also suffered the constant worry that they might be excluded from paradise because of something that *somebody else had done*. Cathar sin had a terrible finality. For Perfects, all mortal sins were equally grave. Any transgression would bar one from heaven, from committing murder to eating an egg. This severity was made more worrying by Cathar religious rules. According to these, each Perfect could only be created by another Perfect. Thus Cathars had a line of succession much like that of priests laying on hands in the Christian Church. Unlike the Church, though, Cathars believed that if a Perfect stumbled from the true path, then, in a kind of chain reaction, all the Perfects he had created, and that they in turn had invested, would *also fall*. In effect, a whole wing of the Cathar Church could lose legitimacy because somebody, somewhere, had taken a bite of cheese.

Such a thing happened. In 1167 Cathars both in Italy and Languedoc were converted to a new and radical form of the belief by a Bulgarian Bogomil named Nicetas. Soon afterwards, however, another Bogomil arrived, bringing the grave news that the Perfect who had granted consolamentum to Nicetas had been caught in suspicious circumstances with a woman. In one stroke Western European Catharism was cast adrift. While Languedoc Cathars chose, wisely, simply to ignore the news, those in Italy took it very seriously. Delegations from Italian cities travelled east to be re-consoled. Unfortunately, the rituals were performed by Perfects from different strands of Bogomilism. Italian cities, already intense rivals in other ways, now competed also in their heresy, hosting rival Cathar sects.

In the end, though, it was not the Cathars' divisions that led to their demise. Nor was it the military campaign launched against

them, the Albigensian Crusade, which was more brutal than effective. The Cathars were defeated because the Church renewed its
own self-purification. In 1210 and 1216 two new monastic orders
came into being, both of which were devoted to a life of simplest
poverty: the Franciscans and the Dominicans. The Church's image
soon began to improve. The Dominicans were founded specifically
to defeat the Cathars, and in the early 1230s Pope Gregory IX
created a new institution, staffed by members of the order, that
was dedicated to rooting out heresy: the Inquisition. Slowly people
in Languedoc and northern Italy were weaned away from hopes
of Cathar paradise, not so much by burnings, which were relatively
rare, but by being slowly worn down. The Inquisition kept
meticulous records of their activities, jailed them, confiscated their
property, banned them from employment and humiliated them,
forcing them to wear large yellow crosses on their clothes. By 1300
Catharism was largely extinguished.

By this time heresy was everywhere on the retreat. Yet Church
self-purification did not last very long. In 1309 Pope Clement V
moved the papacy from Rome to Avignon, where leading clerics
lived in infamous luxury. Church authority was further undermined by the farcical events of the Great Schism, when, from
1378, first two and later three individuals all claimed that they
alone were the true pope.

It was at this same moment that a part of Europe which until
now had shown only the dreariest religious conformity finally
entered the heretical fray: England. Here the Oxford scholar,
John Wycliffe, followed the example of Peter Waldo, by criticising
the Church and having the Bible translated into English. Wycliffe,
who managed to die peacefully in his own bed, but was later be
denounced as a heretic, inspired a movement – the Lollards – that
much resembled the Waldensians and endured as tiny, secretive
and persecuted Bible-reading groups. Wycliffe's denunciations

of the Church, though, also had another and altogether more explosive impact. They found supporters, a little surprisingly, a thousand kilometres to the south-east, in Bohemia, where they helped bring about Europe's greatest explosion of heresy. Wycliffe's anger resonated strongly with the Czechs, who were exasperated by the venality of their German-dominated clergy. When the Czech religious leader Jan Huss was duplicitously seized, tried and burned by Church inquisitors, in 1415, Bohemia broke away from the Church of Rome.

With no Inquisition to control it, the country soon became a kind of *Grand Central Station of dissident religion*, where Waldensian Bible readers could rub shoulders with apocalyptic, egalitarian Taborites, who had burned down their own farms so they would escape the sinfulness of wealth. One group, the Adamites, believed, like the Subtle of Spirit, that they were divine and superior to Jesus. In 1421 they set up camp on an island in the river Nezarka, where, until they were killed by appalled Taborites, they went about naked, enjoyed free love, and, having divested themselves of all property, raided nearby villages for food in a self-declared holy war, killing anyone who came into their hands.

Yet even in the fifteenth century, when the Church was most under attack by religious dissidents, the great majority of Europeans continued to follow its rules, turning a blind eye to its failings and quietly accepting its road to heaven. Many followed the Church with the most intense devotion. After the early 1450s, when the last Czech Hussite forces were defeated, almost all Europeans accepted the Church's worldview. Heretical movements shrank away, so much so that the Inquisition was lost for employment (with, as we will see in the next chapter, unfortunate consequences). As the sixteenth century dawned, the Church was a confident as it had not been for centuries.

It was a confidence that would prove unwise.

Opening Pandora's Box

On 31 October 1517, Martin Luther walked up to the door of the castle church in Wittenberg and nailed to it an angry denunciation of Church practices. It was an action that would later be celebrated in school textbooks by the thousand, and yet, at the time, Luther would have been both shocked and profoundly dismayed, had he been told of the full consequences of his action.

Luther is, in many ways, a familiar figure. He was very much a prophet: charismatic, obstinate and strongly aggressive towards all who opposed his views. Like other prophets he had a band of loyal disciples, who jotted down his most memorable remarks, made during meals, and these jottings were assembled after his death in a volume entitled *Table Talk*. Most of all, he had a prophet's disillusionment with the religious establishment of his age – the Catholic Church – which he believed had strayed dangerously from God's expectations. Unlike most earlier prophets, though, he managed to avoid a violent, premature death. But it was a close-run thing. Had it had the chance, the Church of Rome would certainly have burnt him at the stake.

Long troubled by paradise panic, and doubts as to his own spiritual adequacy, Luther was set on the road of the prophet by a key moment when he found himself newly struck by a passage in Paul's epistle to the Romans.

> . . . it is the power of God unto salvation to every one that believeth; to the Jew first, and also to the Greek. For therein is the righteousness of God revealed from faith to faith: as it is written, The just shall live by faith. (Romans 1:16–17)

Ecstatic with relief, Luther concluded that *faith alone* was enough to lead him to paradise. Yet his discovery, arguably, was less radical than he imagined. He had found theological justification for what others had been doing for centuries: finding a new entry criterion to paradise. He was also, though, challenging the role of the Church. What did priestly rules matter if faith alone was enough to cleanse one of sin? It was the mindset of a heretic, and in an earlier age Luther's career would have been a brief one. That it was not was largely down to his good timing.

Since the last great revolt against the Church, in Hussite Bohemia a century earlier, Europe had changed considerably. By Luther's time, printing had existed for more than two generations, and a growing number of Europeans could both buy books and read them. More significant than the copy of his *95 Theses on the Power and Efficacy of Indulgences* that Luther nailed to the door of the Wittenberg church were those which, less dramatically, he sent to influential acquaintances. Even Luther himself was taken aback by their effect. Despite their being written in Latin, within two weeks his theses were known across Germany, and within a month all over Europe.

It was when they were translated into German that, to use a modern phrase, they *went viral*. Printed and reprinted in towns all over Germany, they were sold in the streets and read out aloud at inns and work places. Though the Church replied with pamphlets of its own, Luther's – so passionate, so simply written, so angry – were more far persuasive, winning to his side German princes who protected him from the Church authorities. The Church, having managed to maintain belief control over for more than a millennium, lost it across much of Northern Europe in a matter of months. Without the support of local rulers it found itself all but powerless.

So much for *how* Luther changed beliefs in Europe. The key question, for a book of this kind, is *what* beliefs he brought? Did he devise any ideas that were truly new? He did not intend to do any such thing. Like many other world-changers before him, from Confucius and Jesus to Muhammad, he regarded himself as a conservative, who sought to guide religion *backwards*. His theses had been inspired by his revulsion at a Church money-raising scheme, which was launched in part to pay for the rebuilding of Saint Peter's Cathedral in Rome. A kind of salesman monk, Johann Tetzel, toured Germany, offering people the chance to buy their dead relatives out of purgatory. He wooed crowds with the catchphrase: 'The moment a coin in the coffer rings, a soul from purgatory springs.'

Luther, disgusted at such Church corruption – which, to be fair, was no worse in 1517 than it had been in many earlier eras – sought to return the Church to a purer time. This hope, though, raised a problem. How far back should it go? Paring the Church back to the preaching of Jesus was clearly impossible, as it would require the amputation of the greater part of Christianity. Back to the Christianity of the Bible? This too was fraught with difficulties, as it excluded the Church's convoluted dogmatic invention, the Trinity. Remove this and one would reopen the thorny debate of precisely how divine Jesus had been. Luther compromised. He accepted the Bible, together with Early Church writings, until around the time of the fall of Rome in the fifth century.

Yet Luther's vision of the Church would actually have shocked early Christians. Like all prophets, his religious blueprint was highly *personal*. The theologically trained son of a self-made peasant, he was proud of his simple roots, he was proudly German (and anti-Semitic) and he was also a proud family man. In 1523 he married the plain but loyal ex-nun Catherine von Bora. So in Luther's church, priests became permitted to marry. It was an arrangement that would have been quite unacceptable to celibacy-obsessed early Christians. They would also have been unhappy with Luther's heaven, which lacked the tough entry requirements of their own, and offered a peasant-friendly paradise that was open to all who had faith.

This heaven was very different from that of Luther's main rivals: the Protestant movement that grew up in Switzerland and became strongly influenced by John Calvin, and became known as the Reformed Church. Calvin's heaven was only for a few elect chosen by God. As enthusiasts for the idea that God had already chosen who would be admitted to paradise – the doctrine of predestination – Calvin's followers had no more certainty of a happy afterlife than had the Cathar Perfect. Neither faith nor virtuous living could ensure one's place in heaven, Calvinists believed, as God's will was not something that could be controlled by the actions of mere humans. God had chosen whomever he felt like choosing. Such an arrangement might seem far from reassuring, yet Calvin's followers were optimists. They *assumed* they were on the list.

Furthermore, they *tampered with the evidence*, to add to their own sense of confidence. Calvinists believed that a comfortable, affluent life was a sign from God that they had been selected for paradise. So they worked industriously to accumulate wealth, to ensure the sign of blessing was upon them. Though in their eyes, of course, this was not evidence-tampering at all, as worldly success was not their doing, but had also been preordained by God. From this worldview emerged an enduring feature of Northern European life, that later became known as the Protestant work ethic.

So far the Protestant Reformation may seem a rather dull business, at least in terms of religious imagination. We have seen nothing truly new. Yet Luther was, in effect, responsible for a vast outpouring of invention, though it was the last thing he had intended. As we have seen, his aim had not been to damage the Church but to restore it to purer ways, yet his revolution brought very different results. He broke the Church's monopoly. Europe became religiously divided between Lutherans and their Protestant rivals and the Church of Rome. The power of the Catholic Church to impose its vision on all, through the Inquisition, was ended for good. Suddenly anything went.

Out of the vacuum there sprang up a series of small movements that formed the radical fringe of the Reformation, and which were termed Anabaptists by their enemies, because members of some of them had themselves re-baptised. Yet Anabaptist groups frequently had almost nothing in common with one another, aside from a vague camaraderie, born out of the fact that they were all persecuted by Catholics and mainstream Protestants.

It was the Anabaptists who provided the real religious imagination of the Protestant Reformation, and their little movements followed a whole rainbow of beliefs. Pacifist Swiss Anabaptists felt that Luther had not gone far enough in his march backwards into the past, and insisted that people should take no notice of any authority except the Bible. Spiritualist Anabaptists went in exactly the opposite direction, looking for God within themselves, and declaring that the Bible was not God's word at all, but the work of humans. Mystical Anabaptists believed they could contact God directly, through trances and visions, in which they felt they were addressed by the Holy Spirit. Apocalyptic Anabaptists, as ever, looked forward to the imminent end of the world. Communitarian Anabaptists hoped to reserve their places in paradise by living as equals, and sharing property, to which end they set up their own settlements, first in the Austrian Tyrol, then, after being expelled, in Moravia, and finally in North America. Many of these ideas came together, as we saw in an earlier chapter, in the Anabaptist theocracy that ruled, briefly and murderously, over Münster in northern Germany, and gave Anabaptism a bad name for centuries to come.

It was in England that these ideas took a further leap. Only dragged into the Protestant Reformation because Pope Clement

VII refused to let Henry VIII divorce his queen, the country did not embark on true religious invention until the seventeenth century. During the civil wars of the 1640s and 1650s, when Church authority collapsed, innovation bubbled up from below, and England became Europe's greatest cauldron of religious imagination.

One of the oddest, if smallest new groups of this remarkable time was the *Muggletonians*. This tiny sect did not claim to have found a new road to paradise, but rather that they *knew in advance that they would get there*. The movement was founded by two London tailors, John Reeve and his cousin Lodowicke Muggleton, who believed themselves to be the two final witnesses mentioned in the Book of Revelation. The cousins claimed they had the power to know, at a single glance, who would be taken up to heaven after death and who would be dragged down to hell. It was a simple yet effective idea. Followers who had the tailors' thumbs-up could enjoy the reassurance of guaranteed salvation. As a rule, unsurprisingly, those who accepted the cousins' authority were destined for paradise, while those who did not were damned – although occasionally the cousins changed their minds, damning those they had previously declared saved, after a disagreement. Despite their sect's home-grown nature, the Muggletonians proved surprisingly enduring, and the last known member of the tiny movement died as recently as 1979.

One of the most radical strands of English religious imagination followed a more mystical road, of uncontrolled, trance-like communing with God. The first movement that engaged in such practices appeared three decades before the English Revolution began when, in 1609 a former Church of England clergyman named John Smyth returned, with his little band of followers, from a year's stay in Holland, where they had come into contact with Dutch Anabaptists. In London Smyth set up a new *Baptist church*, which was intermittently suppressed by the Church of

England, until Civil War brought all such suppression to an end. Baptists were known for very long and highly democratic services. Anyone could preach, even – shocking in male-dominated seventeenth-century England – women. Speakers were not even required to talk about the Bible, but could simply express their feelings, and tell, in an intense outpouring of emotion, how the Spirit of God had come to them.

By the late 1630s a related group had emerged, the *Seekers*, who would sit together in silence, waiting for God to take hold of one of them and cause them to cry out in emotion. However, this intensely emotional religion reached its most radical form, though, with the *Society of Friends*, later known as the *Quakers*. These first appeared in 1652, when several charismatic preachers, including George Fox, began to inspire huge gatherings of listeners. The Quakers quickly became a runaway movement. Starting out with a handful, it had some 60,000 followers by 1657. Not yet pacifists, the Quakers filled conservative England with alarm, with their, rapid rise and their vast, emotionally charged outdoor meetings.

At their most radical, the Quakers became a *church without the Bible*. Many Quakers were proud but poorly educated, and highly suspicious of university-trained clergy, whom they regarded as interlopers between themselves and God. Quakers refused to doff their hats before their supposed superiors, disrupted Church of England services, and sought direct connection with God, in the hope of finding what they termed the *inner light*. George Fox insisted that God spoke directly to him, not through any book, while some Quakers claimed that the scriptures themselves were a dead letter and burned their bibles. Their critics claimed, with some justification, that by rejecting the Bible Quakers were barely recognisable as Christians. Certainly it is hard to imagine how Christianity could have been pared down any further, without the removal of Jesus himself.

The group that caused most shock of all, though, were known as the *Ranters*. Members of this short-lived movement of tiny, dispersed groups were famous for indulging themselves in every way. Ranters believed that they had divinity within them, while some took matters further and claimed that they were *themselves* God. In consequence they felt that religious rules did not apply to them and they should do whatever they liked. Ranters were known to swear constantly – even in their sermons – to steal, to be constantly drunk and to freely have sex with anyone who was willing. Their lifestyle being repulsive to everyone except themselves, the Ranters managed to unite all of England's varied new religionists against them. After they were outlawed in the summer of 1650, they quickly faded from sight.

If all of this sounds familiar, it should. The worldview of the Ranters was a mirror of the medieval heretic anarchists we encountered earlier in this chapter, the Adherents of the Free Spirit. Were they directly connected? There is no evidence that they were. It is more probable is that, having begun with the same premise – that they were divine – both groups reached the same pleasing conclusion: that they should do whatever they liked.

Yet the Ranters were by no means the only new group of the Reformation that can be seen as descending from the heretical movements of the Middle Ages. Most of them did. When Luther broke Church encryption of the Bible, and began translating it into German, in 1522, he was echoing the efforts of Peter Waldo of Lyons and John Wycliffe of Oxford. Likewise the Diggers' vision of an egalitarian, property-less kingdom of Jesus on earth was a reprise of that of John Ball, during the English Peasants Revolt, and Bohemian Taborites who burned down their own farms. The true cauldron of religious invention was the medieval era. The novelty of the Protestant Reformation was that it permitted heresies to become religions, as underground counter-culture became accepted culture.

Yet the new churches of the Reformation achieved one innovation that their medieval forebears had singularly failed to do – something that was, arguably, the true religious novelty of this era. They brought about *religious tolerance*. Tolerance of other religious thinking had been lacking in Christianity from Paul's day, and perhaps even from that of Jesus. It was something in which the early Protestants had no interest either. They dreamed of a single, uniform church, but one that expressed *their* ideas. In 1525, one of the first Reformed preachers, Zwingli, had one of the first Anabaptists, Felix Manz, drowned in the Limmat river in Zurich, and in Saxony in the 1580s Lutherans burned several Reformed Protestants at the stake. The Catholic Church found it famously hard to move on from Paul's dream of total ideological control. Even Anabaptist groups were rarely much interested in tolerance, happily anticipating the moment when everybody except them would perish in the apocalypse, or last judgement. Gradually, though, all religions were *forced* to tolerate their rivals. They had no choice, as they lacked the power to destroy them. By the seventeenth century Christians, having demanded that they be tolerated, demanded the acceptance of diverse visions as a matter of principle. For the very first time Christians demanded tolerance of worldviews *different from their own*. The age of inter-Christian persecution was finally beginning to draw to an end.

But not the age of persecution. During the seventeenth century there was a single matter on which *every* Christian church found agreement. Whether they were Catholics, Lutherans or Reformists, Anabaptists or Baptists, when it came to a particular phenomenon, all were united in their fear and hatred.

Sad to say.

9

INVENTING WITCHES

In July 1628, Johannes Junius, Burgomaster of the city of Bamberg in Bavaria, wrote a letter to his daughter.

> Many hundred thousand good-nights, dearly beloved daughter Veronica. Innocent have I come into prison, innocent have I been tortured, innocent must I die. For whoever comes into the witch prison must become a witch or be tortured until he invents something out of his head and – God pity him – bethinks him of something.
>
> I will tell you how it has gone with me. When I was the first time put to the torture, my brother-in-law, Dr Braun, Dr Kotzendorffer, and two strange doctors were there. Then Dr Braun asks me; 'Kinsman, how come you are here?' I answer, 'Through falsehood and through misfortune.' 'Hear, you,' he retorts, 'You are a witch. Will you confess it voluntarily? If not, we'll bring in witnesses and the executioner for you.' I said, 'I am no witch; I have a pure conscience in the matter. If there are a thousand witnesses, I am not anxious, but I'll gladly hear them.' Then the Chancellor's son was set before me, who said he had

seen me. I asked that he be sworn and legally examined, but Dr Braun refused it. Then the Chancellor, Dr George Haan, was brought, who said the same as his son. Afterward Höppfen Ellse. She had seen me dance on Hauptsmorwald, but they refused to swear her in. I said: 'I have never renounced God, and will never do it – God graciously keep me from it. I'll rather bear whatever I must.'

And then came also – God in highest Heaven have mercy – the executioner, and put the thumbscrews on me, both hands bound together, so that the blood spurted from the nails and everywhere, so that for four weeks I could not use my hands, as you can see from the writing.

Thereafter they stripped me, bound my hands behind me, and drew me up on the ladder. Then I thought heaven and earth were at an end. Eight times did they draw me up and let me fall again, so that I suffered terrible agony. I said to Dr Braun, 'God forgive you for thus misusing an innocent and honorable man.' He replied, 'You are a knave.'

Realising that he could not endure the torture much longer, Junius invented a confession. He said he had been approached by a seductive maiden who had then turned herself into a goat, frightening him so much that he agreed to renounce God and be baptised in the devil's name. He claimed he had attended gatherings of witches, and ridden through the sky on the back of a black dog. Even this, though, was not enough for his torturers, and he was forced to name other witches, so the hunt could be continued.

Junius finished his letter with a scrawl in the margin.

Dear child, six have confessed against me at once: the Chancellor, his son, Neudecker, Zaner, Hoffmaister Ursel, and Höppfen Ellse – all false, through compulsion, as they have all told me, and begged my forgiveness in God's name before they were executed . . . They know nothing but good of me. They were forced to say it, just as I myself was.

Junius' daughter never read the letter. It was intercepted and added to the evidence to be used against her father.

It is a powerful story, and yet, it might be asked, what is witchcraft doing in a book about belief? As any serious historian would agree, in medieval and Renaissance Europe there were *no witches*. There were *sorcerers*, who were sometimes accused of witchcraft, but these were something very different. Sorcery was the idea that invisible connections link all natural things. This meant that someone with an understanding of such matters could, for example, harm another person by sticking pins in a doll, or protect crops by throwing herbs into a fire. Sorcery had such a universal presence, in cultures all across the world, that it is likely to have been one of humanity's earliest beliefs and may have grown out of shamanism. In medieval and Renaissance Europe, although on the decline, it was still practised by a good number of individuals. While some clearly enjoyed the idea that they were secretly inflicting harm on their neighbours, most seem to have been concerned not with malice, but self-protection. They cast spells to try and counteract spells that others might have cast against them, in what was a kind of *supernatural insurance*.

Witchcraft, by contrast, was not a belief held by anyone at all, despite the claims of those who conducted witch-hunts. What, then, of *fear of witches*? Tales of witches, which usually closely followed the same lines, could hardly have been better calculated to unnerve. Witches, were mostly female and elderly. They could change their shape and fly through the air. They had intelligent, knowing animal familiars. They met in groups to dance, to have orgies, and to become possessed by evil spirits. Most distressing of all, witches would creep unnoticed into your home as you slept, suck you blood, have sex with you, consume your flesh, make you ill and kill your children. Such a phenomenon does not seem a belief so much as an imaginative rendering of profound human terrors.

Yet there can be no doubt that fear of witches was a *belief*. We know this because, unlike sorcery, witch fear was far from universal. If it had been an instinctive human fear, one would expect it to have existed everywhere, yet witches haunted people's imaginations in only two parts of the world: Europe and Africa. From Scandinavia to Botswana stories were told of groups of wicked, nocturnal flying women, but in China, India, Australia and the pre-Columbian Americas people had to find other creatures to inhabit their nightmares.

Witches, like astrology, were probably a Mesopotamian export. The Mesopotamian goddess *Lamashtu,* who had a lion's head, donkey's teeth, bird's feet and long fingernails and was accompanied by two snakes, was known to prey on sleeping people, kill men, children and newborns, and drink their blood. The Jews had an infertile female spirit called Lilith, who flew through the night, with owls as her helpers, seducing men, drinking their blood and murdering children. The Greeks, too, had a child-eating demoness. Why this nightmare personality migrated westwards to Europe and Africa, but not east, is anybody's guess.

That Europeans and Africans shared fears of such monsters is interesting, but hardly shocking. What *is* shocking, however, is that this belief was taken seriously and witchcraft viewed as an actual form of human activity which posed great dangers to society. Moreover, this view was accepted by the great majority of Europeans, including most of its keenest minds.

How did such a thing happen? To answer that question we need to return to the episode we looked at in the last chapter, when, in 1022, the knight Aréfast exposed a little circle of religious dissidents in Orléans. The group's religious views were enough to convict them, and yet, curiously, these were not the key accusations laid against them. They were charged, instead, of meeting secretly at night, summoning the devil, taking part in sexual orgies, killing the resulting babies and burning their bodies to make a powder which, when consumed by others, would win them over to the devil.

Why were the Orléans group accused of witchcraft? The answer can only be guessed at, and yet we can make a pretty good guess. As I mentioned, the circle's leader, Stephen, had previously been the French queen's confessor, so there was a real danger that the stain of heresy might mark both her and her husband. It was sound politics, therefore, to make the case against the circle as overwhelming as possible. The bishops present may also have favoured such an approach, as it would discourage anyone present from taking the dissidents' views seriously. Their religious ideas would be drowned out by the horror of the crimes of which they were accused and the heresy would be contained. If this was the churchmen's thinking, it proved highly effective. As we saw, feelings against the circle were so strong that they had to be escorted to their place of execution, to prevent them being killed on the spot by infuriated locals.

The trial seems to have set an unfortunate precedent. Having proved so successful at Orléans, witchcraft accusations quickly became standard practice in the growing number of heresy trials that followed. Cathars and Waldensians were routinely accused of meeting at night to summon the devil. Yet it would be a mistake to see these accusations as coldly calculating. In the eyes of those who prosecuted such cases, heresy and witchcraft were much the same thing. Both were the work of the devil, so if you were guilty of one, you were as good as guilty of the other.

Little by little, as ever more religious dissidents, together with a few sorcerers, were found guilty of having sex with the devil, and flying through the night on brooms, a change in thinking began to occur in Europe. An increasing number people came to imagine that this kind of bogeyman belief must be *real*. Matters took a step further – or further back – in the 1230s, when the Church formed the Inquisition, which actively sought out heretics and witches. Witchcraft charges were so hard to disprove, and summoned up such emotion, that they were useful also in political trials, such as the destruction of the cash-rich Knights Templar in the early fourteenth century. Later in the century, as the papacy fell into the farce of the Great Schism, and heresies raged, there were so many witchcraft accusations that they were standardised, for greater convenience. Torture was routinely used and inquisitors were provided with set lists of questions to be asked, all of which – such as How long have you been a witch? – rather assumed guilt. Still, during the Middle Ages it was comparatively rare for people to be accused of witchcraft if they were *not* followers of heretical movements. Many Europeans were sceptical about the existence of witches and the issue could still be calmly argued.

All of this would change. It is a disquieting truth that the great age of witch terror did not occur during the medieval era, which is so often associated with superstition and ignorance. It took place during the Renaissance: a period we associate with learning, printing and new literacy, with reason and love of the classical world, with great literature and art and music, and with scientific discovery. How did such a thing happen? Part of the blame lay with the retreat of heresy. By the 1450s, as we saw, the heretical explosion in Hussite Bohemia had collapsed, and Europe was religiously tranquil as it had not been for two centuries. The Inquisition found itself with little to do. Like any professionals in such a situation, inquisitors looked about for new work. They knew that other work was waiting for than, as it was not as if the devil had retired. If his followers could no longer be found in heretical sects, then they must be elsewhere. So the Inquisition actively began to seek out witches.

It soon found them. After centuries of conducting heresy trials, the Inquisition had finely tuned its methods for obtaining confessions, using shame, torture and the threat of accusing other members of one's family. The same approaches were now employed, with great success, against suspected witches. Particularly active from the 1470s was a German Dominican inquisitor named Heinrich Kramer, who had taken the scholarly name of Institoris. In 1486 Kramer, who was later condemned by his religious order for embezzlement, published a book, *Malleus Maleficarum*, or 'Hammer of the Witches'. In it Kramer offered the world his collected knowledge as to what witches did, and how they might be discovered and caught. So grew up the strange science of *demonology*, which the historian Lyndal Roper described as 'a morass of images, half-articulated convictions and contradictory positions'.

Kramer's book, which was sanctioned by the pope, found an eager audience. Thanks to the new development of printing, and the rise in literacy, it reached a large number of readers. People became familiar with every detail of witches' lives, and could watch for tell-tale signs among their neighbours. These included weight (anyone who weighed less than a copy of the Bible was certain to be a witch), faint spots on the body where the devil had made his mark, and lumps that were known to be spare nipples, from which familiars were nursed. In a continent whose inhabitants abounded in scars, warts and skin diseases, the potential for witch-discovery was considerable.

The publication of *Malleus Maleficarum* sparked the beginning of what has been termed the *witch craze*. With Kramer's manual to guide them, inquisitors began energetically to seek out witches. The methods they used to obtain confessions seem crudely manipulative to modern eyes, and some inquisitors probably were, like Kramer himself, ambitious to obtain a large number of condemnations. A few may also have sought to confiscate the property of their victims. Yet it is doubtful that very many inquisitors behaved cynically. Most seem to have genuinely believed that they were acting for the good of mankind. In their eyes God could never permit innocents to be punished, so if he did not intercede to save a suspect, then he or she *must be guilty*.

Those who were accused, too, often seem to have believed that God would come to their aid. When it became clear that he was not going to do so after all, most confessed their guilt, admitting that they had had sex with the devil, killed and eaten children, and so forth. One can hardly blame them. They confessed to save members of their families from being accused or to save themselves from torture. The Bamberg witch house was particularly well equipped in this respect, with racks, a strappado to hoist people in the air by their arms tied behind their backs, thumbscrews, lime baths and much more. Inquisitors sometimes also offered tempting *sweeteners*, such as death by strangulation rather than at the stake. As it was well known that witches worked in groups, those under investigation, once they had admitted their guilt, were often required to name other witches. So a minor case of spell casting, or malicious rumour-mongering, could burgeon into a cluster of witch burnings. As ever more witches were discovered, naturally the assumption grew that Europe must be infested. Demand rose for more energetic campaigns to deal with this menace, producing, in turn, more confessed witches. The craze developed a momentum of its own. Having begun in north-west Europe, it slowly spread outwards in every direction until, as the historian Jeffrey B. Russell recounts, witches were seen not merely as a local problem but as 'part of a vast plot against Christians'[17].

Matters were exacerbated by outside factors. One of these was, of all things, the weather. For many Europeans witchcraft was, as the historian Lyndal Roper described it, 'an intensely physical experience'. People reported that 'their milk dried up, that their babies became ill and wasted away before their eyes, that they were suddenly pressed down upon as they slept. Their animals sickened, their crops shrivelled.'[18] These impressions, it is now clear, were far from imaginary. Between the 1420s and 1480s Europe's climate began to change, as an intensely cold era, known as the Little Ice Age, began. European farmers, many of whom already lived a marginal existence, suffered increasingly poor harvests. Some, rather than passively accepting their fate, opted for the more satisfying course of finding someone to blame. Tellingly, the witch craze was most intense from the 1560s, when the Little Ice Age reached a peak and many areas of Europe suffered food crises. To add further to tensions, Europe was also struck by the worst outbreak of plague since the Black Death 200 years previously. In both Milan and Geneva people were accused, and executed, as witches who had spread the disease.

Another factor was the Protestant Reformation. One might imagine that Luther's breaking of Rome's religious monopoly would have calmed interest in witch-finding, but no, it made matters worse. As Europe became a hothouse of religious fear and enmity, witch fears flourished. What was more, leaders of the new Protestant churches proved every bit as zealous to root out witches as their Catholic rivals. Luther himself was a staunch believer in witches and Calvin was little better. As the Reformation extended, it inspired vicious wars, adding to the climate of fear. National authorities, which were often the most effective at reining in over-zealous local witch-finders, had more pressing concerns. Expectations of the end of the world added to the mood, as apocalypticists hungered to impress God by cleansing society of undesirables.

Who were these unfortunates? Some were sorcerers, the charges against whom were then extended to witchcraft. Most, though, were simply unlucky innocents. They were accused by malevolent, or mistakenly conscientious neighbours, or – like Johannes Junius, whose letter opened this chapter – by people who had themselves already confessed to witchcraft and were then forced to provide more names. The real crime of many of the accused was that they were *unpopular*. They were elderly widows, or midwives who, having taken part in unsuccessful births, had made enemies. Or they did not fit in. Anyone who stood out from the crowd might find themselves accused, from beggars and drunks to the odd, the ill-tempered, or the sexually different. But victims also included, curiously enough, those who were *too good:* people who were unusually virtuous, perhaps irritatingly so, such as teachers and judges. It was safest to be plainly *ordinary*. Or – and this is no surprise – powerful.

Why, we might ask, were there no calls to sanity? Why did nobody protest, in this age of new thinking, that it was unlikely that Europe was full of child-murdering devil worshippers who rode through the skies on brooms? Some did, though not many. In 1563, at the height of the witch craze, a Dutch scholar, Johann Weyer, published a book, *On the Illusions of Demons, on Spells and Poisons* in which he attacked *Malleus Maleficarum*, and argued that most accused witches were, in fact, women suffering melancholy or mental illness. For his pains, Weyer himself became accused of witchcraft. It was dangerous to try and oppose such a strong tide of panic.

A grumpy, warty midwife's best hope often lay in the efficiency of her local witch hunters. She was most in danger in places where the authorities became obsessed with witch fears. Or where inquisitors put too much trust in children, who, more than adults, tended to mix fantasy with reality. In two areas of Europe, witch prosecutions were markedly more restrained than elsewhere because of inquisitors' caution. In the Jura Mountains of Southern France witch hunters were reluctant to use torture, followed the law and avoided basing cases on children's evidence. They convicted few witches. The same was true in Spain, thanks to, a little surprisingly, the good sense of the Spanish Inquisition, which concentrated its efforts on cases of sorcery.

Then the whole terrible thing simply faded away. In the later seventeenth century this great crime, in which some 50,000 people had been executed, and the same number again tortured, gradually fizzled out. It ended where it had first begun, in north-west Europe. In 1687, Louis XIV of France produced a new and reasoned law on sorcery. For a time the witch craze continued to ripple outwards, with cases in Scandinavia and, infamously, in Massachusetts, with the Salem witch trials of 1692. And then it was gone. From the first it had been very much a *Christian phenomenon*. It had emerged from the lethal mixing of ancient bogeyman fears with a very real fear held by Christianity's rulers: the fear of different thinking.

What killed the witch craze? Put simply, Europe *outgrew* it. At once horrified by the seventeenth century's brutal religious wars and enthralled by new scientific discoveries, Europeans tired of intense religious belief and became increasingly drawn to the rational. There was a new interest in applying the scientific approach, of proof by experiment, to human affairs. The moment logic was applied to witch cases they fell apart.

By the eighteenth century a truly radical change had begun in European thinking. It became possible to question not only different forms of Christianity, but *Christianity itself*. For the first time in almost a millennium and a half, people such as Voltaire could cast doubt on the very existence of God. By the later eighteenth century Christianity found itself under a two-pronged attack: by by geological discoveries, which undermined biblical claims that the earth was only a few thousand years old, and also by agnostic French revolutionaries. In 1859 a new front was opened up, with the publication of Charles Darwin's *The Origin of Species*, which tore a gaping whole in the notion that the world, and humankind, had been created by God.

Was the age of intense belief finally drawing to an end? Not at all. During the last two centuries people continued to feel insecure and to hunger for beliefs that would give them reassurance. If anything, the myriad of new beliefs that sprang up after 1800 were more diverse, more imaginative and often more bizarre than before. These beliefs began to include, for the first time, worldviews that were not actually religious, but – at least in the eyes of their creators – purely political. Two strands of new belief seem to stand out in particular, each trying to answer new kinds of unease that troubled people's days and nights.

10

NEW FEARS, NEW COMFORTS

Balm for New Wounds

One day in 1837 a 23-year-old schoolteacher named Hong Xiuquan travelled to the busy regional capital of Canton to take, for the third time, the Chinese civil service examination. While in the city he was handed a Protestant pamphlet entitled, 'Good Words for Exhorting the Age'. Hong hardly glanced at this, but took it back with him to his home village. There, on learning that he had failed the exams once again – something not helped by his inability to pay bribes – he for several days fell into a delirious state, during which he believed he was in the presence of two men. One, who was middle-aged, told Hong that he was his brother. The other, who was older and bearded, gave Hong a sword and told him to rid the world of demons. The meaning of these visions only became clear to Hong six years later, when, having failed the civil service examinations for a *fourth* time, he again chanced upon the pamphlet.

'Good Words for [Exhorting the Age]' offered an unusual reading of Christianity. It had been written by a Protestant convert named Liang Fa who was much more struck by the Old Testament than the New. Liang saw Christianity as a religion of triumphant rebellion, which celebrated how the Jews, with the help of their God, had overcome their foreign (Egyptian) oppressors. Many Chinese considered that they, too, had foreign oppressors: the Manchu rulers, who had conquered the country from the north two centuries previously. Lately the Manchu regime had become so decrepit that, in Hong's home region of Guangdong, the country had been humiliatingly defeated by an altogether more alien form of barbarian: the British.

Reading and re-reading the pamphlet, Hong had a moment of epiphany. In his visions six years earlier, he concluded, he had been in heaven. The old man had been God and the middle-aged one Jesus. Hong was Therefore *Jesus' young brother*. Hong saw his destiny. After destroying Confucian writings in the village school where he taught and getting himself fired, he began touring the countryside, preaching and gathering supporters to his new movement: the God Worshippers' Society.

Hong's version of Christianity, though inspired by Liang Fa, was very much his own. In effect he reinvented it as a Chinese religion. Hong claimed that, in the time of China's earliest dynasties – many centuries before Judaeans accepted a single deity – the Chinese already worshipped the one true God of the Old Testament. It was only later that, led astray by foreign dynasties, they had lost sight of their single god. If they returned to him, he would bring them greatness. Hong promised to free China from Manchu rule and lead the country into a new golden age, the Heavenly Kingdom of Great Peace (*Taiping Tianguo*).

For all its strangeness, Hong's brand of Chinese nationalist Christianity proved appealing. After seven years of preaching he raised an army of 20,000 disaffected farmers, smugglers and triad warriors, and in early 1851, in the midst of a famine, he launched his campaign. So began a brutal war, known as the Taiping Rebellion, which only ended thirteen years later, when the Taiping armies were finally defeated by the Manchus, and Hong himself died, either from disease or by his own hand. The Taiping Rebellion, which took place in the same era as the American Civil War, has been described as the last, old-style major conflict. While in America armies battled using railways, high-powered rifles, artillery and armoured warships, Taiping campaigns were fought more often than not with swords and famine.

Yet if Hong's military tactics were old, the state he ruled, briefly, in central China, at the height of the revolt, was like nothing the country had seen before. In his capital, Nanjing, he made every effort to impress his father, God. The city's many Daoist and Buddhist temples were burnt to the ground and their personnel chased away or executed. Nanjingers were required to pray each morning and evening, and Hong, who had introduced the Western solar calendar, designated Saturday to be a new *Chinese sabbath*, when huge outdoor services were held (attendance obligatory).

Hong also tried to please God with some *social remodelling*. The Heavenly Kingdom took Christian ideas of chastity to new levels. Total segregation of the sexes was enforced, as Nanjing was divided into separate male and female districts. At the same time sexual equality – never much of a biblical priority – was promoted. Women were appointed as officials and also expected to do hard physical labour. Out in the countryside – most of which, fortunately, the Taiping rebels never managed to control – austerity took on a more bloodthirsty form, as poor farmers were encouraged collectively to murder their landlords and richer neighbours. A century after Hong Xiuquan launched his rebellion, another Sino-Western hybrid – Maoism – would adopt all of his social policies, aside from gender segregation.

Hong's mixing of Western and local beliefs was far from unique. A few decades, later Zulu prophets in Southern Africa, such as Isaiah Shembe adopted their own, unique form of apocalyptic Christianity. One of the strangest of these fusion religions, founded in 1926, and still going strong today, is that of the Cao Dai of southern Vietnam, which combines Daoism, Confucianism, Buddhism and Spiritualism with Roman Catholic organisation. The Cao Dai are governed by cardinals and a pope, and have an impressive list of saints that includes Jesus, Muhammad, Buddha, the Jade Emperor, Pericles, Joan of Arc, John the Baptist, Sun Yat-sen, Julius Caesar and Victor Hugo. What had inspired such mixings of belief? All, I would suggest, arose from *wounded national confidence*. From the French Revolution, patriotism, which had had a presence throughout history, became much more sharply focused. The age of nationalism had begun. As national pride grew more intense, so did national shame when things went wrong. Just one year before Hong Xiuquan began preaching his Chinese Protestantism, China had suffered defeat to the British in the First Opium War. Zulu apocalypticism emerged shortly after Zulu nations were overwhelmed, also by the British. The Cao Dai sect appeared two generations after Vietnam had been colonised by France. It was as if these proud peoples responded to their humiliation by *borrowing a little of the magic* of those who had defeated them, in the hope that this would help bring revival.

The Western belief that would prove most popular as a balm for national despair was not a religion at all. Or at least it claimed not to be. By the 1960s, close to half the world's population lived under Marxist regimes. It is, of course, questionable how many of their inhabitants truly believed in the ideology, as many of these territories were forced to accept the worldview by conquest. In several countries, though, there can be no question that large numbers of people were genuinely won over to Marxism. Notable among these were Russia during and after the First World War, and China in the 1940s. Both countries possessed a strong sense of national pride, and both had been humiliated by military defeat: Russia by the armies of the German Kaiser and China by those of Imperial Japan.

What made Marxism so appealing in these places? One factor was doubtless its modernity, or seeming modernity. Members of the the elites of both Russia and China despaired that their countries seemed for ever trapped in backwardness. Modernity was a Holy Grail. Marx offered the world not just socialism, but *scientific socialism*: a failsafe analysis based on Marx's expert understanding of German philosophy, French revolutionary politics and British economics. Marx had deciphered history as it had never been deciphered before, and revealed it to be a long process of class conflict. Better still, Marx could read the future. Marx's *Communist Manifesto* thundered prophetic certainty. The lower middle classes would never be able to 'roll back the wheel of history'. The bourgeoisie would produce, in the proletariat, 'its own grave-diggers'. Its fall and the victory of the proletariat were 'equally inevitable'.

The *Communist Manifesto* itself was an important part of the ideology's appeal. Although attributed to both Marx and Engels, it seems to have been overwhelmingly Marx's creation. Part of its power lay in its brevity. Marx could be verbose in the extreme, but the *Manifesto*, which he wrote in January 1848, aged just twenty-nine, was very short. Marx had had little choice in the matter, as the small group of exiled German revolutionaries in England that had commissioned the work – during Marx's very brief time as an active would-be revolutionary – were breathing down his neck. The last section seems so hurried one suspected he was still scribbling it down on the train to London.

It ran to just 12,000 words, or around twenty pages. Many world-changing texts were short. Paul's letter to the Romans and his first letter to the Corinthians, which between them set out the heart of his version of Christianity, are together fewer than 20,000 words. Daniel's Dream, which haunted the Western world for two millennia, is far shorter still, at a mere 5,500 words, or the size of long magazine article. Even the Analects of Confucius are a novella-length 27,500 words. Short, punchy pieces catch readers. If Marx had relayed his ideas only through his later multi-tome, *Das Kapital*, it is doubtful anyone would remember his name.

As much as it was short, the *Communist Manifesto* was also *electrifying*. Marx, like Luther two centuries earlier, had a passionate, aggressive and highly readable style. He wrote as he was. His character, like Luther's, was very much that of a prophet: intense of opinion and savage towards anyone who dared disagree with him. He even looked the part, with his 'shock of deep black hair and hairy hands', his movements that were 'dignified and disdainful', and his 'sharp metallic voice', that was 'wonderfully adapted to the judgements that he passed on persons and things . . .'[19]

Here he is, thundering, bishop-like, against imagined bourgeois critics who claim that communists would undermine the institution of the family.

The bourgeois clap-trap about the family and education, about the hallowed co-relation of parent and child, becomes all the more disgusting, the more, by the action of modern industry, all family ties among proletarians are torn asunder, and their children transformed into simple articles of commerce and instruments of labour.[20]

Yet I would suggest that perhaps the greatest allure of Marxism, to Russians, Chinese and others was neither its seeming modernity, nor its style, nor even its message that history was a process of class conflict which would lead to proletarian triumph. It was, its vision of *the end of the world*.

Marx the apocalypticist? Surely, as a political thinker, he was nothing of the kind? Or was he? Marx divided history into three eras. First there had been a *bad past*, the aristocratic era, when the society had been ruled by a lazy, privileged nobles. Next came a *worse present*, when it was controlled by ruthlessly acquisitive capitalists. Soon to come, though, was a *golden future*, when, after violent revolution, power would finally come to factory workers and exploitation would be ended for ever. If this sounds familiar, it should do. Zarathustra had had a similar vision. More recently, so had the twelfth-century Calabrian monk and hermit Joachim of Fiore, who had divided human history into an unsatisfactory past Age of the Father, a likewise unsatisfactory present Age of the Son and an joyous, imminent Age of the Spirit. Just as Marx prophesied that the proletarian revolution would be led by a vanguard of inspired intellectuals (like himself), Joachim claimed that the way to the Age of the Spirit would be prepared by a movement of dedicated monks (like *himself*). Like innumerable apocalypticists before him, Marx and his fellow revolutionary Friedrich Engels waited impatiently for the great day. During the 1850s Marx, excited by some promising occurrence in the news, several times declared that *now* the revolution was finally coming. Engels even joined the Cheshire foxhunters to improve his riding skills, so he would be ready to lead a vast *proletarian cavalry charge* across Europe.

Like Daniel's Dream and the Book of Revelation, Marx's apocalypse did not only reward the deserving but also punished trangressors. In Marx's version of the Kingdom of Jesus on

Earth (the Dictatorship of the Proletariat), wicked sinners (capitalists) would be cast into their Lake of Fire (the Dustbin of History). It should come as no surprise that Marx's end of the world was popular with people who felt deep national hurt. The apocalypse had first come into the world as a response to precisely this sentiment, when, back in the second century BC, patriotic Jews, including the author of Daniel's Dream, saw their nation and culture threatened by foreign Greek oppressors.

Yet Marx's apocalypse differed in one important way from its many predecessors. For some people it actually *delivered*. End-of-the-world leaders, from Jesus to Jan Bockelson in Münster, had assured their followers that, as believers, they would become great lords in a new kingdom on earth. Such promises had, of course, always proved something of a disappointment, but lucky Marxist faithful *did* find themselves promoted, if not to great lords, then at least to privileged cadres in the new order. Such as this man, whom the Russian First World War General Brusilov had saved from death by firing squad, and was now forced to share his apartment with.

> Coarse, insolent and constantly drunk, with a body covered in scars, he was now of course an important person, close to Lenin etc. Now I wonder why I saved his life! Our apartment, which had been clean and pleasant till he came, was thereafter spoiled by drinking bouts and fights, thievery and foul language. He would sometimes go away for a few days and come back with sacks of food, wine and fruit. We were literally starving but they had flour, butter, and whatever else they cared for.[21]

During the twentieth century, feelings of profound cultural hurt have, of course, drawn people to a variety of intense beliefs. The same feelings would also, I am sure, have been very much in the minds of Osama bin Laden and his followers, when they launched their jihad against the West, and Muslim governments they considered corrupted by the West. Do members of al-Qaeda have an equivalent of the *Communist Manifesto*: a kind of philosophical *user's guide* to their activities? They do, although, rather surprisingly, few in the West, which is daily bombarded with news reports of al-Qaeda's activities, real or feared, have heard of the book, let alone read. It is *Milestones* by the Egyptian writer Sayyid Qutb.

Qutb wrote *Milestones* in 1964 in Cairo's notorious Tura prison. He had been placed there by the regime of his one-time political collaborator, Egypt's ruler, General Nasr. Qutb did not live long after writing the book. Freed for a few months, during which he became leader of a fledgling Islamic military group, he was then rearrested and hanged in August 1966. Much of the evidence used against him was what he had written in *Milestones*.

Where did his radicalism spring from? It seems to have come more from *within* him than *without*. He showed little sign of it in his younger life. Born in 1906 to a poor family in a remote southern Egyptian village, he did well in his studies – in which he shunned the local religious school – and went on to find work in Cairo as a civil servant. Here he began writing poems, novels, book reviews, journalism and commentaries. He became part of Cairo's literary elite, joining in criticism of the iniquities of British control of Egypt, and was an early patron of Egypt's great writer Naguib Mahfouz.

It was in the 1940s that a change had begun to take place in Qutb. Slowly, at first even a little secretively, he became convinced that Egypt was drifting from its Islamic roots and becoming too Westernized. He felt Egyptians were losing their sense of social justice and women were being exploited. Though this change began within him, it was furthered by events of the time. Qutb was shocked when both the West and the Soviet Union gave their support to a Jewish State in Palestine in 1948. When, in that same year, he was sent on a government-sponsored trip to the United States, unlike other Egyptians, who returned from their visits filled with admiration, Qutb grew more fixed in his disdain. On his return he attacked America as filled with racial prejudice, sexual laxity and an absence of spiritual feeling. His former friend Mahfouz, no friend of puritanical Islamicists, came to regard him as sinister, with his bulging, serious eyes.

It was eight years later that Qutb's radicalism took a new direction. Having fallen out with Egypt's ruler, Nasr, when, to Qutb's disgust, Nasr set up a highly secular regime, Qutb became increasingly allied to Egypt's Muslim Brotherhood movement, and in 1958 Qutb was arrested along with many other members of the organisation. Qutb's previous, bookish existence left him unprepared for what came next. Following his arrest he was beaten up. Some years later, in the hospital of Cairo's brutal Tura jail, where he had been his own ill-health, he watched as dozens of his Muslim Brotherhood friends were brought in, dead or wounded, having been shot in their cells because they had refused to perform forced labour in a quarry.

Milestones can be seen as Qutb's riposte. Or his revenge. Written as part of a huge commentary on the Qu'ran, it was, in effect, every Westerner's and secular Muslim's worst nightmare of radical Islam. Qutb claimed that all states, from the West to Japan, from the Soviet Union to India and China, were 'idolatrous'. He was no less scathing of Muslim states, which he described as being, 'steeped in *jahiliyyah*'.22 *Jahiliyyah*, roughly meaning 'godlessness' was a word used to describe the religious ignorance of people in Arabia before their conversion by Muhammad,. Qutb declared that true Islam had been extinct for, 'a few centuries'. In effect, he claimed no country was worthy of the name Muslim. Even many of Qutb's political allies in the

Muslim Brotherhood were uneasy at this thinking. His *jahilliyah* seemed uncomfortably close to
a long discredited Islamic practice, *takfir*, which resembled Christian excommunication for heresy.

How would this unhappy situation be resolved? Qutb saw room for hope. The world, he argued, was in a similar situation to how it had been in the early seventh century, when Muhammad was about to bring God's word to the Arabs. At that time Arabs had been hemmed in by two powerful empires – Byzantium and Persia – and, with the coming of Islam, they had defeated both. The same would happen again, Qutb promised, now with the Western and Communist empires. But to begin Islam's renewal, Qutb wrote:

> It is necessary that there should be a vanguard which sets out, with this determination and then keeps walking on the path, marching through the vast ocean of jahiliyyah which has encompassed the entire world. During its course, it should keep itself somewhat aloof from this all-encompassing jahiliyyah and should also keep some ties with it.[23]

This vanguard, to whom *Milestones*, was addressed, should begin very small, and should initially remain secret, to escape being destroyed by the forces of jahiliyyah. When it had grown strong enough, this force of 'true Muslims' had a right to wage war not only defensively, to protect Islam, but also aggressively, without provocation, in peacetime. Quoting, as ever, from the Qur'an, Qutb also justified martyrdom, insisting that death in support of Islam was a good outcome, as it would take the martyr directly to paradise.

Eventually the vanguard would grow large enough to wage a jihad – Holy War – against all non-Muslim states, by which Qutb meant *all states*, as he considered no regime of his time to be truly Muslim. Qutb insisted that Islam needed to 'move' and expand, just as the very first Muslims had done. It also had a duty to 'annihilate' non-Muslim powers, because only then would humanity have freedom to 'choose' whether to accept Islam: a choice which he claimed non-Muslim rulers would never permit. Eventually all of the world would be conquered and would be governed by shari'a law, which Qutb considered the whole world *should* accept, as it was the only law that came from God. In this way, Qutb urged, humankind would achieve a simpler, morally better society, similar to that of Arabia in the earliest days of Islam.

This vision soon found supporters. One of the first to be won over was the fifteen-year-old Ayman al-Zawari, who, on hearing of Qutb's execution, vowed to create a small, secret vanguard to renew Islam, just as Qutb had urged. Zawari's group later became part of Islamic Jihad, and later again, in Afghanistan, was merged with the organisation of Osama bin Laden, who had also been much influenced by *Milestones*. The actions of 9/11 – a *first strike* at the heart of the West by a small, secret organisation – precisely followed Qutb's suggestions. At the time of writing this book, in 2013, Zawahari is al-Qaeda's leader.

Yet Qutbism has never won a mass following in the Muslim world in the way that Marx's thinking did, for a time, in Russia and China. What *were* popular, at least with some Muslims, were the actions of the groups his writings had inspired. For some the activities of al-Qaeda offered release, if of a fleeting kind, from their feeling of cultural hurt. Yet it is doubtful that many Muslims hunger to return to early medieval ways.

As for Qutb's prescriptions, these show no sign of coming to pass. His dream of a return to the values of Muhammad's day seems further away now than ever. There is no indication that a great warrior movement of pure Muslims is about to spring to life. Those who followed his guidance remain a small and secretive vanguard. Shari'a law shows no sign of becoming a worldwide export. Westerners, Chinese and Russians remain obstinately outside Islam. All the while, rather than growing simpler and more traditional, the Islamic world has become ever more complex. It now includes citadels of modernity, such as Dubai. It is Qutb's nightmare, not the West's, which has become more real.

Then again, Qutb suffered the disadvantage of offering a political programme that has failed in the here and now. Because, despite its Qu'ranic quotes, it was just that: a programme of military action to topple regimes he disdained. Political dreams are so easily measured. Hong Xiuquan's revolt – another religious movement with political aims – failed to deliver its promise of overthrowing the Manchus. Marxism, too, became discredited by its record, when, rather than creating bountiful social justice, its regimes produced economic stagnation and widespread poverty. A religious programme that promises paradise, by contrast, may save itself from judgement, as disappointment will at least be less evident.

Had Qutb lived, would he have been shocked at the direction the world has taken? I am not so sure. A close reading of *Milestones* reveals, behind the calls to action, a background note of pessimism. The book includes a short passage on European 'material inventions' in which Qutb admires Western achievements and seems gloomily resigned to the Islamic world's limitations, remarking that 'Europe's creative mind is far ahead in this area, and at least for a few centuries to come we cannot expect to compete with Europe and attain supremacy over it in these fields.' Later on, he insists that Islam should be open to scientific progress, but urges Muslims to limit themselves to 'learning purely scientific and technological subjects'. He warns them to be on their guard against Western scientific 'philosophical speculations', which are 'generally against religion and in particular against Islam', and that 'a slight influence from them can pollute the clear spring of Islam'.

Qutb had good reason to be wary of Western scientific theory. He had identified what was surely the greatest threat to his beliefs. We can see him as the latest in a very long line of devout thinkers who, for more than two millennia, had struggled to retain their beliefs in the face of reason. Some of the Middle Ages' greatest minds, including the Christian Thomas Aquinas, the Jewish Maimonides and the Muslim Abu ibn Sina, tried to square their scriptures with Greek philosophy. Yet the results were never very satisfactory. However one might rearrange the jigsaw pieces, reason and faith obstinately refused to fit together. Qutb's answer was to urge Muslims to accept Western scientific practice but stay clear of the theory. It was a suggestion, though, that was hardly doable: Western practical science had grown out of Western scientific theory. One could not have one without the other.

Qutb's biographer John Calvert sees him, in his younger years, as a 'type well represented in European Romantic and Existentialist literature,' and 'a young man at odds with the banality of existence, who reaches for and sometimes catches a glimpse of a higher spiritual truth.' Romantics often have a certain incendiary potential. When their dreams are disappointed, trouble follows. A sprinkling of cynicism makes for a safer mix. When the world failed to live up to Qutb's ideals, he rejected it and devised a programme for its wholesale replacement.

His growing disgust left him single-minded to the end. Following his release from jail, in 1965, Calvert reports that 'Beneath his tired and broken visage, he remained a man on fire.' Rather than take a back seat from activism, he did the opposite, holding court to

Islamists from across the Muslim world and becoming The informal leader of a tiny, barely armed Egyptian revolutionary group. In his last days of freedom, in a beach chalet on Egypt's Mediterranean coast, he sensed that he would be soon be arrested his biographer thinks he was already focused on martyrdom. In this, at least, he would not be disappointed.

So much for beliefs that offered a cure for cultural wounds. The last two centuries have also seen the rise of a quite different kind of intense belief that seeks to answer a quite different kind of pain. From this strand has grown up a veritable rainbow of imaginative inventions.

Filling the Great Vacuum

One night in September 1827 a young man by the name of Joseph Smith climbed Cumorah Hill near his home in New York State. Smith, so he claimed afterwards, was guided in his ascent by an angel named Moroni, whom Smith had seen repeatedly in visions during his teenage years. On the hill, according to Smith's account, he levered up a boulder, beneath which he found a kind of stone receptacle. Inside this he discovered a set of gold-coloured plates covered with ancient-looking letters. He also found, conveniently, two devices with which the text could be translated. One was a pair of stones called 'interpreters', the second was a seerstone.

During the next days and months, Smith set to work. At first he used the interpreters, peering into them and then at the mysterious words, which he was then able to decipher. Later he was able to dispense with everything, even the written plates, and just use the seerstone. With its help he sometimes managed to set down 3,500 words in a day.

It was a rate of progress that most fiction writers would be delighted with, and the 140-page result rather resembled a novel. *The Book of Mormon*, as it came to be known, offered adventure and heroism, betrayal and escape, a great voyage and desperate battles, along with, at times, rather leaden moral instruction. Like the Bible, it was made up of a series of books, ascribed to different authors, but these Mormon prophets, unlike their biblical counterparts, introduced themselves, and even explained how they were related to one another, creating a much more pleasingly coherent narrative than the Bible's.

The book was written in a style closely resembling the standard English Bible of this time, the King James Authorised Version, and in particular that of the Book of Isaiah, with a great number of sentences beginning with 'And it came to pass'. (Mark Twain, rather unkindly, remarked that it was like 'chloroform in print'.) Though *The Book of Mormon* claimed to tell the true story of some of the North America's earliest inhabitants, it opens, rather surprisingly, in the Middle East. In 600 BC, the book's first protagonist, a wealthy inhabitant of Jerusalem named Lehi, has visions of God, and, more remarkably, of Jesus, a full six centuries before his birth. Lehi is told that Jerusalem will soon be attacked and destroyed by the Babylonians (as it indeed would be). When his fellow Judaeans refuse to heed his warnings, he flees with his family to Arabia. Here his son Nephi finds, outside his tent, a device called a 'Liahona', which is a kind of combined directional and moral compass.

> And now, my son, I have somewhat to say concerning the thing which our fathers call a ball, or director – or our fathers called it Liahona, which is, being interpreted, a compass, and the Lord prepared it. And behold, there cannot any man work after the manner of so curious a workmanship. And behold, it was prepared to show unto our fathers the course which they should travel in the wilderness. (Alma 37:38–9)

The Liahona leads the little clan far across the seas, to a seemingly uninhabited North America, where Lehi's descendants live over the next 1,000 years. Split into two rival tribes, one virtuous and one wicked, they fight each other and, in the case of the virtuous Nephites, struggle to retain their faith. This faith is renewed when Jesus, resurrected after his crucifixion, pays the Nephites a brief visit, to preach, heal and praise them for maintaining their belief in him over the long centuries before he was born. The account ends, a little hurriedly, with the demise of the Nephites, in the fifth century AD, which is described in two books attributed to Mormon and his son Moroni. Moroni – who would appear 1,300 years later as the angel who guided Smith to the hidden golden plates – writes as the very last survivor of his people, to tell how everything has gone wrong.

> And the army which is with me is weak; and the armies of the Lamanites are betwixt Sherrizah and me; and as many as have fled to the army of Aaron have fallen victim to their awful brutality. (Moroni 9:17)

Joseph Smith was the first true *American prophet*, and his career mirrored those of other prophets we have examined. He won converts and enemies, endured triumph and struggle, became exiled – repeatedly – and finally met a violent end. Like other prophets Smith's ideas diverged steadily from the religion with which he had grown up. In 1832, after leaders of other Christian churches obstinately insisted that *The Book of Mormon* was a fake, Smith asserted that God had sent him to earth to create a new true Church, to replace all the rest, which had long ago been lost in false belief.

Further radical pronouncements followed. In 1833 Smith told his followers that they must abstain from all stimulants, from tobacco and alcohol to coffee and tea. He also proposed the almost Hindu-like concept of *pre-mortality*: that people experienced life before birth, as 'Spirit Children'. These innovations, and *The Book of Mormon* itself, caused Smith's movement to be denounced as alien to Christianity and won it a steady stream of enemies. Smith and his followers found themselves repeatedly expelled by angry neighbours, and to be pushed ever further westwards. When, in the early 1840s, Smith advocated polygamy, some of his own followers turned against him, and in 1844 he was murdered by an angry mob in Carthage, Illinois.

His religion, though, lived on. Just three years after his death, his supporters founded their new and permanent home, in Salt Lake City, Utah, which remains their heartland to this day. As for the Book of Mormon, although for a time it was rather on the back burner in the movement, is now more important than ever, and is cited and taught in Mormon schools almost as much as the Bible itself.

What was the appeal of Joseph Smith's vision of the world – an appeal strong enough to keep the loyalty of his followers, even though they were forced to abandon their homes and saw fellow believers killed? Mormonism offered a new road to paradise at a highly troubling moment. The 1820s and 1830s were a time when many Americans were bewildered by the country's rapid changes, as the market grew tougher and politics rougher, immigration increased tenfold in twenty years, and life for the poor became increasingly harsh. Americans were also intensely proud of their new nation. Smith offered them a uniquely *American Christianity*, complete with American angels, anciently American scriptures, and, of course, an American-born prophet, sent by God to overturn corrupt and decrepit Old World churches.

Mormonism, though, was by no means unique in offering

epic narratives of the past. Another movement that did so emerged six decades after Joseph Smith climbed Cumorah Hill. This was the work of our very first *female prophet*. Helena Petrovsky Blavatsky, better known simply as Madame Blavatsky, seems to have found inspiration early on for her highly unusual vision of the world. Born in 1831 in Ekaterinoslav in the Ukraine, she spent much of her childhood reading from her great-grandfather's extensive library of books on the occult. The life she then led was highly unconventional for her times. Married aged seventeen to an aristocrat twenty years her senior, she abandoned him on her honeymoon (though she kept his name, Blavatsky). Thereafter she became an intrepid world traveller, and even went to war, being wounded in the 1865 battle of Mentana, in Italy, when supporting Garibaldi's struggle for Italian unification. She also won admirers for her skill at contacting spirits of the dead, and her apparent ability to cause strange noises and make pieces of furniture move

At the end of the 1860s, she later claimed, she made a truly remarkable discovery. In 1868 she received word from her 'master', Morya, a tall Hindu she had met previously at the London Great Exhibition and who now told her she must travel with him to Tibet. By her own account she spent two years with Morya and another master, named Koot Hoomi, at the Tibetan monastery of Tashi Lhunpo at Shigatse. She could not have been in better company, as both had superhuman powers and were not subject to the rules of ordinary monks. With their help Blavatsky gained access, as she had in her childhood, to a highly unusual library.

Before we see what she purported to have found there, I would like to stop for a moment and glance at some other new beliefs that sprang up around this time, as Madame Blavatsky's new religion cannot easily be understood without them. Around

1850 there occurred quite an explosion of radical new notions. Although these ideas frequently contradicted one another, pamphlets promoting them were often sold on the same book-stalls and read by the same people. These readers were often reasonably educated, but felt themselves excluded from a more privileged world. In other words, they were not unlike the poor independent artisans and tailors who had supported radical new beliefs in Europe for the last thousand years, from Tanchelm to the Muggletonians. For that matter it was just such people who had lately commissioned Marx to write the *Communist Manifesto*.

The beliefs of this new wave were often not religious, and yet they had something in common with religions. They offered reassurance in a rapidly changing and insecure age. Europeans and North Americans became fascinated with improving their health through vegetarianism, mesmeric healing and popular hygiene. They followed Mary Eddy Baker's Church of Christ, Scientist, and ceased to visit doctors, happy in the discovery that pain, disease and even death *did not exist*. They believed they had an invisible connection with the whole cosmos through animal magnetism, and that they might converse with dead loved ones through spiritualism. They hoped to learn they had a bright future, through palmistry, and through that old chestnut astrology. They believed that carefully measuring the shape of bumps on their heads – phrenology – would show them to be morally superior to aristocrats and monarchs.

Or they took pleasure in believing that they and their country-men belonged to a superior race. At almost precisely the same time that Marx was hurriedly writing his *Communist Manifesto*, a disgraced, former grave-robbing Scottish surgeon, Robert Knox, was working on the racialist equivalent of Marx's work: *The Races of Men: A Fragment*. The book, published in 1850, asserted that Northern Europeans were more advanced than other races because they gestated in the womb for longer periods. Knox argued that interracial marriage was doomed, while he showed a particular disdain for members of the 'Norman Race', whom he denounced as the parasitical rules of Britain (and, whom I suspect, he blamed for his ejection from the medical profession). He prophesied a vast race struggle, culminating in an apocalyptic and cleansing race war, which would establish white dominance over the world. Unlike the *Communist Manifesto, The Races of Men: A Fragment* was an instant bestseller.

When Madame Blavatsky unveiled her new creed, the Theosophy Movement, in New York in 1875, she announced it to be 'perennial religion': a final combining of ancient doctrines from across the world. Yet this was a misleading claim. Theosophy was very much of its time, and drew from many of the new beliefs just described from racism to spiritualism. A leading source from which she gained her insights, Blavatsky reported, was a spirit she had been in touch with, named John King, who was on good terms with a group of Egyptian masters from the 'The Mysterious Brotherhood of Luxor', which was part of a larger body named 'The Universal Mystic Brotherhood'.

With this expertise to help her, Blavatsky wrote, in her New York apartment, a wandering 1,300-page attack on Western rationalism and materialism entitled *Isis Unveiled;* Unkind critics noted that large sections of the text showed an uncanny resemblance to books on her shelves. It was a decade later, Though, that Blavatsky produced her seminal work, the 1,500-page *Secret Doctrine.* Published in 1888, Blavatsky claimed that it drew heavily on a remarkable ancient and secret text that she had discovered during her earlier visit to the monastery of Tashi Lhunpo in Tibet: 'The Stanzas of Dyzan'.

'The Stanzas of Dyzan' made *The Book of Mormon* seem positively staid. It recounted nothing less than the *whole of human history* from the very beginning of time. Blavatsky, as she relayed this lost narrative to a wider audience, recounted that there were seven forms of planet, and seven earths, only one of which was visible to human eyes. She listed seven 'root races', each of which had created seven subsidiary races. The very first, the Astral root race, had lived in a sacred, imperishable and invisible land, while the Atlantean root race had created beautiful, towering buildings, until their home vanished beneath the Atlantic Ocean. Though early races had been superhuman giants, an episode of disastrous interracial breeding then reduced most of humanity to sinful inferiors. Yet hope was not lost. A small, pure race, descended from priest kings, had survived: the Aryans. Humans might yet hope to reach the highest level of development, as spiritual beings.

Blavatsky's vision may now seem eccentric, to say the least, and yet in its way it was highly influential, and fragments of it would later emerge in all kinds of places. It inspired a number of imitations, notably by two self-proclaimed Viennese aristocrats, both of whom took Blavatsky's epic invention of the past into a much more German direction. One of these, Guido List, was the son of a leather goods maker and got himself into difficulty in snobbish Vienna, for appending a *von* to his name. With his long woolly beard and staring eyes, List can be seen as a modern version of that timeless phenomenon, the wandering prophet, though, rather than losing himself in the wilderness, List was a keen Alpine walker. Like Blavatsky he claimed to have rediscovered a lost religion: the worship of the German pagan god Wotan.

Almost nothing is known about early German religion, but, as Nicholas Goodricke Clarke describes, in his seminal book *The Occult Roots of Nazism*, this did not discourage List. The classical Roman writer Tacitus, who is virtually the only source on the subject, mentioned that the ancient Germans had been divided into three tribes. List claimed that these had, in fact, been three social castes, the highest of which – Tacitus' Hermiones, which List Germanized to Armanen – had been the priests of the sun king, Wotan. It was List's realisation that he himself was a direct heir of this ancient aristocracy that led him to add a *von* to his name.

From 1900, List steadily built up his reinvention of ancient Germany, which he recounted in journalistic articles. Sometimes he 'interpreted' German place names or old songs and sayings. More often he drew directly from his imagination, or borrowed from the imagination of Madame Blavatsky. Her Atlantean giants found a place in List's vision, as did her Aryan master race, and also her fondness for a Hindu sign that she had discovered during her visits to India, and which she had included in the seal of the Theosophical Society: the swastika. List also took on notions from another reinventor of the distant past, this time from Berlin: Max Ferdinand Sebaldt von Werth, who claimed that the ancient Aryans had practised a *sexual religion,* so they could maintain their racial purity.

List then reconstructed the Armanen religion's unhappy later history. Wotan's followers, he reported, had been brutally attacked by the Church of Rome, aided by Charlemagne. Bereft of their sexual religion, Germans' precious racial purity had become degraded. All was not lost, though. The old Armanen belief had been secretly preserved by a collection of diverse groups, which included medieval Knights Templar, Renaissance Humanists and Freemasons.

As he reinvented the past, List also foresaw the future. He warned of a grand conspiracy against Germans by what he called the Great International Party. Despite his scorn for Christianity, List enthusiastically took on one of its key ideas: the notion of the end of world. He predicted an imminent racial apocalypse, which would usher in a cleansed Aryan-ruled world, in which the Armanen religion would finally return to its past glory. He foretold a new pan-German empire, ruled by a priestly elite of limitless power. In this new Germany, Aryan families would be required to keep records to prove their racial purity, and racial inferiors would be brutally suppressed, performing drudge work, so pure Germans could enjoy a lifestyle appropriate to their status. To help make this vision a reality, in 1911 List founded a new elite, the High Armanen Order, or HAO.

List's ideas were taken further again by our next visionary, a friend of List's, named Jörg Lanz von Liebenfels. Another self-proclaimed aristocrat, Lanz claimed to have been born in Sicily, the son of a baron, though he was in fact the son of a school-teacher from suburban Vienna. If List was a modern version of the wilderness prophet, Lanz, too, was a familiar figure, whom we have met in Tanchelm of Flanders and Martin Luther: the ex-monk prophet. After spending six years in the Cistercian Heiligenkreuz monastery near Vienna, Lanz returned to the wider world filled with new ideas. In 1905, he recounted these in a book with the arresting title of *Theo-Zoology or the Lore of the Sodom-Apelings and the Electron of the Gods*.

Like Guido List, Lanz reconstructed the ancient past from pieces of fragmentary evidence and large doses of pure imagination. He claimed that reliefs and inscriptions found in Mesopotamia showed that the Assyrian king, Ashurbanipal II, had once received several strange-looking creatures as tribute from the ruler of a minor state close to the Red Sea. Drawing on quotations from the Old Testament, Lanz concluded that these creatures, which Ashurbanipal kept in his private zoo, had in fact been African pygmies. Lanz asserted that the hitherto pure Aryan Assyrians had made the grave mistake of sodomising these sub-humans, and so bringing to life a new inferior race. Lanz insisted that the whole Old Testament had been written as a warning to Aryans against such behaviour.

Another of his discoveries concerned the Aryans' special power. Lanz maintained that the original, pure Aryans had been able to communicate telepathically with one another using electronic signals. He argued that Jesus, as a leading Aryan, had performed his miracles by means of his electronic powers. These superhuman qualities, though, had been steadily eroded as Aryans interbred with inferior humans. Sometimes such inbreeding was forced upon the Aryans, and Lanz claimed that the gospels' accounts of Jesus' last hours did not, as was generally supposed, describe his trial and execution by the Jerusalem authorities, but rather depicted Jesus' attempted rape by satanic, pygmy sodomites.

The Aryans' situation was grave, but Lanz still had high hopes for the future. In his book, and later in articles in his own magazine, *Ostara*, he insisted that Aryans could regain their old electronic powers if they took care to breed only among themselves and so enhance their racial purity. Matters would also be helped by an imminent apocalyptic war, in which inferior humans would be destroyed, and after which Jesus would return, to rule over a kingdom of his rejuvenated people. In the meantime, Lanz urged the prompt extermination of all inferior pygmy races. In an epic struggle of the blonds versus the dark-haired, he recommended that inferior races should be castrated, sterilised, enslaved, transported to Madagascar or simply incinerated as offerings to God. German women, who as the weaker sex were prone to finding their pygmy inferiors sexually attractive, should be subjugated utterly by their Aryan husbands.

Lanz, like List, was keen to do his part in creating a new Aryan elite to lead Germans in their racial crusade. In 1907, four years

before List created his copycat HAO, Lanz founded the Order
of the New Templars, which was a kind of society of racialist
monks. Members of the order had to accept rigorous racial
examination, by methods Lanz had outlined in his magazine,
Ostara, after which they were allocated places, according to their
purity, in a strict hierarchy. Associate New Templars included
Guido von List and also, more surprisingly, the Swedish playwright
August Strindberg. With the help of wealthy Viennese supporters,
Lanz bought a ruined castle, Burg Werfenstein, for his new racial
aristocracy. Having ranked and housed them, Lanz devised rituals
for them to practise, psalms to sing and splendid vestments to
wear. Above the castle he flew a swastika flag.

Finally there was also a third Viennese visionary, Karl Maria
Wiligut. Wiligut, a career soldier, was no writer, and his claims
were recorded by a member of Lanz's New Templars order,
Theodor Czepl, who interviewed him in 1920–21. Wiligut felt no
need to seek evidence for his vision of Germany's ancient past,
relying purely on what Goodrick-Clarke terms his 'ancestral clairvoyant memory'.24 Wiligut's claims easily trumped those of List.
His remembrances extended back to 228,000 BC, when, Wiligut
related, the world had had three suns and had been populated by
giants and dwarfs. He also reported that he was a representative
of a German religion that was far older than the upstart Armanists.
This was the priesthood of the Irminists proclaimed in 12,500 BC.
It was later attacked by List's Wotanists and, after a 10,000-year
struggle between the two religions, followed by war with the
Church of Rome, Wiligut's ancestors – who happened to include
a considerable number of the most famous figures from Germany's
past – became dispersed across Europe. Yet they had kept the
torch of their ancient faith.

Unfortunately, Wiligut felt his priestly ancestors' imagined
persecution by rivals too keenly. Living in Salzburg after the First

World War, he became convinced that, because of his Irminist priestly status, he was the victim of a conspiracy by Jews and Freemasons, whom he blamed both for the failure of a business venture and for the collapse of the Habsburg Empire. In 1924, he grew violently threatening towards his wife. In November of that year she had him committed to a Salzburg mental asylum, where he remained for two years, diagnosed with grand delusions and paranoid schizophrenia. However, as we will see, this was far from the last that would be heard of him.

Where did these strange notions of Germany's distant past come from? Clearly they did not originate from Germany's prehistory, as was claimed. Yet they had roots that were altogether older than one might suppose, and far older than Madame Blavatsky's Theosophy. They sprang, in some ways, from *medieval heresy*. We saw earlier how apocalyptic texts evolved the idea of a superhuman Christian emperor, who would usher in Jesus' kingdom on earth. In thirteenth-century Germany this Christian emperor was thought by some to be an *actual*, living emperor, Frederick II. The belief continued to linger after Frederick's death, and from the 1280s a number of fake Fredericks appeared, inspiring brief, excitable followings.

In the fifteenth century these beliefs moved into more xenophobic waters. A text called *Gamaleon* prophesied that Frederick II would defeat the pope and the king of France, crush the Slavs, Hungarians and Jews, exterminate all those employed by the Church of Rome and rule as a kind of pope-emperor from Mainz. An early sixteenth-century text, 'The Book of a Hundred Chapters' took matters further still. It claimed that Germans had been God's chosen people but had become poisoned by foreign influences – the Old Testament and the Church of Rome – which had put them under the yoke of inferior Latin peoples.

Fortunately all was not lost, as a figure called the Emperor of the Black Forest would soon correct matters, by exterminating the rich and sinful, then leading German armies against the Turks, the king of France and the pope, conquering Jerusalem, and ruling for a thousand years, again from the city of Mainz. The Book of a Hundred Chapters was unpublished in its own time and survived only as a handwritten text, gathering dust on a shelf of the library of Colmar, but was rediscovered in the 1890s, just when Guido List began devising his new vision of the world. List's ideas, like those of Lanz and Wiligut, seem to have drawn on a distant mindset that mixed confidence in national superiority with a deep fear of the foreign.

So much for the origin of these notions. The key question is, did anyone take any notice? Most Austrians, unlike List and Lanz, were not interested in a pan-German empire. They were loyal to the Habsburg state. Likewise, as faithful Catholics, they certainly did not see the Catholic Church as a malign, foreign influence that had destroyed Germans' true religion. Most serious-minded Viennese had no time for Lanz or List, whom they regarded as the cranks they were. When, in 1903, List sent a manuscript outlining some of his notions to the Austrian Imperial Academy, it was returned, scornfully, without so much as a comment.

Yet if List and Lanz's supporters were not very many, they were influential. The rejection of List's manuscript brought a complaint in parliament. In 1905 a List Society was established whose membership included many high-profile anti-Semitic figures, in both Austria and Germany, from politicians and academics to newspaper editors. As we saw, Lanz's New Templars also included many high-profile Viennese, whose contributions bought him Berg Werfenstein.

How, it might be asked, would *anybody* take seriously claims that a caste of pagan German high priests had secretly survived for thousands of years, or that Jesus had been an Aryan with superhuman electronic powers?

List and Lanz, like Hong Xiuquan and Marx, offered reassurance in the face of *national* panic. Not that Austria-Hungary had been shamed by foreign occupation, but some Austrians were highly uneasy about the future. German-speakers, who had formed the Habsburg Empire's ruling class for centuries, could see their advantage ebbing away. Hungarians, Czechs and others were demanding, with growing success, full and equal rights, as the empire threatened to become something like a Middle European EU. List was furious when, in the late 1890s, Czech-speakers gained rights to government jobs in their homeland. German triumph in an apocalyptic race war would solve such problems for good.

After her defeat in the First World War, Germany felt a similar sense of national panic. Here List and Lanz's claims found new followers. There is some evidence that Hitler himself had been a keen reader of Lanz's magazine, *Ostara*, during his days as a struggling artist in Vienna, though if he had been, he kept quiet about the fact during his rise to power. Another figure's interest in the Viennese visionaries, though, is quite unequivocal. This was the Reichsführer-SS, Heinrich Himmler.

We know of this because Himmler gave one of the Viennese trio a job. In 1933 he employed Karl Maria Wiligut – who, after his embarrassment in the Salzburg asylum, had taken the pseudonym of Karl Maria Weisthor – in the SS, where he was put in charge of the Race and Settlement Main Office. Wiligut was required to recount his memories of Germany's prehistory, and also tell the remarkable story of his family, the preservers of the lost Irminist religion. Regularly consulted by Himmler, with whom he exchanged birthday presents, Wiligut introduced a like-minded confederate, Günther Kirchhoff, who offered his own revelations of the past, such as how Europe had once been ruled by three great kings, one of whom was 'Arthur of Stonehenge'. Himmler had Wiligut design the SS *Totenkopf* (death's head) ring, and he helped devise new Irminist religious rituals for the SS, to celebrate SS marriages, the birth of SS babies and the solstices. Until, in 1938, Wiligut's great days came to an abrupt end, when a member of Himmler's staff tracked down Wiligut's wife. Learning of his spell as a lunatic, Himmler had him quietly sacked.

Not only Wiligut's ideas made their way into Nazi thinking. Himmler's SS – an all-male hierarchy of, supposedly, racially pure Germans, intended to renew the race and crush inferiors – was, in effect, a combination of List's High Armanen Order and Lanz's order of the New Templars, if with the latter's Catholic influences removed. Himmler became so convinced by Blavatsky's and List's claims of an ancient Aryan world empire that he sent expeditions to Finland, Iceland, Iran and Tibet in search of proof.

As we saw, List had suggested a number of measures to preserve German racial purity: Germans should be banned from breeding with non-Aryans and should keep documentary proof of their racial purity, while their racial inferiors should be relegated to drudge work. All of these arrangements became law under the Nazis. Lanz had urged that inferior races should be castrated, sterilised, enslaved, transported to Madagascar or incinerated as offerings to God. All of these possibilities were considered by Nazi leaders and all, except transportation to Madagascar, were put into effect, leading to the deaths of millions of Jews, Roma, Slavs and homosexuals.

If the results had not been so horrific, this succession of events would be laughable. In effect, political polices of the government of the second most powerful economy in the world were partly inspired by a former lunatic, the editor of a tiny, poisonous Viennese equivalent of the *National Enquirer*, and a man who believed himself to a member of a secret caste of pagan German high priests and whose visions resembled a kind of toxic Tolkien.

Did epic reinvention of the past end with the collapse of the Nazi state in 1945? Not at all. The most remarkable and colourful such worldview emerged into history shortly afterwards. Unlike any belief that we have encountered until now, this one was *publicised in advance*. In late 1949 an issue of *Astounding Science Fiction* magazine announced that one of its leading contributors, the writer of westerns, adventure stories and science fiction, L. Ron Hubbard, was completing a new system for the total eradication of all neuroses. The system was fully described the next spring, in Hubbard's book *Dianetics: The Modern Science of Mental Health*.

The life of L. Ron Hubbard – the very last of our prophets – is a little elusive. He told his followers that he grew up adventuring on his grandfather's ranch, which covered a quarter of the state of Montana. From the age of fourteen, he wandered across China and the Pacific, communing with magicians and bandits, and sometimes learning a new language in a single night. In the Second World War he fought in all five theatres and won twenty-one medals, until, badly wounded, he ended the conflict in Oak Knoll Naval Hospital in California. Here, crippled, blind, and abandoned by friends and family alike, he regained his health through pure self-will.

Hubbard's unauthorised biographer, Russell Miller, offers a rather different picture. In his unsparing account, *Bare-Faced Messiah: The True Story of L. Ron Hubbard*, Miller reports that Hubbard's grandfather owned not a quarter of the state of Montana, but a veterinarian practice and horse and buggy hire business. Likewise, Hubbard's knowledge of China derived not from years of teenage roaming, but a couple of tourist visits with his parents when his father was stationed in the Pacific as a naval supply officer. As to Hubbard's wartime career, he briefly commanded a submarine chaser, only to be dismissed after a few weeks for hunting non-existent Japanese vessels and inadvertently firing on Mexico. He won not twenty-one but four medals, two of which were given to all military personnel who had served throughout the war. Though he *did* end the war in Oak Knoll Hospital, he was not blind and crippled from war wounds, but was admitted for a minor gastric complaint, probably an ulcer.

Fortunately, when it comes to the *beliefs* of Hubbard's movement, the picture is much clearer. These grew out of Dianetics, which, as we saw, claimed to offer a cure for all mental health problems. Dianetics' key idea was that, unknowingly, humans remembered absolutely *everything*, even before their birth. Hubbard claimed that people could remember events from twenty-four hours following their conception. But from memories came trauma. During stressful moments the analytical mind ceased to operate, and memories became lodged, instead, in what Hubbard – whose theories were crammed with strange terminology and acronyms – called the *reactive mind*, where they lurked as harmful *engrams*, causing later neuroses. Yet help was at hand. A Dianeticist *auditor* could cause patients (optimistically termed *preclears*) to remember their *engrams*, after which these traumatic memories would take their proper place in the analytical mind and cease to cause trouble. Hubbard claimed a 100 per cent success rate for his new system.

Despite being savaged by *The New York Times*, the *Scientific American* and the American Psychiatric Association, *Dianetics* was a huge hit. It was easy to understand why. As Russell Miller recounted, 'The techniques were easy to learn, were available to everyone, and best of all, always worked.'[25] Hubbard's book topped the *LA Times* bestseller list for several months during 1950, as multitudes of Americans – many of them science fiction fans – audited one another, drawing out painful moments from the past. Enthusiasts crossed the country to join Hubbard's high-priced lecture courses on auditing, at the new Dianetic Research Center in Elizabeth, New Jersey.

Often, as Hubbard's book explained, harmful engrams sprang from behaviour by bad mothers. Hubbard recounted cases that he himself had audited, where preclears, during their foetus days, had listened as their mothers had adulterous sex, or – far more traumatising – tried to do away with their unwanted baby with knitting needles. These submerged memories, Hubbard explained, were the cause of all kinds of later problems, from ulcers (Hubbard's own affliction at the end of the war) to depression, and from hair loss to having an overlong nose.

Dianetics, though, did not only promise to solve individuals' problems. It also offered, in an angst-ridden age, to *enhance world sanity*. So, almost from the very beginning, Dianetics had an element of prophesy. Hubbard, like other struggling prophets, began by winning over a small but dedicated group of followers, which included a GP, a book publisher and, most usefully of all, the editor of *Astounding Science Fiction* magazine. With their help he quickly inspired a passionate following.

The movement's full transformation came in the early spring of 1952. Just as Dianetics was beginning lose its novelty, and its enthusiasts, Hubbard announced, to a gathering of supporters in a hotel in Wichita, Kansas, that he had now devised another wholly new science, which extended far beyond Dianetics. Scientology had been born.

How was Scientology different from Dianetics? All was made clear in L. Ron Hubbard's book *Scientology: What to Audit*, which was soon retitled *Scientology: A History of Man*. The work's introduction opened with the striking phrase, 'A Cold-blooded and Factual Account of your last 60 Trillion Years'. Put simply, Scientology vastly extended the reach of people's forgotten memories. Hubbard asserted that humans had the ability not only to recall the entirety of their own lives, but also previous lives, which Hubbard termed *the whole track*. These lives had several distinct origins. Firstly, people could remember their earlier existence as a *Genetic Entity*, or *GE*. GEs, which entered a preclear's body several days before conception, and were to be found in the region of their stomach, had dwelt in people's ancestors' bodies for millions of years. Thus a preclear might recall his or her GE's time as a medieval aristocrat, or, going further back still, as an ape or fish.

These distant recollections were as nothing, though, compared to what else people might remember. Hubbard explained that between 70,000 and 35,000 years ago Earth had been visited by an immensely superior form of beings called *Thetans*. Thetans had inhabited millions of beings across the universe for trillions of years. They could travel at high speeds unaided through space, communicate using telepathy, and, though they were generally peaceable, sometimes fought one another with energy flows. Bored with their endless life, they had become fascinated with inhabiting lesser mortals (*MEST beings*), including humans. As Hubbard explained,

> Where is the thetan? Contrary to any past practice, his second-best place is just outside the MEST body monitoring it with direct contact on the MEST body's motor controls, on either side of the head . . . The thetan, in most cases, is behind and above the MEST body.[26]

Naturally these revelations – which Hubbard acknowledged had wholly rewritten Darwin's theories – offered a vast new wealth of sickness and neurosis-causing memories to be rooted out. Thus if a preclear had a fear of heights this reflected his order GE memories as a sloth, frightened of falling out of the tree. A preclear's inability to cry reflected an earlier existence as a particular type of shellfish called a 'Weeper', which Hubbard explained was 'originally called the *"Grim Weeper" or "Boohoo."*'

> The plights of the Weeper are many and pathetic. Still obtaining its food from the waves, it yet had to breathe. Waves are impetuous and often irregular. The Weeper would open up to get food from the water and get a wave in the shell. It would vigorously pump out the water and try to get some air and then, before it could gulp atmosphere, be hit by another wave. Here was anxiety.[27]

Preclears drawn to masochism were recalling past lives when they had passively endured being eaten. Preclears who smoked were remembering a time when the world had been much subject to volcanic eruptions. Preclears who suffered semi-paralysis from strokes were in fact recalling being blasted by a thetan's 'half-light, half-black gun which shot out a wave' which then split them into two people (a *halver*). A preclear who suffered cold hands and feet remembered being transported across the universe in ice before being dropped into an ocean to thaw. To further complicate matters, preclears might be traumatised by memories that were not from their own past, but from *somebody else's*. Thetans could be mischievous, and would sometimes steal the past lives of another thetan's human host, for entertainment, 'just like a Homo sapiens likes TV'.

Even a single cell in one's body could retain traumatic recollections of earlier lives.

> The pulp of a tooth, for instance, tracks back, cell by cell, to early engrams; when these are relieved a toothache in that tooth becomes

all but impossible, no matter how many nerves are exposed, a matter which brings about quite a revolution in dentistry.[28]

So, like the founder of Christian Science, Mary Eddy Baker, eighty years earlier. Ron Hubbard saw physical ailments as non-existent. In the foreword of *Scientology: A History of Man*, he declared that, 'This is useful knowledge. With it the blind again see, the lame walk, the ill recover, the insane become sane and the sane become saner.' What Hubbard offered to his followers, though, went far beyond health matters. With a course of intense auditing, and careful use of a device called an *e-meter*(a kind of psychic stethoscope, comprising two metal cans attached to a box with a dial, which measured electrical changes in the skin), a preclear could be cured of physical and mental ailments and even become taller. He or she could even become a *Mest Clear*, who, as Hubbard explained, was 'about a skyscraper higher than Homo Sapiens'. Yet this was only the start. The next stage was to become a *Theta Clear*: a superhuman being who could knock hats off heads at fifty yards and 'read books a couple of countries away'. Finally, there was the highest state of all, the *Cleared Theta Clear*, which was, quite simply, unimaginable.

Yet, for all its dazzling promises, the Church of Scientology's history proved a chequered one. For a time it thrived, so much so that Hubbard was able to buy an English mansion for himself, in East Grinstead, Sussex, where he alarmed servants by reading them with his e-meter. The good times, though, did not last. Like so many prophets before him, Hubbard found himself beset by enemies – although unlike Zarathustra or Jesus, these were not priests, but rather US government employees. Hubbard's chaotic accounting brought increasing interest from the IRS. In spite of the fact that he had patriotically denounced a good number of people as probable Communist sympathisers – including his ex-wife and her lover – the FBI also regarded Hubbard with growing concern, doubting his sanity.

After an Australian board of inquiry denounced Scientology as a threat to the community, and the State of Victoria banned it outright, Hubbard bought a number of ships and took his movement to the oceans, as the *Sea Organization*. On occasion he appointed as his ships' captains followers with no sea experience, trusting to their nautical recollections from previous lives. Russell Miller recounts how, withdrawn from the world, Hubbard became increasingly subject to bursts of anger and paranoia. He ordered punishment of anyone suspected of being a *Suppressive Person*, or *SP*, and, having decided that his dogs were clears, he came to believe that anyone they barked at must have committed an *Overt* (malicious act) against him and his family.

Hubbard escaped the violent end of many another prophet, but it was a strange end. He spent his final years, in the mid 1980s, as a recluse, unknown to his neighbours and surrounded by fences, on a ranch in central California, which he repeatedly tore apart and rebuilt. Yet his movement endured, and continues to do so. What was, and is, its appeal? Because there can be little doubt that it has one. According, admittedly, to its official website, the Church of Scientology is now the world's fastest-growing religion, and at the time of writing in 2013 it has almost 500 churches and centres across six continents, disseminating Hubbard's message to the world.

It is not hard to discern the insecurities that first sent people in Hubbard's direction. The early 1950s were a time of great anxiety. This was the age of the Korean War, of McCarthyism and suspicion of secret Communist conspiracies. Most of all people feared atomic war. For the first time in their history, people were quite right to worry about the end of the world. The Soviet Union detonated its first atomic bomb in August

1949. Hubbard's new science of Dianetics was announced later that same year. Drawing on the contemporary fascination with psychoanalysis, Dianetics' chief claim was to cure individuals of their neuroses, but it also, as we saw, promised to enhance world sanity. At a time when the world seemed anything but sane, it was an appealing prospect. Scientology made atomic war *unimportant*. What did such a thing matter if the being within one had the power to travel unaided through space, to communicate telepathically and survive almost any cataclysm? What did the bomb matter if one had existed for trillions of years and would exist for trillions more? Hubbard offered *total reassurance*.

Yet Scientology, I would say, also offered something else. Along with Mormonism, Theosophy and the worldviews of List, Lanz and Wiligut, and also of Karl Marx, it attempted to *fill a great vacuum*. Having had such a tight hold on people's imaginations for so many centuries, Christianity, now that its grip was finally loosened, left a disquieting feeling of emptiness. Certainty was gone. These new beliefs each offered a replacement. In particular they produced new and apparently unquestionable substitutes for the biblical creation story: the very belief where Christianity had suffered its first body blow. Mormonism gave the world the story of Lehi and his descendants, which for believers had the authenticity of having been found in a stone container on a hill in New England. Marx's vision of history as a progression of class conflicts was rendered indisputable thanks to his method of scientific analysis. Madame Blavatsky, Guido List and Jörg Lanz offered new accounts of the distant past, verified by numerous sources, from texts supposedly found in a Tibetan monastery to their own clairvoyant memories. L. Ron Hubbard went further again and helped people remember their own distant days as immortal, superhuman beings, seventy trillion years ago, with the help of an e-meter.

So much for beliefs of the past, distant and recent. What of the future? Is the great age of religious imagination finally over? It is sometimes claimed these days that humankind is on the verge of a post-religious world. Certainly religion, at least in parts of the West, is now regarded with great wariness. In the past people were fearful of other people's religion. Now, in some areas of Europe, many are suspicious of *all* strongly held religious beliefs, which they view as akin to madness. In Britain a politician with even modest religious belief is regarded with deep distrust. An increasing number of people now prefer to navigate through life without believing in supernatural forces. They find they can get by with the cooler comforts of science. Even in parts of the world seen as intensely religious, such as the Middle East, the world is becoming obstinately more complex, and old certainties more elusive.

Will we continue along this road? Throughout this book I have argued that people adopt intense beliefs from a hunger for reassurance, to ease their insecurities. These insecurities, naturally, have changed a good deal since the days of hunter-gatherers, who feared bad weather, disease and failure to find animals to hunt. Insecurities, though, remain very much with us, and will doubtless continue to do so in the future. So I suspect there will be a few more invented worldviews. What fears will they answer? This will depend on us. It will depend on *how safe our world feels*.

And that, needless to say, is anybody's guess.

ACKNOWLEDGEMENTS

If a book of this kind can be justified, it is because it brings diverse beliefs together in a way that, I hope, readers may find illuminating and surprising. Studies of all of these beliefs have been provided by professional historians, who have done the hard work, digging away at the pit face of history and presenting the world with their gold. Without their efforts, it goes without saying, I could not have completed a single page.

I would like to thank all those whose writings I have listed, at the end of this book, as sources and further reading. I would also like to pick out a few of these, to offer my particular thanks for their outstanding, and often drily funny, accounts. I would like to thank Jean Bottéro for his wonderful examination of ancient Mesopotamian religion. Robin Lane Fox for his dazzling analysis of the Bible, and also of classical paganism and early Christianity; E. P. Sanders for his marvellously lucid account of Jesus's life; Norman Cohn for his remarkable examination of apocalyptic movements during the Middle Ages; both Christopher

Hill and Andrew Bradstock for their rich portraits of radical religious groups during the English Civil War; and finally Nicholas Goodrick-Clarke for his extraordinary unveiling of pre-Nazi occult religion.

I would also like to thank Bryan Ward-Perkins and Gervase Rosser for their invaluable suggestions as to reading. I would like to thank my agent, Deborah Rogers, both for her wise understanding of books and for her being always supportive, though thick and thin. And I would very much like to thank my two editors at the Bodley Head, Jörg Hensgen and Katherine Ailes, for their dedication, wise judgement and impressive knowledge of this huge subject.

Finally, and most of all, I would like to thank my wife, Shannon, and our children, Alexander and Tatiana, for putting up with me as I tried, and tried again, to write this book.

NOTES

1 Jean Bottéro, *Religion in Ancient Mesopotamia*, London, University of Chicago Press, 2001.

2 From Benjamin R. Foster (trans. and ed.), *Before the Muses: Myths, Tales and Poetry of Ancient Mesopotamia*, Bethesda, CDL Press, 1995.

3 From James Vanderkam and Peter Flint *The Meaning of the Dead Sea Scrolls: Their Significance in Understanding the Bible, Judaism and Christianity*, London HarperCollins, 2002, p. 352.

4 E. P. Sanders, *The Historical Figure of Jesus*, Harmondsworth, Penguin Books, 1993.

5 Josephus, *The Jewish War*, trans. G. A. Wilkinson, rev. edn, Harmondsworth, Penguin Books, 1981, p. 357.

6 Tacitus, *The Histories*, trans. Kenneth Wellesley, Harmondsworth, Penguin Books, 1975, pp. 281–2.

7 Josephus, *The Jewish War*, trans. G. A. Wilkinson, rev. edn, Harmondsworth, Penguin Books, 1981, p. 362.

8 W. H. Shewring (trans.), *The Passions of SS. Perpetua and Felicity*, London Sheed and Ward, 1931.

9   Robin Lane Fox, *Pagans and Christians, in the Mediterranean World from the Second Century* AD to the Conversion of Constantine, Harmondsworth, Viking, 1986.

10 First epistle of Clement, in Joseph Barber Lightfoot (trans.), *The Two Epistles to the Corinthians*, London, Macmillan, 1869.

11 Ibn Ishāq, *The Life of Muhammad, Apostle of Allah*, trans. Edward Rehatsek and ed. Michael Edwardes (Given to Royal Asiatic Society, London, 1898), London, Folio Society, 1964.

12 Jonathan Berkey, *The Formation of Islam, Religion and Society in the Near East, 600–1800*, Cambridge, Cambridge University Press, 2003, p. 65.

13 Albert Hourani, *A History of the Arab Peoples*, 1991, London, Faber, p. 20.

14 David N. Keightley, 'The Environment of Ancient China', in *The Cambridge History of Ancient China*, Cambridge, Cambridge University Press, 1999.

15 From Edward Gilman Slingerland (trans.), *Confucius: Analects: With Selections from Traditional Commentaries* (Analect b.22), Cambridge, Hackett Publishing Co., 2003.

16 From account by Paul of Saint-Père de Chartres, from Edward Peters, *Heresy and Authority in Medieval Europe: Documents in Translation*, Philadelphia, University of Pennsylvania Press, 1980, p. 71.

17 Jeffrey B. Russell and Brooks Alexander, *A New History of Witchcraft: Sorcerers, Heretics and Pagans*, London Thamas and Hudson, 2007, p. 113.

18 Lyndal Roper, *Witch Craze: Terror and Fantasy in Baroque Germany*, London, Yale University Press, 2004, p. 9.

19 From Pavel Annenkov, 'A Wonderful Ten Years', in *Reminiscences of Marx and Engels*, Moscow, Foreign Languages Publishing House, (n.d.), pp. 269–72.

20 Karl Marx and Friedrich Engels, *The Communist Manifesto*, p. 24.

21 Orlando Figes, *A People's Tragedy: The Russian Revolution, 1891–1924*, London, Jonathan Cape, 1996, p. 695.

22 Sayyid Qutb, *Milestones*, English translation by Islamic Book Service, 2001, pp. 10–11.

23 Ibid.

24 Nicholas Goodrick-Clarke, *The Occult Roots of Nazism: Secret Aryan Cults and their Influence on Nagi Ideology*, London, Touris, 1998, p. 46.

25 Russell Miller, *Bare-Faced Messiah: The True Story of L. Ron Hubbard*, London, Michael Joseph, 1987.

26 L. Ron Hubbard, *Scientology: A History of Man*, 1988 edition, p. 89.

27 Ibid., p. 34.

28 Ibid., p. 12.

SOURCES AND FURTHER READING

Arnold, John H., *Inquisition & Power: Catharism and the Confessing Subject in Medieval Languedoc*, Philadelphia, University of Pennsylvania Press, 2001

Barbour, Hugh, *The Quakers in Puritan England*, London, Yale University Press, 1964

Bennett, Judith M. and C. Warren Hollister, *Medieval Europe: A Short History*, London, McGraw-Hill, 2006

Berkey, Jonathan P., *The Formation of Islam: Religion and Society in the Near East 600–1800*, Cambridge, Cambridge University Press, 2003

Bottéro, Jean, *Religion in Ancient Mesopotamia*, London, University of Chicago Press, 2001

Boyce, Mary, *A History of Zoroastrianism*, Leiden and New York, E. J. Brill, 1975

Bradstock, Andrew, *Radical Religion in Cromwell's England: A Concise History from the English Civil War to the End of the Commonwealth*, London, I. B. Tauris, 2011

Bushman, Richard Lyman, *Mormonism: A Very Short Introduction*, Oxford, Oxford University Press, 2008

Calvert, John, *Sayyid Qutb and the Origins of Radical Islamism*, London, Hurst, 2010

Cantor, Norman E., *The Civilization of the Middle Ages*, New York, HarperCollins, 1993

Chadwick, Owen, *The Reformation*, Harmondsworth, Penguin Books, 1964

Clothey, Fred W., *Religion in India: A Historical Introduction*, London, Routledge, 2006

Coe, Michael D. and Rex Koontz, *Mexico: From the Olmecs to the Aztecs*, London, Thames and Hudson, 2002

Cohn, Norman, *The Pursuit of the Millennium: Revolutionary Millenarians and Mystical Anarchists of the Middle Ages*, London, Secker & Warburg, 1957

Cooter, Roger, *The Cultural Meaning of Popular Science: Phrenology and the Organization of Consent in Nineteenth-Century Britain*, Cambridge, Cambridge University Press, 1984

Dalton, Rex, 'Lion Man Takes Pride of Place as Oldest Statue', *Nature*, 4 September 2003

David, Rosalie, *The Ancient Egyptians: Beliefs and Practices*, London, Routledge & Kegan Paul, 1982

Drew, David, *The Lost Chronicles of the Maya Kings*, London, Weidenfeld & Nicolson, 1999

DuBois, Thomas David, *Religion and the Making of Modern East Asia*, Cambridge, Cambridge University Press, 2011

Dunbar, Robin, *The Human Story: A New History of Mankind's Evolution*, London, Faber and Faber, 2004

Economist, The, 'Social Media in the 16th Century: How Luther Went Viral', 17 December 2011

Fairbank, John King and Merle Goldman, *China: A New History*, London, Belknap Press, 1998

Figes, Orlando, *A People's Tragedy, The Russian Revolution, 1891–1924*, London, Jonathan Cape, 1996

Fischer, Steven Roger, *A History of Writing*, London, Reaktion, 2001

Foreign Languages Publishing House, Moscow: *Reminiscences of Marx and Engels* (n.d.)

Frend, William H. C., *The Rise of the Monophysite Movement: Chapters in the History of the Church in the Fifth and Sixth Centuries*, Cambridge, Cambridge University Press, 1972

Gaskill, Malcolm, *Witchcraft: A Very Short Introduction*, Oxford, Oxford University Press, 2010

Givens, Terryl L., *The Book of Mormon: A Very Short Introduction*, Oxford, Oxford University Press, 2009

Goodman, Martin, *Rome and Jerusalem: The Clash of Ancient Civilizations*, London, Allen Lane, 2007

Goodrick-Clarke, Nicholas, *Helena Blavatsky*, London, North Atlantic Books, 2004

—, *The Occult Roots of Nazism: Secret Aryan Cults and Their Influence on Nazi Ideology*, London, I. B. Tauris, 1985

Heun, Manfred et al., 'Site of Einkorn Wheat Domestication Identified by DNA Fingerprinting', *Science*, 278, 5341 (14 November 1997), 1312–14

Hill, Christopher, *The World Turned Upside Down: Radical Ideas during the English Revolution*, London, Temple Smith, 1972

Hourani, Albert, *A History of the Arab Peoples*, London, Faber, 1991

Hubbard, L. Ron, *What to Audit / A History of Man*, 1952

Jones, Brian W., *The Emperor Domitian*, London, Routledge, 1992

Karlen, Arno, *Man and Microbes: Disease and Plagues in History and Modern Times*, New York, Putnam, 1995

Kuhn, Dieter, *The Age of Confucian Rule: The Song Transformation of China*, London, Belknap Press, 2009

Lambert, Malcolm, *Medieval Heresy: Popular Movements from the Gregorian Reform to the Reformation*, London, Edward Arnold, 1977

Lane Fox, Robin, *Pagans and Christians in the Mediterranean World from the Second Century* AD to the Conversion of Constantine, Harmondsworth, Viking, 1986

—, *The Unauthorized Version: Truth and Fiction in the Bible*, Harmondsworth, Viking, 1991

Lewis, Bernard, *The Arabs in History*, London, Hutchinson, 1950

—, *The Jews of Islam*, Princeton, NJ, University of Princeton Press, 1984

Lewis, Mark Edward, *China Between Empires: The Northern and Southern Dynasties*, London, Belknap Press, 2009

—, *China's Cosmopolitan Empire: The Tang Dynasty*, London, Belknap Press, 2009

—, *The Early Chinese Empires: Qin and Han*, London, Belknap Press, 2007

Lewis-Williams, David, *The Mind in the Cave: Consciousness and the Origins of Art*, London, Thames and Hudson, 2004

Lewis-Williams, David and David Pearce, *The Neolithic Mind: Consciousness, Cosmos and the Realms of the Gods*, London, Thames and Hudson, 2005

Livi-Bacci, Massimo, *A Concise History of World Population*, Oxford, Blackwell, 1992

Loewe, Michael and Edward L Shaughnessy, eds., The Cambridge History of Ancient China: From the Origins of Civilization to 221 BC, Cambridge, Cambridge University Press, 1999

Lonsdale, Henry, A Sketch of the Life and Writings of Robert Knox, the Anatomist, London, Macmillan, 1870

Marx, Karl and Friedrich Engels, The Communist Manifesto [1848], trans. Samuel Moore and intro. A. J. P. Taylor, Harmondsworth, Penguin Books, 1967

Mieroop, Marc van de, A History of the Ancient Near East, c. 3000–323 BC, Oxford, Blackwell, 2004

Miller Russell, Bare-Faced Messiah: The True Story of L. Ron Hubbard, London, Michael Joseph, 1987

Mithen, Steven, After the Ice: A Global Human History, 20,000–5000 BC, London, Weidenfeld & Nicolson, 2001

Münzel, Susanne C. and Nicholas J. Conard, 'Cave Bear Hunting in the Hohle Fels, a Cave Site in the Ach Valley, Swabian Jura', Revue de Paléobiologie, Genève, 23, 2 (December 2004), x–xx

Newby, Gordon Darnell, A History of the Jews of Arabia: From Ancient Times to Their Eclipse under Islam, Columbia, SC, University of South Carolina Press, 1988

Pagels, Elaine, The Gnostic Gospels, London, Weidenfeld & Nicolson, 1981

Payton, James R., Jr, Getting the Reformation Wrong: Correcting Some Misunderstandings, Downers Grove, Ill., IVP Academic, 2010

Penton, M. James, Apocalypse Delayed: The Story of Jehovah's Witnesses, Toronto, University of Toronto Press, 1985

Pinker, Steven, The Blank Slate, London, Allen Lane, 2002

Poewe, Karla, New Religions and the Nazis, London, Routledge, 2006

Portier-Young, Anathea E., *Apocalypse Against Empire: Theologies of Resistance in Early Judaism*, Cambridge, William B. Eerdmans, 2011

Pringle, Heather, *The Master Plan: Himmler's Scholars and the Holocaust*, London, Fourth Estate, 2006

Qutb, Sayyid, *Milestones*, 1964

Roper, Lyndal, *Witch Craze: Terror and Fantasy in Baroque Germany*, London, Yale University Press, 2004

Rowe, William T., *China's Last Empire: The Great Qing*, London, Belknap Press, 2009

Russell, Jeffrey B., *A History of Witchcraft*, London, Thames and Hudson, 1980

Sanders, E. P., *The Historical Figure of Jesus*, Harmondsworth, Penguin Books, 1993

Sardesai, D. R., *A History of India*, 2008

Saunders, J. J., *A History of the Mongol Conquests*, London, Routledge & Kegan Paul, 1972

Schäfer, Peter, *The History of the Jews in the Greco-Roman World: The Jews of Palestine from Alexander the Great to the Arab*, London, Routledge, 2003

Schiffman, Lawrence H., *Reclaiming the Dead Sea Scrolls: The History of Judaism, the Background of Christianity, the Lost Library of Qumran*, Philadelphia, Jewish Publication Society, 1994

Shaw, Ian, ed., *The Oxford History of Ancient Egypt*, Oxford, Oxford University Press, 2000

Skilton, Andrew, *A Concise History of Buddhism*, Birmingham, Windhorse, 1994

Smith, Huston and Philip Novak, *Buddhism: A Concise Introduction*, New York, Harper, 2003

Stepan, Nancy, *The Idea of Race in Science: Great Britain 1800–1960*, London, Macmillan, 1982

Tacitus, *The Histories*, trans. Kenneth Wellesley, Harmondsworth, Penguin Books, 1964

Thomas, Keith, *Religion and the Decline of Magic*, London, The Folio Society, 1971

Twitchett, Denis and Michael Loewe, *The Cambridge History of China: The Ch'in and Han Empires*, Cambridge, Cambridge University Press, 1986

Ullmann, Walter, *A Short History of the Papacy in the Middle Ages*, London, Methuen, 1972

Vanderkam, James and Peter Flint, *The Meaning of the Dead Sea Scrolls: Their Significance in understanding the Bible, Judaism and Christianity*, London, HarperCollins, 2002

Vine, Aubrey R., *The Nestorian Churches: A Concise History of Nestorian Christianity in Asia from the Persian Schism to the Modern Assyrians*, London, Independent Press, 1937

Wheen, Francis, *Karl Marx*, London, Fourth Estate, 1999

Wigram, W. A., *The Separation of the Monophysites*, New York, AMS Press, 1978 [1923]

INDEX (10 PP BLANK)

Index (10 pp blank)

Index (10 pp blank)

Index (10 pp blank)

Index (10 pp blank)